The Saints
of Ireland

*A Chronological Account of
the Lives and Works of
Ireland's Saints and Missionaries
at Home and Abroad*

by
Mary Ryan D'Arcy

THE IRISH AMERICAN CULTURAL INSTITUTE
St. Paul, Minnesota

Published by
The Irish American Cultural Institute
683 Osceola Avenue
St. Paul, Minnesota 55105

© Copyright 1974 by the Irish American Cultural Institute

PRINTED IN THE UNITED STATES OF AMERICA
AT THE NORTH CENTRAL PUBLISHING COMPANY
SAINT PAUL, MINNESOTA

Library of Congress Catalog Card Number: 74-83242

TO
KATHLEEN, BRIAN, PATRICK
AND KIERAN, WITH LOVE

Contents

Introduction ix

I. Early Irish Saints 1

II. Irish Saints in Scotland 71

III. Irish Saints in England 89

IV. Irish Saints on the Continent 112

V. The Post-Viking Period 171

VI. Henry II to Henry VIII in Ireland 177

VII. The Martyrdom of Ireland 190

VIII. Modern Irish Missionaries 210

Postscript 228

Selected Further Readings 230

Feast Day Index 234

Alphabetical Index 238

Acknowledgements

Permission to reprint material is hereby gratefully acknowledged to the following publishers: to Yale University Press (*Crosses and Culture of Ireland* by Arthur Kingsley Porter); to Charles Scribner's Sons (*Tara* by R.A.S. Macalister); to Oxford University Press (*A Study of History* by Arnold J. Toynbee); to the *Chicago Tribune* for the "Unveiling of Lincoln's Statue"; to the London *Daily Telegraph* for the "Trinity College Art Exhibit"; to the many Irish publishers and writers whose books out of copyright I have used so extensively; and, finally, to the many individuals who have in so many and in such varied ways contributed to bringing this book to publication. To every one my deepest appreciation and my most sincere thanks — and most particularly to Dr. Eoin McKiernan.

M.R.D.

Introduction

It all began with a prayer book from Ireland that had a litany of the Irish Saints. There were all of those names I had never even heard of. I soon found out that not only is their importance little to be gathered from the material one may find in available general lives of the saints, but, also, for the average reader, the really good books on the Irish saints are very scattered and far from easily obtainable. With that fact in mind and in the hope that my years of research may make a worthwhile record I made this tabulation.

Pre-Christian Ireland had a highly developed culture. It had its brehons, or law-givers, its richly remunerated bards. Its poets ranked only below the king. It was from this educated class that Patrick recruited his clergy. The poet Fiacc is said to have mastered the Alphabet (or brief exposition of Christian doctrine) and the ecclesiastical Ordo (or method of administering the Sacraments and celebrating the Holy Sacrifice) in fifteen days. By Patrick's death Ireland had become Christian. Within a century after his death, the Irish became a phenomenal missionary people.

During the 5th and 6th centuries, when barbarians were threatening the very existence of Christian Rome, great monastic schools grew up from which the Irish were soon to begin their great march over England and the Continent. "The Irish Miracle," as Daniel-Rops calls it, "is this second setting out of Christianity, from a country which had just been baptized, and which was immediately dreaming of giving Christ back to the world. Ireland, between the 5th and the 8th century, was like a second Palestine, a new cradle of the Christian faith." Of the Irish monasteries, he continues, "whilst culture was sinking in the West, each of these centers was lighting a torch whose flame would soon be carried everywhere."

The Irish phenomenon, if we may call it that, has intrigued writers of diverse nations and times. A Yale professor, Arthur Kingsley Porter, wrote, "The success of the Celtic Church was a religious and political event of the first magnitude. From Ireland came the learned and the fervent; the Irish clergy enjoyed unrivalled prestige throughout Europe. Countless abbeys looked to Ireland as their head. Even in Italy herself the most important monastery was the Irish Bobbio'' (in Northern Italy, in whose Cathedral crypt lie the honored remains of Columban, the Irish saint from whose greatness the importance of Bobbio arose).

The adoption of Irish script, for instance, so distinctive a modification of the Roman, gives lasting testimony of the importance and influence of Irish teachers in Europe and in England. Porter states, "To Ireland belongs the credit of having been the first to develop a minuscule in the true sense of the word." And concerning this influence upon England he tells us "it was not from Rome, notwithstanding the models sent, but from Ireland that England learned her later writing."

The Italian scholar Tommasini was equally generous in his tribute to the Irish: "At the end of the 5th century an army of saints of heroic stature and original character arose in that privileged land and thence marched over the world, bringing to the remotest lands their unwearying apostolic fervor and humble aspiration after martyrdom." He was joined by the French writer Montalembert: "It has been said and cannot be sufficiently repeated, Ireland was then regarded by all Christian Europe as the principal center of knowledge and piety — superior to anything that could be seen in any other country of Europe."

The English, too, were to acknowledge their debt. The Venerable Bede, for example, wrote of crowds of Anglo-Saxon youths who "forsook their native island" to go to school to Ireland where "the Irish most willingly received them all and took care to supply them gratuitously with daily food, as also to furnish them with books to read and with their teaching without making any charge." So many of them were at the School of Armagh, one district of the city was called the Saxon Quarter. And a later English churchman, Bishop Milner, was equally grateful: "The Irish clergy were the luminaries of the western world. To them we are indebted for the preservation of the Bible, the Fathers, and the Classics. Then, a residence in Ireland, like a residence at a university, were almost essential to establish a literary reputation."

Toynbee in his *Study of History* makes this evaluation: "The literary studies which Christian liturgical requirements kept alive everywhere during the post-Hellenic interregnum bore fruit in Ireland in a greater mastery of the Latin Classics than was retained by the Christian Church in the *ci-devant* Roman provinces on the Continent where Latin remained the vernacular language. More remarkable still, the Irish ecclesiastical scholars contrived to recapture a command of the Greek language and literature, at a time when the knowledge of Greek was extinct in Latin Christian countries that were much less remote geographically than Ireland was from the living reservoir of Greek that survived in the East Roman Empire. . . . the genuineness of the ninth-century Irish Hellenists (e.g. Johannes Scotus Erigena) is beyond question.'' Concerning Erigena Toynbee affirms: ''Johannes Scotus Erigena: the giant of the Carolingian Renaissance whose like was not seen again in Western Chritendom until the Italian Renaissance of the fifteenth century.''

In order to recognize the work of the Irish in Britain and on the Continent, one may find it helpful to remember what Toynbee terms that well known curiosity of history, the fact that originally the term ''Scot'' meant an Irishman. Anciently a Latin name for Ireland was Scotia. (Another, of course, was Hibernia.) When an Irish colony was established in northern Britain, it was first called Scotia Minor, then the Land of the Scots, and finally, Scotland. The dynasty of Scottish kings — and the Gaelic language of the Highlands — descend from the ancient Irish colony of Argyle. During Ireland's long centuries of persecution, organized learning went down in the common debacle of blood and ruin. A forgetful world — Rome included — was soon extending to the later Scots the achievements of the earlier Irish ''Scots.'' Errors multiplied from this semantic shift as, for instance, when the foundations of Marianus Scotus in Germany were mistakenly credited to the latter-day Scots. Thomas Dempster (dubbed the Saint-Stealer) made a pious attempt to claim for Scotland all of the olden Irish Scots. Even today, tourist guide books not only label the Irish Scots as Scottish but often set them down under the general term English.

One by one these misconceptions fall before modern-day scholarship, as evidenced by Benedict Fitzpatrick, J. F. Kenney, the Benedictine Dom Gougaud, Tommasini, and Pope Pius XI. Daniel-Rops, author of some 70 books on the history of the Roman Catholic Church, deemed it necessary and right to pay homage to that important element in Christian history, *''The Miracle of Ireland.''* He makes this comment: ''The history of this Celtic Christianity is a history which has not always met with the notice it deserves, but anyone who studies it fairly will find it is of capital importance.''

M.R.D.

November 6, 1973
Feast of All the Saints of Ireland.

I

Early Irish Saints

Ireland commemorates a number of native pre-Patrician Irish saints. Prosper of Aquitaine tells us that, in the year 431, Pope Celestine sent "to the Scots believing in Christ" their first bishop, Palladius. Scholarship generally accepts that Palladius (July 7) was in Ireland a very short time; that he went to what is now Scotland and died there. So, even though Christianity came to Ireland before Patrick, the title "Apostle of Ireland" belongs to Patrick, the patrician youth who found his vocation in servitude on the hillsides of Ireland and later returned as a bishop to minister to his adopted people. He was to head a distinguished group of men and women whose zeal became a byword in European Christianity.

Abben (Abban)
May 13*   Second century

O'Hanlon, citing old martyrologies and chronicles, records the now generally accepted opinion that the English city of Abingdon in Berkshire derived its name from a religious monk named Abbenus who came from Ireland into Roman Britain and was there baptized. "Summe Chronicles sey this was in yere of oure Lord 165." Having faithfully preached the word of God as the Holy Ghost inspired him and having requested and received a generous grant of land in Berroccense, now Berkshire, the Irish pilgrim "happily founded a monastery." Other-day allusions to this place called it Abbandun. The modern *don* is a corruption of the Gaelic *dun*, fortress or seat.

In 685, in Anglo-Saxon times, on the spot called Abba's Hill where previously had stood a religious center, there arose at Abingdon a new monastery destined to be "hardly second to any in England." Generously endowed by the local prince Cissa, the founder of this establishment was Hean; his successor as abbot was Conon, both distinctively Irish names.

In the reign of Henry II during the 12th century, when Laurence O'Toole, ambassador from Roderick O'Connor, the last monarch of Ireland, found

*Feast days are given under the saints' names.

himself a victim of Henry's displeasure, a virtual prisoner in England forbidden to return to Ireland, the place in which he chose to wait out his time was Abingdon. It was not by chance, perhaps, that these three weeks of Laurence O'Toole's ebbing life were spent in a cloister of Irish traditions before he followed Henry to France where he died.

O'Hanlon, V: 236; Fitzpatrick, I: 253; Butler-Attwater, IV: 343.

Mansuy (Mansuetus)
September 24   Fourth century

One of the earliest Christians to be explicitly assigned an Irish origin was Fethgno, whose Gaelic name was Latinized into Mansuy or Mansuetus. According to tradition, he was sent from Rome to be the first bishop of Toul in Lorraine in France about 338–350. His 10th century biographer, the ecclesiastical writer Adso, educated in Irish-founded Luxeuil, is credited with having derived his information from a written source. Abbot Adso wrote "Hibernia's soil was rich in Christian grace. There Mansuy saw the light, there lived his noble race."

Kenney, 161; Benedictine Monks, 390; McManus, 104.

Grimonia (Germana)
September 24   Fourth century

The Christian Irish woman Grimonia, who fled her country and especially her pagan father, is venerated in the diocese of Soissans. She was martyred in the forest of Thierache and when her grave became famous for miracles, a church was built over it. Around the church the town of La Chapelle developed. In the 13th century, Grimonia's relics and those of Proba, or Preuve, the Irish companion who died beside her, were enshrined at Lesquilles; in the 16th century they were removed to the abbey of the Canons Regular at Henin-Lietard near Douai.

Benedictine Monks, 276; Butler, IX: 73, 617; *Catholic Encyclopedia*, XIV: 131.

Eliph
October 16   c. 362

Eliph was an Irish prince who chose "to serve Christ the Lord in poverty" in the city of Toul in France. He was imprisoned there, but was set free miraculously. His preaching converted some 400 people before Julian the Apostate had him beheaded. Sharing in his martyrdom were Eliph's sisters and his brother Eucharius. Their place of burial, Mount Eliph, still commemorates the saint. In the 10th century his relics were removed to Cologne.

Benedictine Monks, 196; McManus, 104; note, 237.

Ailbhe

September 12   Fifth century

Four native pre-Patrician Irish bishops, who are said to have received consecration in Rome, are famed as having been active in Ireland before the coming of Patrick: Ailbhe, Ibar, Declan, and Kieran of Saigher.

Moran, in tracing Irish saints in Britain, quotes the Bollandists that St. David of Wales was born of an Irish mother. He states that Ailbhe of Emly baptized David.

Ailbhe built his church at Emly, 14 miles west of historic Cashel. The monastic school that arose in connection with it became important in the 6th century. It flourished for 300 years, until it was plundered and burned by the Vikings.

Benedictine Monks, 21; Ryan, 118; 325; Moran, 29.

Ibar

April 23   Fifth century

Although Ibar is said to have been at first reluctant to submit to Patrick, peace was eventually made between them. According to the story tellers, Patrick threatened to banish Ibar from Ireland and Ibar answered, "Wherever I shall be, I will call it Ireland." Ibar had his church, his school and many disciples on a little island in Wexford harbor, Beg-Eri ("Little Ireland"). Foreign as well as native students enrolled there.

Beg-Eri was long a holy shrine and a place of pilgrimage. Writings of the 17th century adventurer Colonel Solomon Richards refer to Iberian, as he calls Ibar: ". . . in the little chapel there was a wooden image of the saint and people go there to worship him, and settle any cases of controversy that may arise amongst them by oath before the image of the saint. Moreover if any false charges were made against a man, the parties take boat to the island, the suspected man swears the charge is false, and this oath before the saint is at once readily accepted as satisfactory proof of innocence. Once or twice, 'idle fellows who love not wooden gods' stole away St. Iberian, and burned him, but the image was miraculously restored as the silly people believe, once more to its place."

Ryan, 118; Benedictine Monks, 302; Healy, 158.

Declan
July 24   Fifth century

Fosterage was an educational system practiced in ancient Ireland whereby a youth was sent into the home or family of an outstanding person whose virtues he was to emulate. Declan, a prince of the Decies and one of the four pre-Patrician bishops, was given into fosterage to a Christian guardian. He went to Rome to study, was ordained and consecrated bishop there. Patrick later confirmed Declan in his seat at Ardmore, in Waterford, which it is claimed was a bishopric before Patrick came to Ireland.

Ardmore is rich in memorials of its former glory. Declan's resting place is his own 9′ by 13′ oratory, reroofed in 1716. The cathedral, a very ancient building that evidences much repair and alteration, has an 11th century nave and a 13th century Gothic choir, together with scriptural and other sculptures and many other curious much older features. Within it are two Ogham stones, one with the inscription "the loved one." The round tower, 95′ high, is perhaps the best surviving example of this type of architecture in the whole country. Another group of buildings includes St. Declan's Well and the ruins of a church.

Ryan, 118; Benedictine Monks, 168; Healy, 153; *Benn*, 225.

Kieran of Saigher
March 5   Fifth century

All the dioceses of Ireland keep the feast day of Kieran of Saigher, but on Clear Island, at the most southerly point of Ireland, there is very special commemoration every March 5. Here is Kieran's birthplace and the remains of a church he is said to have built there, though it is obviously of centuries later date.

Kieran, who was of Munster royalty, studied at Tours and Rome and came home a bishop. Out of his cell in upper Ossory in the midlands grew the monastery of Saigher (Seirkieran) and a convent for women which he placed in the care of his mother, Liadan.

In Brittany Kieran appears under the name Sezin, and in Cornwall as Piran. In Wales, in the most ancient extant list of the Abbots of St. Illtud's Monastery, the second name is that of Kieran of Saigher. The most interesting of many memorials connecting Kieran with Cornwall under the name Piran is the chapel at Perranzabuloe or "St. Piran's in the Sands." After being embedded in the strand for 800 years it was brought to light, almost perfect in its solid masonry, with its sculptured corbels and zig-zag ornaments so complete "one might imagine it was one of our old Irish oratories transplanted to the Cornish shore.''

The identification of Piran with Kieran has been rejected. Unfortunately, if Piran and Kieran are not the same, Piran has no life of his own, only the borrowed life of Kieran of Saigher, only Kieran of Saigher's feast day, March 5.

The Irish tradition is that Kieran died at Saigher.

Ryan, 118; Butler-Attwater, I: 489; Healy, 194; O'Hanlon, III: 147; Moran, 32; Neeson, 53.

Sedulius
?February 12   Fifth century

In 1922, George Sigerson of Dublin brought out an English translation of "Carmen Paschale," entitling it "The Easter Song, being the First Epic of Christendom, by Sedulius, the first Scholar-Saint of Erinn." The publication was the first translation in whole or part into a modern language.

The earliest Vatican documents, according to the Spanish writer Arevalus, tell briefly that Sedulius was gentile, a poet who taught philosophy in Italy, a convert to Christianity and the founder of a school of poetry in Athens where he wrote his great poem in A.D. 430. He was a "gentile" — i.e., in the ecclesiastical meaning of that day, one who was not of the Continental classical world of Romans, Greeks, Gauls, Spaniards, Syrians, Africans.

Some authorities assert Sedulius was Irish, others question it. Meager though the reference to Irish nationality may be, there is no evidence anywhere that he was a native of any other country. The 8th century Irish geographer Dicuil, for example, speaks of Sedulius as "noster" or "our own" Sedulius.

The German writer, Abbot Trithemius of Spanheim, in the 15th century, describes the poet as "Sedulius a priest, a Scot [i.e., Irish] by nation, a disciple of Hildebert, Archbishop of the Scots. . . . [who] left Scotia through love of learning and came to Gaul; then he travelled through Italy and Asia; finally departing the confines of Greece, he shone in the city of Rome." Colgan identifies the Archbishop of the Scots as Ailbhe, one of the four pre-Patrician saints, his name Germanized into Hildebert.

Sigerson points out the characteristically Irish structure of the verses of Sedulius — exact, complete, and varied examples of Irish meter in Latin verses. They are, he declares, as irresistible as evidence of the Irish authorship as would be an interlaced illuminated illustration from an Irish manuscript.

"Carmen Paschale," composed about 430 A.D., has been acclaimed throughout the centuries. Its earliest editor was Asterius, a Roman Consul in 449; an Emperor, Theodosius, declared himself grateful for its dedication; the Decree of the First Roman Council of the Church in 494 distinguished "by signal praise the Paschal Work of the Venerable man, Sedulius." Today, a passage from it salutes the Mother of God in the Introit, or Entrance Antiphon of the Mass of the Blessed Virgin: *Salve sancte parens*, Hail holy Mother, who gave birth to the King who rules heaven and earth forever.

About 70 manuscript editions of Carmen Paschale" are extant, 14 of them in the Vatican. Almost all are on parchment, many of them examples of the ancient art of illumination. The oldest copy in existence is in Turin, a parchment volume written in the square lettering of the 6th century, inscribed on the first page, in letters less ancient than the text, "The Book of Saint Columban of Bobbio." The Bobbio library yielded several copies of the poem.

Every century from the 6th to the 16th produced a manuscript edition of the Easter Song, sometimes several. In the 15th century literary revival, Sedulius along with other Christian writers was elegantly reproduced. With the invention of printing, his works were prominent among those first chosen for reproduction in print. An undated Paris edition and the 1475 Utrecht edition are considered the earliest editions. A 1475–1886 tabulation lists 75 editions, an average of one edition in every five and a half years. France, Spain, Italy, Germany, Holland and Switzerland have published editions. Edinburgh is represented once. England is missing.

Sigerson; Hoagland, 8; Healy, 29; McManus, 105, 257; Concannon, II: 35.

Patrick
March 17   461? 493?

ˏ St. Patrick's "Breastplate"

Christ be with me, Christ be before me
Christ be behind me, Christ be within me
Christ be beneath me, Christ be above me
Christ be at my right, Christ be at my left
Christ be in the fort, Christ be in the chariot
Christ be in the ship
Christ be in the heart of everyone
                who thinks of me
Christ be in the mouth of everyone
                who speaks to me
Christ be in every eye that sees me
Christ be in every ear that hears me.

From 55 B.C. to 427 A.D. the Roman Eagle flew over Western Europe as far as and including Britain. Ireland not only remained free, it kept up a formidable raiding of Roman frontiers. The poet Claudian, writing about 400 A.D., tells that Rome sent her best general, Stilicho, to protect Britannia when the Irish moved all Ireland against her "and the sea foamed beneath the weight of their oars." Christianity came to Celtic Britain with the Roman occupation. Almost nothing is known of the infiltration of Christianity into Ireland.

One of the Irish invasions of 5th century Britain brought back, among "many thousands" of captives, the 16-year-old Patrick. After six years in slavery, "voices" told him he was to return to his fatherland. Later, other "voices" calling from Ireland besought him "to come and walk once more among us." He went back as a missionary.

The precise chronology of Patrick's apostolate has eluded historians and writers through the ages, from 7th century Tirechan and Muirchu to today's galaxy of expert Patriciologists. Binchy, in "Patrick and his Biographers, Ancient and Modern," likens the story of the saint to a jigsaw puzzle with all the important pieces missing.

The man himself, however, is saved for us by his own writings, his *Confession* and his *Letter to Coroticus*, two great documents of strong and lasting appeal. Beautiful and touching words attest to a nobility of mind and heart and soul, and a great abiding charity, especially toward those who had injured him. From first to last he is a missionary with an insatiable desire for souls. The conversion of the Irish is the "epistle of salvation" which he had written by deeds, not by words, "not with ink, but with the spirit of the living God."

The saint calls himself Patricius. He says his father was Calpornius, a deacon and a decurion, with men and maid servants; that his grandfather was Potitus a priest. He was neither very religious nor very studious, he says, and "before he knew what to pursue and what to avoid," he was taken captive along with many others from the family estate near the town of Bannavem Taburniae, which speculation locates somewhere in Wales. Where he was born has never been determined.

In captivity in the northeast of Ireland, he had to tend sheep in the woods and on the mountainside. But the love of God came to him more and more. A hundred times a day and as many times in the night, he tells us, he prayed and he felt neither frost nor snow nor rain, so warm burned the spirit of God within him.

After six years, in obedience to a voice in his sleep, he made his escape. Trusting God to direct him, he travelled 200 miles to the ship his voices had said awaited him. After a first harsh refusal, the captain took him aboard.

Three days of sailing carried them to the Continent, and for 28 days they were without food in desert country somewhere in Gaul. In their plight, the pagan captain asked Patrick to pray to his God for them, and from then on the party had food and fire and fine weather.

After a few years Patrick was once again in Britain with his people. They urged him not to leave them. But persistently in visions of the night came pleas from the Ireland that had made him its own. In his dreams, a man from Ireland, Victoricus, brought him countless letters, "the voice of the Irish." Voices from Foclut Wood by the western sea beseeched him to return, the spirit of God spoke to him in the same vein. Patrick's own writings say nothing about the interval between his escape from slavery and his return to Ireland, nothing about the districts in which he preached, nothing about the clerics who worked with him in Ireland.

The saint has long been believed to have studied under St. Germanus at Auxerre in France. In 1961, the city of Auxerre held a three day celebration to mark the Patrician year. St. Patrice, a village near Tours which has a church containing a statue of Patrick and a window depicting him above the altar, claims that he came there in midwinter tired and cold and that the frost-covered thorn tree under which he slept burst into soft and warming bloom above him. In December every year, with everything else bare, the flowers of St. Patrick as people called them, bloomed at St. Patrice. About 1890 a chapel-like monument surmounted by a statue of Patrick was erected near the now destroyed, miraculous thorn tree. Into our own century, the phenomenon was testified to by the curé of the parish and by archaeological and agriculture societies.

There is a tradition, too, that Patrick studied at Lerins, a tradition proudly perpetuated in the Lerins Island of St. Honorat, in the Mediterranean, off shore from Cannes in France. An engraved stone on the side of the main monastery records that St. Patrick, Apostle of Ireland, came there in the 5th century to study the sacred sciences in preparation for his mission to Ireland.

St. Germanus was in Britain in 429 and a mission to Ireland was contemplated at that time. Actually, it is not known just when Patrick's mission to Ireland began. Some scholars hold that he arrived in Ireland in 432, others say as late as 456. Years as widely separated as 461 and 493 are given for his death. That there were pre-Patrician missionary efforts, we know. One such missionary bishop was Palladius, ordained and sent to Ireland, according to the Chronicle of Prosper, by Pope Celestine in 431. However little we know about Patrick and the 5th century, we know at least that the great conversion of Ireland took place in his time and has always been attributed to his efforts.

The saint's most active apostolate is believed to have been in the north. The

See of Armagh, two miles from Emain Macha, was founded, some scholars hold, while the fortress was still the capitol of the most powerful kingdom in Ireland. There is question of Patrick's Eastertime confrontation with King Laoghaire at Tara, the capitol of Meath in the midlands. The day was Holy Saturday (?432) which, that year, coincided with the great druid festival at Tara when no fire might be lighted in all Erin before the new lighting of the sacred pagan fire. Outraged druids saw the Christian Patrick's campfire which was plainly visible at Tara. According to tradition, they warned Laoghaire that, if that fire were not stamped out, it would never after be extinguished in Erin. And when Patrick was brought before Laoghaire, affronted druids assailed him fiercely. Although Patrick won from Laoghaire an invitation to Tara for the morrow, Laoghaire died a pagan. Laoghaire's brother, Conal Gulban, prince of the north and ancester of Colmcille, appears to have been Patrick's staunch disciple, protector and helper. The cross on the coat-of-arms of his descendants, the O'Donnells, represents the Sign of the Cross Patrick is said to have traced on Conal's shield.

In his *Confession*, Patrick tells he did everything lovingly and gladly. He was God's debtor, he says, for the great grace of baptism given to so many thousands, for the multitude of people reborn in God and afterward confirmed, with clerics ordained for them everywhere. The sons and daughters of the kings of the Irish became monks and virgins of Christ. Women who lived in slavery followed him bravely, though they were forbidden to do so. "Wherefore may it never happen to me from my God that I should lose His people whom He hath purchased at the ends of the earth."

"Not wishing to bore his readers," Patrick mentions, without elaboration, persecution even unto bonds, twelve dangers to his life, numerous plots against him. February 9 commemorates Odran, his charioteer who, tradition says, aware of impending danger, feigned weariness and asked the apostle to take the reins. Riding in the place of honor, Odran was killed by a lance meant for Patrick.

St. Patrick's great legacy to the Irish people is the faith of the Irish in Ireland and the missionary spirit of the Irish as it has been manifested in every part of the modern world.

Armagh, Patrick's primal See, spans the centuries to the present. From the 6th to the 12th century, the *Annals of the Four Masters* make frequent reference to noted scribes, professors, rectors and others of Armagh. Plunderings, burnings and slaughter came to Armagh with the Norsemen. Turgesius the Dane enthroned himself, in 831, in the place of highest prestige in all Ireland, the high altar at Armagh. The conqueror of the Norsemen, Brian Boru, in 1004 laid 20 ounces of gold upon the altar in "the apostolic city which in Irish is called Ardmacha,'' signing himself as ''Emperor of the Scots'' (that is, of the Irish).

In 1126 the great church of St. Peter and St. Paul was restored to more than former splendor. The Augustinians were introduced there. Armagh was primarily a great theological seminary. In 1162, in order to insure uniformity, it was enacted no person be allowed to teach divinity in any school in Ireland who was not accredited by the school of Armagh.

In 1169 King Roderick O'Conor, last monarch of Ireland, made grants in perpetuity, from himself and every king who should succeed him forever, to Armagh in honor of St. Patrick and to instruct the youths of Ireland and Alba in learning. Under the Primate Gelasius who died in 1174, Armagh reached its short-lived zenith. The Donation of Ireland by Pope Adrian IV to Henry II opened the floodglates to Angevin adventurers. Year after year DeCourcy, DeBurgo and DeLacy swooped down on St. Patrick's city and in 1178, ''the sun of Armagh's ancient glory set in darkness and in blood.''

Not until 1854 was it discovered that under the name Concord, Armagh's 55th primate, Conchobar MacConchaille, pilgrim to Rome in 1175, was venerated as a saint in Savoy in France. But Armagh's woes culminated in the Penal centuries. Any priest found in Ireland was charged with treason. Irish prelates were ''on the run'' or in exile. Richard Creagh spent 18 years in the Tower of London, where he died in 1587. Edmund MacGauran was slain at Tulsk in 1593. The next five primates lived in exile. Oliver Plunket died on the scaffold in London in 1681.

Today the flag of a foreign nation flies over the ecclesiastical capital of Ireland, the Primatial See of Armagh.

The oldest copy of St. Patrick's *Confession* is contained in the *Book of Armagh*, which, under the title *Canoine Patriacc* came to be held in the greatest reverence. And the *Canoine Patriacc* and the *''Baculus Jesu''* (Patrick's crozier) together were considered the very title deed to the See of Armagh. Armagh's great Book was transcribed about 807 by ''Ferdomnach sapiens et scribus optimus Ardmachae.'' It is an illuminated manuscript precious as a work of Celtic art. The illuminations are described as fine pen drawings, its text as penmanship of extreme elegance, admirable throughout for its distinctiveness and uniformity. It was enshrined in 937 in a now missing gem-studded cumdach (book-shrine) by Donnchad, son of Flann, King of Ireland. An endowment of eight townlands supported a keepership for its safety, with the name of the hereditary stewards of the canon, maor na canon (MacMoyre) deriving from the office. After the Reformation, the endowment came to an end with the English Confiscation of the eight townlands and the MacMoyre residence. The keepership itself ended in 1681 with one Florence MacMoyre who pawned the Book of Armagh for five pounds to pay his way to London to testify against Blessed Oliver Plunket. Subsequent transfers brought the Irish classic finally to its present home, Trinity College Library, Dublin.

Patrick's crozier, called the "Baculus Jesu," or "Staff of Jesus," was Ireland's most precious treasure for more than a thousand years. St. Bernard mentioned it, gold covered and adorned with precious stones. Gerald Cambrensis called it the most famous and wonder-working crozier in Ireland. It was publicly burned in Dublin in the reign of Henry VIII in 1538.

However, today the National Museum preserves two great Patrician treasures, the saint's own hand bell and an ancient reliquary. According to the *Tripartite Life* (an 8th century work in three parts designed for use in the three day celebrations anciently observed in honor of the saint for his feast day) Patrick gave MacCartan of Clogher a case for relics. And tradition declares that the inner yew box of the Domnach Airgid is that very relic case. The famous reliquary is made up of three cases, centuries apart in their respective ages: the real treasure, the primitive yew box; the 8th century silver-plated box of Celtic ornamentation; the richly embossed outer case of silver plated with gold and set with precious stones which the inscription tells was made by John O'Barrdon at the order of John O'Karbri, successor of Tighernagh of Clones, who died in 1353.

Patrick's little iron hand bell reposes in a gem-studded shrine made for it in 1091 by Domnal MacAuley, King of Ireland. The bell, which was long safeguarded in the hereditary keepership of the MacBeolans of Galway, once travelled the length and breadth of Ireland with the Primate. It was brought out, and heard around the world via radio, at the time of the Eucharistic Congress in Dublin in 1932. Gilbert Keith Chesterton, present for the occasion, describes the effect: "It was as faint as the sound of a far-off sheep-bell and as weak as the bleat of a sheep; but there was some thing in it that was not only weighty but curiously hard; almost dead . . . it was the Bell of St. Patrick which had been silent for 1500 years . . . From far away in the most forgotten of the centuries, as if down avenues that were colonnades of corpses, one dead man had spoken and was dumb. It was Patrick; and he only said 'My Master is here.' "

And Patrick's memory is vividly preserved in the annual pilgrimage associated with the ancient tradition that he fasted and prayed on Cruachan Aigli, the hill of the eagles, now called Croagh Patrick, 2500 feet above Westport Bay in County Mayo. From time beyond memory, oratory after oratory has been built on its peak, and each summer, on the last Sunday of

July, pilgrims in thousands, many bare-footed, make the long penetential climb to attend Mass on the summit.

O'Fiach; Binchy; Bieler; Hayes; Sweeney; Needham; Healy; Stokes, 52; Curtis, 28; Chesterton.

Benignus (Benen)
November 9   Fifth century

Benen was very young when Patrick and his missionary band came to the home of his father, Sesgne, won all there to the faith and, then and there, destined Benen for the See of Armagh as his successor.

As for Benen, he was so attentive to the apostle, following him everywhere, bringing flowers when he rested, that the others remonstrated. But Patrick said to them, "Restrain him not, that youth shall yet heir my kingdom." At the leavetaking, Benen, refusing to be parted from his new-found friend, sat on Patrick's foot, arms locked around the saint's knee. And so it happened that Sesgne gave Benen into Patrick's keeping and that from boyhood on, Benen travelled and studied with Patrick on his missionary journeying. As time went on, Benen became Patrick's psalm-singer in charge of the music for religious services, was ordained to the priesthood and eventually became the second bishop of Armagh. He was the most prominent and the most important of Patrick's native-born Irish bishops.

Benen appears in the legend of the Breastplate, "Christ be with me . . ." which Patrick is said to have recited on the way from Slane to Tara on Easter Sunday when King Laoghaire had stationed soldiers along the road expecting to intercept Patrick's arrival at Tara. But the soldiers saw no missionaries, only a herd of deer and a little fawn. The *Triparte Life* tells that "Patrick went with eight young clerics and Benen as a gillie with them, and Patrick gave them his blessing before they set out. A cloak of darkness went over them so that not a man of them appeared. Howbeit, the enemy who were waiting to ambush them, saw eight deer going past them, and behind them a fawn with a bundle on its back. That was Patrick with his eight, and Benen behind them with his tablets on his back."

Ryan, 83, 95; Healy, 114; Bieler, 14, 104; Concannon, I: 117.

Fortchern
February 17   Fifth century

One of Patrick's bishop-disciples was the British Lommán: "likely from his name to have been an Irish Briton. The Britons proper affected Latin names"

John Ryan, S.J., tells us. Lommán came into the district of Ath Truim, the ford of the elder-tree, now Trim, and he met there and won for the Mission another holy young recruit, the princely little boy Fortchern, grandson of the High Ling Laoghaire. Fortchern's father was Feidlimidh, Laoghaire's son; his mother the British princess Scothnoe. "And Feidlimidh believed . . . and he offered up to Lommán and to the holy Patrick his territory with all his goods and with all his race." When Lommán felt his death was near, he named Fortchern his successor. But it was Fortchern's view that as bishop of Trim he would be taking back the gift his father had made to the Church and after three days he handed over his see to "Cathlaid the pilgrim." However, Trim soon reverted to Feidlimidh's descendants, of whom eight bishops are of record.

Trim's great treasure was the celebrated image of the Blessed Mother. For centuries the shrine of Our Lady of Trim was a place of pilgrimage, of great miracles of healing wrought through Mary's intercession, of graces dispensed beyond number. Henry VIII's relic-burning archbishop of Dublin, George Brown, about 1554, at first disavowed any intention of destroying the famous shrine at Trim: "There goeth a common bruite among the Irishmen that I intend to ploke downe Our Lady of Tryme with other places of pilgrimage as the Holy Cross and such like, which indeade I never attempted though my conscience would right well serve to oppress such idollys." His "conscience" would not be denied, however, and the wooden statue was soon thrown on the fire in the market place at Trim.

It is believed that the statue was rescued before being badly harmed and that it was kept in great reverence in a Catholic home in Trim. In 1642, Sir Charles Coote came to garrison Trim and lodged himself in the residence that housed the holy relic. He complained of cold and his son hit upon the great ancient sculpture of Our Lady hidden there, a treasure above price in the Irish church. He chopped it up for firewood. But before Sir Charles got to warm himself, the Irish advanced on the city and Coote fell in action defending Trim for the Parliamentarians.

Ryan, 98; Concannon, I: 107; II: 69; Benn, 71; Benedictine Monks, 239, 372.

Fiacc (Fiach)
October 12   Fifth century

When Patrick was proceeding through Leinster, he went to Donaghmore to see Dubthach, the royal bard of Ireland and the first to believe at Tara. He wanted Dubthach to find him a man of good family and good morals, the husband of one wife and with one child only, that he might ordain him bishop of Leinster.

Dubthach suggested the young poet Fiacc, already a distinguished man of letters and next to Dubthach in the Bardic Order. Fiacc offered himself at once, whereupon Patrick gave him an Alphabet, or brief manual of Christian doctrine, and an Ordo for the sacraments and the Holy Sacrifice of the Mass. "And Patrick conferred the degree of bishop upon Fiacc; and he gave to Fiacc a cumdach [box] containing a bell, and a minister [relics] and a crozier, and a poolire [leather satchel]." He gave Fiacc seven of his family of religious as the nucleus of a community.

During a long life time, Fiacc founded churches and taught the Faith. Together with his son St. Fiachra, he is buried at Sletty in Leix where "three twenties of his disciples" preceded him to the grave. Apparently Fiacc put his bardic training to good use, for he is credited with a metrical *Life of Patrick* or *Genair Patraicc*, always called the "Hymn of Fiacc." Scholars may dispute its authorship and date of composition (Eoin MacNeill dating it about 700, Fr. Francis Shaw holding for an even century later), but it is regarded by all as one of the cherished documents of the early Irish church.

Ryan; Concannon; Healy.

Ethna and Fidelma
January 11   Fifth century

Cruachain, now Rath Crogan, was the site of the palace of the pagan kings of Connacht until Tara became the political capital of Ireland. In the time of St. Patrick, King Laoghaire's two beautiful young daughters, Ethna and Fidelma, were at Rath Crogan. Maol and Coplait, the wisest druids in Erin, were there to educate the princesses in the knowledge and graces proper to their royal station.

Ethna and Fidelma and their handmaidens early one morning came upon Patrick and his missionaries at the fountain of Clebach at the edge of the wood of Rath Crogan. They asked many questions. They listened to Patrick's story of the one true God. They asked to see Him face to face. The saint instructed them, baptized them and gave them Holy Communion. "And they received the Eucharist of God and they slept in death," Muirchu tells us.

There was great lamentation in Erin. Maol and Coplait bitterly reproached Patrick, Coplait especially crying out against him. But the saint exhorted Coplait and Coplait believed, and Patrick tonsured him. Then Maol came, more insulting than ever. But in the end, he, too, listened to the apostle and came to believe and was also tonsured. Afterwards there was a proverb in Ireland, "Maol is like Coplait."

MacCartan
March 24   Fifth century

MacCartan, long the companion and bodyguard for Patrick on his missions into pagan territory, was consecrated bishop by the apostle and assigned to the druidic stronghold, Clogher in Tyrone. According to Tirechan in the Book of Armagh, MacCartan's neice Brigid was present for the founding of Clogher. And in connection with Clogher is to be found the only mention of Brigid in the lives of St. Patrick. After founding the church at Clogher, Patrick preached for three days and three nights at a nearby place called Lemain and Brigid fell asleep during his preaching. It spoils the story to tell she afterwards described a long prophetic dream she experienced during that nap and that the apostle explained it as symbolic of the present and future state of the Irish Church.

Preserved at Clogher today is the Cloch-oir, or Golden Stone, once a ceremonial stone sacred to the druids. Legend has it that the old pagan noble reigning at Clogher subjected the Christian saint to every possible harassment but in the end was won to the faith. His grandson, Tighernach of Clones, succeeded MacCartan as bishop of Clogher.

The *Tripartite Life* tells that Patrick gave MacCartan a case for relics, his own staff and his own bible. Tradition claims that the inner yew box of the famous reliquary, the Domnach Airgid now in the National Museum, is the very relic case Patrick gave to MacCartan. The manuscript Bible, apparently not originally so encased, but found folded within the yew box when opened, is also traditionally ascribed to MacCartan.

Kenney, 351, 639; Healy, 65, 130; Needham, 2; *Benn*, 126.

The Children of Miluic
?   Fifth century

Soon after his return to Ireland, Patrick went "with such gracious purpose" to see Miluic with whom he had spent his six years of captivity. Rather than meet with a former slave, the pagan Miluic locked himself in his house and set it on fire. Miluic's family is a far happier story.

Patrick educated Miluic's son Guasacht and consecrated him bishop of Granard in County Longford. He is commemorated January 24. Two of Miluic's daughters, the two Emers, were given the religious veil by Patrick and placed in a convent said to be the first in Ireland. Their feast day is December 11. A son of Miluic's daughter Bronach, Colman Muilinn (Colman of the Mill) is commemorated January 1. At June 26 is listed another son of Bronach, Caylan or Mochae, founder of the monastery of Nendrum, who when just a boy was blessed and destined for the church by Patrick himself.

A lovely poetic fantasy, retold by Aengus and O'Cleary, was inspired by the beauty of the life of this Mochae, Nendrum's founder.

Mochae was enchanted for 150 years by heavenly psalmody so wonderful he felt not the flight of time or the withering of the years. He had gone into the woods with the brethren to cut wattles to build his church, and just as he finished his load, he heard a most beautiful bird singing in the boughs of the blackthorn bush beside him. The bird said he was an angel of God from heaven and sang three songs before saying farewell. Mochae returned home to find his church built and he saw only strange faces. But when he told them his strange story, they believed him and they built a shrine at the spot where he had seen God's angel and heard the heavenly song. The bird sang three songs only but each lasted 50 years. "If one Angel's song can be so sweet and so beguiling, what a joy to listen to the chorus of all the heavenly choirs."

Ryan; Benedictine Monks; Healy, 144; O'Hanlon, January 24; Concannon I.

Sinell of Killeagh
March 26   Fifth century

Sinell of Killeagh, of Leinster nobility, was one of Patrick's earliest converts. The community he founded at Killeagh was second only to Brigid's monastery at Kildare in north Leinster.

Irish annalists hand down the account of Sinell's great feast day celebration, March 26, 1443. Margaret, daughter of O'Carroll of Ely and wife of Calvagh O'Connor, Prince of Offaly, invited to Killeagh all the bards and sages of Ireland and Scotland, "2700 persons besides the gamesters and poor men." Margaret inaugurated the proceedings by placing on the altar of Sinell's great church two massive chalices of gold, and by taking into her charge two orphans to care for and educate. All who came were entered in a Roll by MacEgan, chief brehon to Calvagh O'Connor, who remained outside on horseback to see that all were welcomed and assisted on arrival. Seated in one of the galleries of Sinell's church, the nave of which had been converted into a banqueting hall for the occasion, was the queenly Margaret "clad in cloath of gold, her deerest friends about her, her clergy and judges, too," shedding a lustre on the scene below. "Meate and moneys" and all manner of gifts were bestowed upon all who came. And for those unable to attend there was a second inviting for the feast of the Assumption of Our Blessed Lady Mary, and the second day was nothing inferior to the first day.

Mentioned in connection with Sinell is his "Pious Rules and Practices" written in the native Gaelic language. His community at Killeagh flourished down to the 16th century when Lord Leonard Gray dismantled the church and took its organ and stained glass windows for the church at Maynooth.

Tommasini, 192; Benedictine Monks, 545; McManus, 350; Sullivan, 184.

Attracta (Adhracht)
August 11   Fifth century?

Poetry and legend tell us that Attracta, daughter of Talan, received the veil from Patrick. She was venerated throughout Ireland as a holy nun who devoted her life to the poor and the sick.

Attracta sent her servant Mochain in search of a site, one near seven roads that it might be more easily accessible to as many as possible of the needy. Mochain found such a spot at Lough Gara in Sligo and there arose Killaraght — cell of Attracta. Her hospice there flourished for more than a thousand years, until 1539.

The saint's cross, preserved through the Middle Ages in the hereditary keepership of the O'Mochain family, is noted in an entry in the Calendar of Papal Letters dated 1413, which tells that the cross and cup of St. Attracta were then venerated in the church of Killaraght in the diocese of Achonry.

After 1829, when the Catholic religion was no longer banned in Ireland, Pius IX authorized the Mass of St. Attracta to be celebrated in the diocese of Achonry, of which she is the patroness. The prayer and proper lessons for her Office were drawn up by Cardinal Moran. Attracta continues in use as an Irish baptismal name.

Catholic Encyclopedia, II: 22, 62; Benedictine Monks, 77; Carty, I: 51.

Mel
February 6   c. 490

Mel was one of 17 sons and two daughters of Conis and Darerca, all of them in religion. He was the first abbot-bishop of Ardagh in Longford, where his richly endowed monastery flourished for centuries. One of the stories told of Mel is that through error during Brigid's profession, he read over her the episcopal consecration, and that Macaille protested. But Mel, with a saint's serene conviction that all that happens is the will of God, insisted it was the work of providence and should stand.

At Longford today there is a St. Mel's Cathedral, a St. Mel's College and a St. Mel's Crozier. Originally partly gilt with a number of colored settings, the now darkened bronze reliquary was executed in the 9th century to contain the oaken core which is supposedly the crozier once used by the saint. It was found in the 19th century at Ardagh near the old cathedral of St. Mel and is now the possession of St. Mel's College.

Ryan, 78; Benedictine Monks, 418; Healy, 131; Curtayne, 70; Henry II, p. 118.

Tassach
April 14   C. 490

Tassach was one of Patrick's artificers, the maker of crosses, croziers, shrines and other ecclesiastical articles, even the builder of churches for the apostle. Patrick placed Tassach first bishop over Raholp in County Down and at the time of his death asked Tassach to give him the last Sacraments. Some historians think it is possible that Assic of Elphin and Tassach may be the same person.

Benedictine Monks, 557; Catholic Encyclopedia, XIV: 463; Healy, 66; O'Hanlon, IV: 511.

Asicus (Assic)
April 27   C. 490

Asicus, patron of the Elphin diocese, was the first bishop over the church and monastery at Elphin in Roscommon. 7th century Tirechan tells that Bishop Assic, Patrick's artificer, made altars and square book cases and patens. Tirechan himself had seen three Assic patens, one in the church of Patrick in Armagh, another in the Elphin church and the third in the church of Donough Patrick. Elphin became an important school of art under successors of Asicus.

It is known from the Annals of Lough Cé that, in 1123, Donal O'Duffy was bishop of Elphin. In that year ''a portion of the True Cross came into Ireland'' and was enshrined in the superb processional Cross of Cong by order of Turlough O'Connor, King of Ireland. One of the five inscriptions along the sides of the Cross reads ''Pray for Donal O'Duffy . . . under whose superintendence the shrine was made.'' The Cross received its name from what is now a picturesque ruin, the Monastery of Cong in Mayo, founded by Turlough O'Connor, King of Ireland, and further endowed by Roderick O'Connor, last monarch of Ireland. The relic, hidden away in the Reformation, was found early in the 19th century by the parish priest of Cong in an oak chest in the village. It is now in the National Museum, Dublin.

There are no inscriptions to tell the respective origins of two of Ireland's finest examples of Christian art, now in the National Museum, Dublin. The Tara brooch, found by a child near the coast of Bettystown south of Drogheda in 1850, and the Ardagh chalice, found in 1868 by a boy digging potatoes near a rath in Ardagh; neither gives name of king or ecclesiastic, nor asks a prayer for artist. The history of these masterpieces may well go back through a line of artist abbots to Asicus of Elphin.

Concannon, I; Ryan; Healy, 564; Stokes, 88; *Benn*, 12, 13, 14.

Domnoc (Modomnoc)
February 13   c. 500

Domnoc, of the royal line of O'Neill, studied under St. David of Menevia in Wales and then returned to become a solitary at Tibraghny in Kilkenny. He had taken care of the bees at Menevia and at the time of his departure they swarmed determinedly about his boat. He tried three times to return them to their hives, all to no avail. At last David told him to be gone, bees and all, with God's blessing. This is supposedly the beginning of the cultivation of honey in the monasteries of Ireland.

Moran, 30; Neeson, 42; Benedictine Monks, 429.

Sinach MacDara
September 28 (also July 16)   Fifth-Sixth century

Down the centuries, until outboard motors, fishermen dipped sails three times in salute to MacDara's island off the Connemara coast. Now they sign themselves with the Cross. September 28 is given as the main feast day of the saint, but July 16 is the special day of local fishermen whose currachs still carry a small bottle of holy water in the prow. It is a day of reverent pilgrimage with the celebrant of the Mass bringing the Blessed Sacrament to the island in a special currach. Marking MacDara's monastic settlement today are the famous remains of the little almost roofless ancient oratory built of massive stone. A wooden statue of the saint was preserved there for many centuries.

Fifth-century MacDara's name Sinach is met with again in 12 century Irish religious history. Ceallach of the Clann Sinach brought his "great name and influence" to the cause of renewal in the Irish church. Long a favorite name locally, MacDara is recently coming into greater use. It is interesting to note that Patrick Pearse, poet-patriot of modern Ireland, chose MacDara as the name of his hero in *The Singer*, his classic play of Irish patriotism.

Nor has MacDara's little stone oratory ever lost its appeal. Its gable shape stands as the prototype of features noted in important Irish art treasures such as the gabled top of the Monasterboice Muireadach sculptured Cross and the gable shape of the Moneymusk reliquary (a case for relics of Colmcille, preserved from 1315 in Moneymusk House and now in the Edinburgh Museum.)

O'Hanlon; Joyce, 83; Benedictine Monks, 383; Canfield, 236; Curtis, 40; Rice, 249; McLaren, 360; Porter, fig. 94.

Dabeoc

January 1   Fifth or Sixth century

Every summer, thousands of pilgrims spend three days in exercises of medieval severity at St. Patrick's Purgatory in Lough Derg in Donegal, a tiny island smaller than the average city block. Barefoot, they pray continually throughout the day and night and get one meal a day of dry bread and black tea. Tradition claims that Patrick fasted and prayed and saw visions of the torments of purgatory there.

The patron of St. Patrick's Purgatory is Dabeoc who came from Wales to Donegal in the 5th or 6th century. He is held to have been the original founder of a monastery on the island. Dabeoc was of Irish blood on his father's side, of the family of Brecan that gave Brecknockshire in Wales its name. The family is reckoned in the Welsh Triads as one of the "three holy families of Wales." An old 5th or 6th century stone, now preserved in the wall of the Basilica at St. Patrick's Purgatory, records a pilgrimage made to Lough Derg by MacNessi (September 3), the first bishop of Connor.

A great amount of literature has been inspired by St. Patrick's Purgatory. The earliest mention of a lay pilgrimage occurs in the story of Dervorgilla, the beautiful wife of Tiernan O'Rourke, Prince of Brefny, who in 1151 sent word to Dermot MacMurrough, King of Leinster, to come to take her away while her husband was absent on a pilgrimage "to the cave of St. Patrick's Purgatory," the incident that was to lead to the Norman invasion and Ireland's eventual loss of independence.

About the same time the legend of the Purgatory merged with Henry of Saltry's greatly embellished account of the soldier Owen's penitential pilgrimage into the cave. Soon the story with variations was appearing in all the languages of Europe, eventually finding reference in Ariosto and Dante (and, possibly, Shakespeare: some scholars believe the ghostly oath "by St. Patrick" in *Hamlet* is such a reference).

In Italy, one Nicholas told of his adventures in the Purgatory in the work called *The Golden Legend*. From Hungary in 1353 came the nobleman George Crissaphan, whose account of his visions enjoyed a long popularity even to publication in the Czech language at the end of the 19th century. A Spanish noble was specific even to the names of acquaintances he recognized among the dead in the Purgatory, one of them a kinswoman of whose death he had not before known. She was punished chiefly for spending so much time "trimming and painting her face." In 1406, the Englishman William Staunton said he was escorted through the Purgatory by the saints John of Bridlington and Hilda of Whitby. The drama, *El Purgatorio de San Patricio*, written by the Spanish poet-priest Calderon, was considered one of the best religious plays of the Spanish theatre in the 17th century.

At the end of the 15th century a Dutch monk visited the cave, saw no visions, and complained to Rome that the place was a fraud. Pope Alexander ordered the cave closed, but did not ban the pilgrimages. In 1503, Pope Pius III granted liberal indulgences to the pilgrims and faculties to the monks in charge of the pilgrimages. In 1517, Chierecoti, Papal Nuncio in England, wrote of his intention, afterwards reported accomplished, "to see St. Patrick's Purgatory and all the other things written about that island." In 1632, the English government outlawed Lough Derg and demolished all the buildings, and in the reign of Queen Anne, the pilgrimages were declared "riotous" and unlawful, punishable by fine or whipping or both. The people continued to come. No real interruption of the Purgatory pilgrimage has ever been known throughout the 1500 years of its existence. Today, thousands repair there each year, and the church on the islet has the status of a basilica.

O'Hanlon; Benedictine Monks, 100, 382; *Catholic Encyclopedia* XII: 580; Salmon, 195; McKenna; Tommasini, 175.

Erc
November 2   C. 512

The young pagan nobleman Erc, a brehon by profession and one of King Laoghaire's inner circle, was present at the storied confrontation with Patrick on the Hill of Slane on Easter Saturday when the apostle was brought before the king and the druid priests assailed him bitterly. Erc alone paid him homage. Patrick blessed him then and afterwards ordained him priest and bishop.

Of the number of localities in which Erc preached the Gospel, his church at Tralee is memorable for his best loved disciple, Brendan the Navigator, whom he tutored from the age of six until ordination. Erc's hermitage at Slane grew into a monastic school that flourished for centuries. It is the school scholars designate as the one in which was educated a future king of France, 7th century Dagobert II.

Today, some curious old gravestones and ivy-covered ruins of a 16th century church mark the once considerable foundation. Viking marauders in 948 plundered the Round Tower there destroying "the best of bells" and Erc's crozier and shrine. In 1170 the church was plundered also by Diarmuid MacMurrough and Strongbow. The church has not been in use since 1723. South of the church is an early tomb which could be that of St. Erc.

O'Hanlon, V: 619; Healy, 65, 213, 589; Ryan, 169; Concannon, I: 115.

Modwena (Moninne, Edana)
July 6   c. 516

The name is Edana with the prefix Mo (a prefix of endearment used with many saints' names). Convents in Ireland, in Britain and in Scotland are credited to this earliest of several Irish saints named Modwena. Her foundation at Killeavy near Newry in Down continued until the 12th century. In legend and popular tradition Modwena is associated with Patrick from whom she is said to have received the veil; with Ibar whose guidance she sought for her nuns at Beg-Eri; and with Brigid whose gift of a silver shrine to Moninne is recorded in Irish Annals.

Skene in *Celtic Scotland* identifies the modern names of Edinburgh and Maiden Castle with the maiden saint of Ireland, Medana or Mo-Edana, who is commemorated in the Breviary of Aberdeen at November 19. He says Edinburgh, commonly and mistakingly supposed to have been named for a fort erected there by King Edwin, was long before that time Edana's sanctuary and a place of pilgrimage.

Ryan, 136; Skene, II: 36; Moran, 139.

Conleth
May 3   c. 519

Conleth was famous as an artificer in metals and as a copyist and illuminator before he entered Holy Orders. Afterwards, as Brigid's bishop and head of the Kildare school of metal-work and penmanship, Conleth, Tassach, Patrick's craftsman, and Daigh, craftsman of Kieran of Saigher, were acclaimed the "three chief artisans of Ireland" of their time. Cogitosus in his description of the Kildare church pictures the golden crown suspended above Brigid's tomb and a silver crown above Conleth's resting place. Preserved to this day in the Royal Irish Academy in Dublin is a crozier said to have belonged to Finbar of Termon-Barry and to have been made by Conleth.

Curtayne, 78; Neeson, 90; Benedictine Monks, 150.

Fanchea
January 1   C. 520

In his *Confession*, Patrick speaks of "the sons and daughters of the kings of the Irish who became virgins of Christ." Fanchea, abbess-foundress of a convent at Rossory in Fermanagh, was a daughter of Conall Derg, king of Oriel. She was an older sister of Enda and is said to have persuaded him to study for the priesthood. With his own hands, he helped erect a sturdy convent wall for her and ruins of a wall are still visible in the old cemetery there (although they are, no doubt, ruins of a later structure). Fanchea died at Killeany in the convent she founded close to a monastery Enda built there after obtaining the grant of the Aran Islands.

Benedictine Monks; Neeson, 15; Healy, 164.

Buite
December 7   C. 521

Buite founded Monasterboice in County Louth. Earlier, he preached in Scotland. On a return from Rome, when he arrived at the royal court there, Nectan, the King of the Picts, was dying and Buite's prayer raised the king to life. The grateful Nechtan granted him several building sites. Among his foundations, the church the saint erected near the royal fort was called Kirkbuddo, or Church of Buite.

The monastery Buite founded in his native land about 500 was not one of the great schools in its early days, but became very important in the 9th and 10th centuries. The wanton destruction of Ireland's books by the Vikings was accompanied by a great flowering of sculpture when native artists turned to the representation of Biblical and other subjects in stone crosses. Two of the sculptured Crosses at Monasterboice are among the finest in Ireland. The taller and older West Cross, dated about 923, is named for the Monasterboice Abbot Muireadach who "caused this Cross to be made." An easy visit from Dublin, the crosses are now included in the itineraries of thousands of tourists each year.

Surviving also is a literary monument of 11th century Monasterboice, the historical poems of the Abbot Flann. Fourteen of his works are extant in manuscript in old Gaelic books, especially in the *Book of Leinster*, works whose historical value, scholars claim, it would be hard to overestimate.

Kenney, 372; Porter, 28, 110; Skene, I: 135; Stokes, 15, 17; Simpson, 70; Moran, 167; Healy, 628.

Brigid (Bridget, Bride, Brigit)
February 1   C. 525

Brigid was beautiful, she was holy, she was beloved. After Patrick, Brigid of Kildare is the most famous of the Irish saints. Irish writers have called her "the Prophetess of Christ," "the Queen of the South," "the Mary of the Gael." Irish missionaries carried her name and devotion to Scotland, to England, to the Continent. Gougaud, writing in 1922, could still say, "The Saint of Kildare enjoys a remarkable popularity all over western Europe." There is a Bride's Peak in the Himalayan mountains, an island named Bride off the coast of Japan. One of the prettiest legends concerning the saint tells us that as St. Bride she was the patroness of the Knights of Chivalry, that they began the custom of calling the girls they married their brides and that from the Knights of Chivalry the word bride came into general usage in the English language. Brigid is rightly remembered as a model for women of every age.

Cogitosus and Ultan, her earliest biographers, writing more than a hundred years after her death, state that her father was Dubthach, a powerful pagan nobleman of Leinster. They do not agree concerning her mother, the Christian Brocessa, daughter of Dalbronach. One of them says Brocessa was of noble parentage, the other that she was a beautiful slave girl in Dubthach's household, banished to Faughart near Dundalk in County Louth before Brigid's birth. As for Brigid's early years in the home of a druid, her subsequent career suggests she may have been there in fosterage, the old Irish system of education.

In due time, Dubthach interested himself in a husband for his beautiful daughter, selecting for her "a man of chaste life, a poet." It was a high choice; poets in ancient Ireland ranked next to the king. But Brigid chose the religious life. Seven other girls, all in the white home-spun wool which became the distinctive garb of Irish nuns for centuries, came with her to make their vows before Bishops Mel and Macaille, a ceremony that inaugurated the first formal community of nuns in Ireland. Far from being a solitary, or leading a cloistered life, the white-robed Brigid (in the same home-spun báinin tweed featured in today's better dress shops) was a familiar figure coming and going on the historic Curragh of Kildare, famous even then as the place where the Irish kings raced their horses. She was an indefatigable traveller, organizing convents everywhere, obtaining freedom for captives, counselling the great of her day. Her feast day, February 1, is a Christianized pagan festival, Imbolc — one of the four great pagan festivals marking the beginnings of the four seasons.

Very little personal history can be found in any of the so-called Lives of Brigid. There is the strange anomaly that she is named for the pagan goddess Brigid. Writers such as J. F. Kenney and the archaeologist Macalister offer a very plausible explanation. In pagan Ireland Brigid was the Goddess of Fire and Song, a deity worshipped by the filid, the pagan poets. At the place afterwards named Kildare (Church of the Oak) from a tree believed to have been sacred to the druids, there was a pagan sanctuary with a perpetual fire, a pagan ritual fire. This sanctuary was tended by vestal virgins whose high priestess was regarded as an incarnation and successively bore the name Brigid. Macalister's theory is that the last of this succession, Brigid and her companions, accepted the Christian faith and Brigid in her new enthusiasm swept all before her, even to the tremendous feat of transforming the pagan sanctuary into a Christian shrine and of rededicating all of its pagan monuments into Christian memorials.

Along with her very name, all of the prerogatives of the pagan goddess fell to the Christian saint. Brigid became the special patroness of Irish schoolmen, especially seminarians. The great oak, rededicated under Christian auspices, was a cherished landmark long after it was reduced to a broken stump. Brigid's nuns tended Kildare's perpetual fire, a religious symbol unknown anywhere else in Ireland. It was maintained in a 20 foot enclosure at Kildare all through the centuries until the suppression of religious in the Reformation.

Brigid's charity to the poor knew no bounds. There was the time she was waiting in her father's chariot and handed over his sword to a leper that came begging and then tried tearfully to make the "mightily enraged" Dubthach see that it was because it *was* his best sword she wanted to give it to God. For just such openhandedness the pagan Dubthach had already threatened to sell her to the king of Leinster. But the king had been baptized and he said "Leave her alone, her merit before God is greater than ours." The King of Leinster gave Brigid the site for her convent at Kildare. Brigid never changed. After Bishop Conleth's death she gave the cherished vestments he had brought from Rome to a poor church that had no vestments. Another time her nuns had all in readiness for visiting prelates. But when beggars came clamoring at the convent gates, they got the choice repast. Fortunately, Blathe (January 29), the lay sister in charge of Brigid's kitchen, was a saint, too. And bread and bacon in Brigid's company were better than a banquet elsewhere.

The Book of Lismore tells that "the comradeship of the world's sons of reading was with Brigid" and that the Lord gave them through Brigid's prayer every perfect good they asked. The saint herself, according to Cogitosus, was trained in letters from childhood. It is believed that a prayer in the Irish language now preserved in the Burgundian Library at Brussels is of Brigid's authorship.

Kildare ranked with the greatest of the monastic centers of Ireland. Actually, it had two separate cloisters, side by side, one for the nuns, one for the monks, with Conleth the first resident abbot-bishop. It had its own great Book, the Kildare Gospels. Legend claims an angel brought the incomparable designs achieved in it by the Kildare scribes. This now lost masterpiece was seen and described in the 12th century by Gerald Cambrensis who, although notorious for maligning Ireland, declared the Book of Kildare was so beautiful it could only have been the work of angels.

Brigid was at first laid to rest in her own church at Kildare, in a casket of precious metals and jewels under a suspended golden crown at the right of the high altar. Later, in 835, because of the Norse marauders, for greater safety, the remains of Brigid, Colmcille and Patrick, we are told, were interred in one grave in Downpatrick, though there is no scholarly proof for this. Finally, three Irish knights who set out for the Holy land in 1283, carried with them the head of St. Brigid. The journey ended at Lumiar in Portugal. A stone in the wall of the ancient church three miles from Lisbon, records the coming of the knights and their internment therein. The Lumiar church enshrines the precious relic in a chapel to St. Brigid with a statue of the saint dressed in a white habit.

Brigid's popularity was not confined to Ireland. In Scotland in the 6th century, Nechtan-Mor "offered Abernathy to God and St. Brigid," making Brigid patroness over all the Abernathy territory, a designation that continued in Brechan when it became a separate diocese. Moran lists more than 20 dedications along the western coast and in the Orkneys. Brigid was the patroness of the great family of Douglas and St. Brigid's Church at Douglas was, until 1761, their burial place.

Brigid is also invoked in the ancient litany the 8th century English scholar Alcuin composed in Paris, a litany Charlemagne recited as part of his daily devotions. When Gunelda, sister of Harold the last Anglo-Saxon king of England, fled to Belgium, among the valuables she took with her was a cloak said to have been worn by Brigid. Authentication of the relic states that on her death in 1087, the princess willed Brigid's cloak along with a magnificent set of jewels to the Bruges Cathedral.

There are of record 19 pre-Reformation dedications to Brigid in England. The 1969 brochure of the now Episcopalian St. Bride's in Fleet Street, London, suggests it may have been the first place of Christian worship in London and that Bride herself may have paid a visit there. In 1205, the principal Court of the realm was held in St. Bride's. King John held his

Parliament there. The martyr Thomas-a-Becket was born in that parish and Cardinal Wolsey once served at St. Bride's. Bridewell Palace (named from the nearby holy well dedicated to Bride) was where Emperor Charles V was lodged on his visit to England in 1522. In 1764, George III called in Benjamin Franklin for advice when lightning struck the steeple; the two fell out over it.

Under the aura of the Irish patroness of poetry and learning there gathered English men of letters, hardly a writer of England missing in the annals of St. Bride's in Fleet Street. The first commercial printing press of London located close to St. Bride's because that was where the best customers were. After four centuries it is stated "History has made St. Bride's the focal point of print." The Communications building of Southern Illinois University has a broken angel retrieved from a destroyed former St. Bride's of Fleet Street, London.

"Devotion to Brigid in Europe," according to Abbe MacGeoghegan, "is evidenced by an Office of nine lessons in her honor found in several breviaries in Europe: in an ancient Roman one printed in Venice in 1522; in that of Gein in Italy; in that of the Regular Canons of the Lateran; in an ancient breviary of Quimper of Armorica; in a church bearing her name at Cologne; in a chapel dedicated to her at Fosse, diocese of Maestricht. An Office to Brigid is to be found in the breviaries and missals of Maestricht, Mayence, Würzburg, Constance, Treve, Strasburg and other towns of Germany." The Divine Office of Paris commemorated Brigid until the year 1607.

The French Gougaud in his *Gaelic Pioneers of Christianity* lists myriad dedications and memorials to Brigid. Beginning in long past centuries, he names Reichenau and Echternach; Nivelles, St. Gall, the St. Omer district; Walloon, Liege, and Cologne. He found Brigid's title "Protectress of Travellers" taken from the old Irish prayer of St. Moling, in a 15th century German Reisesegen. He relates the frustration and subsequent resignation of a new pastor of a little church in the Brittany countryside when he made the mistake of replacing an old badly deteriorated statue of Brigid of Kildare with a nice new one that turned out to be Bridget of Sweden.

Tommasini, in his list of memorials to Brigid of Kildare in Italy, also describes a confusion of dedication. A Piasco chapel that now honors the widow of Sweden, has a fresco depicting the saint that is earlier than the 14th century, and so is earlier than Bridget of Sweden. In the 14th century in a time of hail and frost disaster, the dioceses of Fossano, Monrovia and Saluzzo, at the persuasion of Blessed Oddino Barroti, chose as their protectress "St. Brigit, venerated in Ireland next after the Virgin Mother of God . . . and famous throughout the whole Latin Church." Tommasini enumerates the cities of Fossano and Pinerolo, a number of parishes, hospitals, some twelve churches and chapels in northern Italy of which Brigid of Kildare is the patron and which are dedicated in her name. In Rome, the Canons Regular of the Lateran name Patrick and Brigid members of their Order. St. Brigit's Church at Piacenza, built and personally endowed in honor of the saint by the Irish Donatus, Bishop of Fiesole, is a foundation which has been accorded privileged status for more than 1100 years. Among many historical events, the Peace of Constance was ratified within its doors by all the deputies of the Lombard League in 1185. In 1911, St. Brigit's was scheduled a national monument of Italy.

In 1807, when only "hedge schools" could teach the Catholic religion because of government restrictions, the Bishop of Kildare, Daniel Dulaney, founded the Congregation of St. Brigid, beginning with six catechists dedicated to Christian education. The Order has now grown to some 800 members. In 1884, after his appointment in Rome as Archbishop of Sydney, Australia, Cardinal Moran made a special trip to Cologne, a once famous center of Irish missionary activity, to obtain a relic of Brigid for his Brigidine nuns in Sydney. The Sisters are now organized in three provinces, one for Ireland and Britain, two for Australia and New Zealand. Since 1953, the Order has been in the United States, where a novitiate was established in San Antonio in 1960.

Kenney, 356–63; Macalister, 197; Gougaud; Curtayne; Moran, 173; Skene, I: 134; II, 136; Tommasini; *New Catholic Encyclopedia* 2: 803.

Cannera
January 28   C. 530

Irish sailors through the centuries have saluted at Cannera's resting place on Scattery Island (Inis Chathaigh). 16th century poetry invokes Cannera, patron of seamen, in Gaelic verse "Bless my good ship, protecting power of grace. . . ." Until modern times it was believed that pebbles from Scattery Island protected the bearer from shipwreck.

Cannera was a holy recluse with a cell near Bantry. Shortly before her death, a vision convinced her that Senan's church on Scattery was the holiest place in Ireland. She abandoned her cell at once and travelled without rest to arrive at Senan's foundation. He was adamant in his rule that no woman should enter his monastic enclosure. But Cannera won from him the promise he would give her Communion at her death and that he would have her interred on the extreme edge of the holy island. To Senan's objections that the waves would undermine her grave, Cannera replied she would leave that to Divine Providence and would not expect her remains to be disturbed by the sea. She died on that visit and at high tide, the brethren dug a trench for her grave. Today, the traditional spot of her burial, although washed by the tide, is not effaced.

Benedictine Monks, 126; O'Hanlon; *Catholic Encyclopedia*, XIII: 713.

Enda
March 21   C. 535

Enda of Aran, the patriarch of Irish monasticism, is described as a famous ex-warrior who abandoned the world in mature life. He had succeeded to the kingdom of his father, Conall Derg of Oriel, and was contemplating marriage with a lovely girl in his sister Fanchea's convent. She died suddenly and, soon after, Fanchea persuaded Enda to study for the priesthood. At her suggestion he went to Candida Casa, or Rosnat, in Galloway.

Sometime about 484, Enda obtained a grant of the Aran Islands from Aengus, King of Cashel, who was married to another of his sisters. Aengus would have settled him in a fertile spot in the Golden Vale. But the lonely, unproductive Aran islands were more to Enda's idea for a religious life. On Aran he lived a rule of astonishing severity with his monks. Fed and clothed by the labor of his hands, his day given to prayer, labor, sacred study, with only the scantiest of fare to sustain him, no fire ever tempering the stone cells, however cold — "if cold could be felt by those hearts so glowing with love of God" — such was the ideal the Irish monk set for himself.

Ryan in *Irish Monasticism* tells us "With Enda, as far as can be ascertained, monasticism in the strict sense (of embracing vows, complete seclusion from the world and a stern system of discipline) began in Ireland. How much he adopted without change from his teachers at Candida Casa is not clear, but there is reason to believe he did not rest content with slavish imitation. The organization at Aran had a character very much its own."

Many saints are named in Aran Annals. Brendan the Navigator took Enda's blessing with him on his great voyage. Others who came to Aran were: Finian whose school at Clonard later rivalled Enda's; Jarlath of Tuam; and Carthage the Elder of Saigher. Colmcille called Aran the Sun of the West, another pilgrim's Rome, under whose pure earth he would as soon be buried as close to the graves of Saints Peter and Paul. Five graves, two of them larger than the others, all of them covered with flagstones, lie side by side on the island of Aran. One of the headstones has the inscription "VII Romani" (Seven Romans). Britons, driven out of Britain by the Angles and the Saxons; Gauls, driven out of France by the Franks; and Romans, all took refuge in Ireland and continued to come to it in the centuries when Ireland was the haven of saints and scholars.

Enda lived out his long life on Aran, his abbot's quarters a cell of hard narrow stone. There he rests beside the sea, his grave sometimes exposed, sometimes covered by the shifting sands. Some hundred and twenty seven saints he loved and taught and sanctified surround him. Aengus in his *Féilire* (Saints' Calendar) says it will never be known until the day of judgment the countless number of saints whose remains are mingled with the soil of Aran.

Ryan; Butler-Attwater, I: 656; Healy, 164; Kenney, 373.

Munchin
January 2   ? Sixth century

Under Munchin and succeeding abbots, Mungret attained a reputation for no less than 1500 brethren within its cloisters. (According to the *Tripartite Life*, Mungret goes back to St. Patrick, who founded it for the youth Nesson whom he ordained deacon.)

A munster saying "as wise as the women of Mungret" recalls the strategem resorted to by Munchin's community when challenged to a test of erudition by another monastic school. Fearing to be worsted in the encounter, the men of Mungret dressed some of the young monks as women and set them washing clothes in a stream that crossed the approach to the college. The ladies conversed only in Latin interspersed with Greek. And when the astounded opposing team saw even the women so learned, they retired from further confrontation, leaving the victory to "the women of Mungret."

Munchin presided at Mungret for many years. In his old age he retired to a cell, and an oratory called Kill-Munchin near which eventually grew up the city of Limerick. Two of Munchin's sisters had convents adjoining his monastery, Rose of Kilrush, and the more famous Lelia, or Liadhain, of Killely, commemorated August 11.

Cormac MacCullinan in 908 bequeathed to Mungret three ounces of gold, an embroidered vestment and his blessing. In 1102, another scholar, Mugron O'Morgair, St. Malachy's father and chief lector at Armagh, died at Mungret and was buried there. St. Munchin's church in Limerick lost cathedral status in 1180 when Donal O'Brien, King of Thomond, built the existing (now Protestant) St. Mary's Cathedral. It is of interest for the tomb slabs of Donal O'Brien and other personages and for the mutilations of Cromwell's time when his troops stabled their horses in it. It is especially notable for its surviving original 19 prebendaries stalls and the fanciful, wonderfully rich carvings that support the misericords — mute witness to the artistry lavished upon Ireland's churches before the devastations of the Reformation. They are believed to date from the time of Bishop John Folan in 1489.

The Mungret school declined under the Viking raids, came to an end with the advent of the Anglo-Normans, but true to form, it has arisen again. Since 1884, Mungret has been a Jesuit institution. There are two churches of Saint Munchin in Limerick City: St. Munchin's Catholic Church and the now Protestant St. Munchin's (Church of Ireland), Castle Street, which was the Cathedral of Limerick before the foundation of St. Mary's. Within the Castle Street St. Munchin's may be seen the original stone Bishop's Throne with the arms of the diocese of Limerick carved upon it.

Healy, 506; Benedictine Monks, 432; Bulfin, 251.

Mobhi
October 12   C. 545

Neeson tells us Berchan was the saint's real name, that Mobhi was a nickname, with "Mo," the Gaelic term denoting endearment (prefixed to the names of many Irish saints). Mobhi was one of Finian's earlier disciples at Clonard. Although less well known than others so designated, his name comes down as one of the "twelve apostles of Ireland." It was routine in his time for seminarians or newly ordained clergy to spend periods of varying duration with different outstanding abbots and to Mobhi at Glasnevin came four of Ireland's future greatest saints, Colmcille, Comgall, Kieran of Clonmacnoise, Cainnech of Aghaboe. A tradition pictures Colmcille and his companions, in a time of high flood waters, swimming the river Tolka to vespers in the church on the other side. Mobhi died of the plague about 545 and his foundation did not survive long after.

Neeson, 92; Kenney, 716; Graham, 39; Healy, 296; McManus, 161.

Kieran of Clonmacnoise
September 9   C. 545

> In a quiet watered land, a land of roses,
>   Stands Saint Kieran's city fair;
> And the warriors of Erin in their famous generations
>   Slumber there.
>
> There beneath the dewey hillside sleep the noblest
>   Of the clan of Conn.
> Each below his stone with name in branching Ogham
>   And the sacred knot thereon.

> There they laid the seven kings of Tara,
>   There the sons of Cairbre sleep —
> Battle-banners of the Gael that in Kieran's plain
>   of crosses
>   Now their final hosting keep.
>
> And at Clonmacnoise they laid the men of Teffia,
>   And right many a lord of Breagh;
> Deep the sod above Clan Creide and Clan Conaill
>   Kind in hall and fierce in fray.
>
> Many and many a son of Conn the Hundred-Fighter
>   In the red earth lies at rest;
> Many a blue eye of Clan Colman the turf covers,
>   Many a swan-white breast.

For long centuries, Clonmacnoise was a living monument to Kieran. Kings endowed it, scholars taught at it, saints followed in Kieran's footsteps. At Clonmacnoise, says Father Cotter, there are more saints slumbering than ever made illustrious the pavements of the Coliseum.

Kieran's birthplace was in Connacht. He was tutored from boyhood by the deacon Justus and received his later training at Clonard under Finian, who offered him the master's chair, and at Aran under Enda, who wept when he blessed him in the farewell parting.

Clonmacnoise is where the ancient chariot road through Ireland crosses the Shannon. As Kieran set about his building there, Diarmuid MacCearbhail came sailing down the river and Kieran called to him "Come to me for you are a king and mark out the church and offer the harbor to me." "I am not a king," Diarmuid told him. The saint replied prophetically, "You will be king tomorrow." Four centuries later, Clonmacnoise artists in stone sculptured on the Cross of the Scriptures the kilted prince and the tonsured saint with their hands joined in setting the first stake.

After only seven months (Macalister says seven years) Kieran died of the plague. But his name and his memory hovered blessedly over Clonmacnoise. His Eclais Beg, or Little Church, in which he was buried became one of the most sacred spots in Ireland. The Imda Chieran, or cow-skin, that had been his bed was one of its holiest relics.

Kieran's father, Beoit, was a chariot-maker from Antrim; his mother the Kerry-born Darerca. And this background of moderately gentle birth, of northern and southern parentage, guided the policy of his school which drew its abbots from different sections and more often than not from the craftsman class. After Armagh, Clonmacnoise was the greatest of the monastic schools of Ireland, laying claim through the league of churches of which it was the head, to ecclesiastical rule over half of Ireland. As a center of learning and literature, it played an equally important part in the amalgamation of secular and ecclesiastical, Gaelic and Latin, and in the preservation both of old Irish literature and of records of national events. The Book of the Dun Cow, the Annals of Tighernach (Tierney), the Annals of Clonmacnoise, all were compiled within its walls.

Important names at Clonmacnoise were legion. Fogartach (Fogarty), the Sage of Clonmacnoise, was one of those commemorated with an important sculptured Cross. There was Arno, who succeeded Virgilius as bishop of Salzburg in Austria; Colgu the Wise, teacher of Alcuin, England's scholar at the court of Charlemagne. Graham identifies Suibhne (Sweeney), teacher of geographer Dicuil, as abbot of Clonmacnoise who died in 810. (Dicuil's works, finished about 825, were published in Paris in the early 19th century from a manuscript preserved in the Imperial Library in Paris. Information in it, said to be found nowhere else, about the Nile and a canal to the Red Sea, came from 8th century Irish pilgrims to Jerusalem; data on Iceland was given to Dicuil by Irish monks who had been there before the year 825.)

In the belief that Kieran would bring safely to heaven the souls of all those buried in his holy churchyard, "those of the royal blood divided it among themselves." King Diarmuid made large grants to Clonmacnoise in thanksgiving for a victory over Guaire, stipulating that no king of Meath forever might take so much as a drink of water therefrom without paying for it. Diarmuid and Guaire are both buried at Clonmacnoise. For 10th century Flann who built the great stone cathedral at Clonmacnoise, the abbot erected as his tombstone the famous Cross of the Scriptures. Connacht King Fergal O'Rourke built the oldest now existing part of the round tower. Eleventh century Conchobar, asking to be buried at Clonmacnoise, brought his gift of many townlands. King Ó Ceallaigh (O'Kelly) about 1167 added a sepulchral chapel for his family, and handsome endowments. Dervorgilla erected the beautiful Celtic Romanesque Nuns Church. Ireland's last High Kings, Turlough and Roderick O'Connor, generous patrons like all the other royal occupants, lie buried in Clonmacnoise.

Clonmacnoise suffered greatly in the two centuries of Viking incursions. In one of them, Turgesius the Dane, having chosen Armagh for himself, installed his wife Ota as priestess to deliver oracles on the high altar of the next most important place in Ireland, Clonmacnoise. But in spite of the Danes, and the aftermath of internal political disorders that brought fresh troubles, Clonmacnoise rebuilt to new heights and to a preëminence as a school of Celtic art. It was not permanently impaired until the advent of the Anglo-Normans, whose repeated plunderings, begun in 1178, reduced the fine old monastery to poverty and obscurity. Finally, a thousand years after its founding, the soldiers of Elizabeth completed the destruction of Kieran's City. The real treasure, the faith it had nurtured, remained beyond their reach.

Ryan; Kenny; Porter; Stokes; Healy; McManus, 217; Graham, 174.

Finian of Clonard
December 12   c. 549

With Enda of Aran, Finian stands at the head of the patriarchs of Irish monasticism. He founded Clonard about 520.

Born into Leinster nobility, Finian studied for many years under Fortchern, grandson of King Laoghaire. He also spent some time with a holy recluse, Coemhan, on an island in Wexford harbor.

Irish tradition claims Finian enrolled, or visited, at the monasteries of two celebrated abbots of Wales who had Irish ties. They were David of Menevia who had been baptized by Ailbhe of Emly, and Cadoc of Llancarfan whose teacher was the Irish Tathai. Clonard is older than Llancarfan but Finian is believed to have patterned his Rule on the Lerins tradition of strict observance he learned, or saw, at Llancarfan.

It is certain that Finian corresponded with Gildas on matters of monastic discipline, Gildas of the diatribe against the British bishops of his day: Gildas believed that the worldly position, wealth and power then attaching to the episcopal office were great obstacles to perfection.

Whether because of the influence of Gildas on Finian, or as a natural outgrowth of the Irish inclination to the monastic life and the Irish political formation into small kingdoms, the Irish church became monastic rather than episcopal in government, a departure from the ordinary hierarchy established by Patrick.

Finian was a bishop as well as abbot, but some of his greatest abbot-disciples chose never to advance above priestly Orders. Of lesser importance than the abbot, monastic bishops, along with the abbot, lived the life of the brethren. The monastic concept of the episcopal office was that a bishop should be a saint, not a ruler.

Clonard was one of Ireland's all-time great monastic schools, and Finian trained up so many of Ireland's greatest saints he was called the Tutor of Saints. Twelve of his outstanding disciples were named the twelve apostles of Ireland: Kieran of Saigher, Kieran of Clonmacnoise, Brendan the Navigator, Brendan of Birr, Colm of Iona, Colm of Terryglass, Molaise, Canise, Ruadhan, Mobhi, Sinnell and Ninidh of Inismacsaint. But it is an elastic dozen. Kieran of Saigher was earlier than Finian, and added for good measure are Finian himself, Finian of Moville and Comgall of Bangor.

Clonard had a long tenure. Migne's *Patrology* contains an excerpt from the writings of Clonard's 7th century Aileran. The old monastery survived Danish onslaughts, native strife, the Norman aggressions, all the way to the 16th century suppression of the Catholic faith by the English.

Now in the Protestant church of Clonard are two antiquities from by-gone days: an 11th century eight-panelled grey marble baptismal font with sculptured scriptural figures, and a head-shaped stone, once a corbel in the abbey, now inserted in the church tower over the door. Gone are all traces of Finian's tomb, all traces of his church. Not even a broken arch or a ruined wall survive to speak of the great Clonard.

Ryan; Healy, 193–208; Benn, 61; Migne, 80: 328.

Colm (Terryglass)
December 13   c. 549

Senach (March 8), who became Finian's successor at Clonard, was often sent by the abbot to make the rounds of the seminarians to see what each was doing. Senach told him about finding one of them kneeling in prayer, oblivious to all about him with his hands stretched to heaven and the birds came and lighted on his shoulders. "He it is," said Finian "who will offer the Holy Sacrifice for me at my death."

The youth was Colm, son of Crimthann of Leinster nobility, and fellow-student of the more famous Colm of Iona, at Finian's great monastic school at Clonard. Colm founded Clonenagh where his disciple Fintan stayed on to become a famous abbot. He founded Iniscaltra (Holy Island, in the Shannon) that is more noted in connection with Caimin. Near to Iniscaltra was Terryglass, a beloved retreat to which Colm often retired for prayer, and where he founded a monastery before his death of the plague in 549. This, too, like his other foundations was soon an important home of religion.

Ryan; Benedictine Monks, 148; Healy, 202, 401, 513.

Gobnait
February 11   Sixth century

At Ballyvourney in County Cork there are many interesting memorials to Gobnait, the nun who from her time to this has always been one of the best known and revered of the saints of Munster.

In 1602, in the historic retreat of O'Sullivan Beare to the territory of O'Rourke of Brefney, he and his fighting men, women, children and servants, paused at Ballyvourney to pay homage to the memory of Gobnait. Until 1843, a 13th century wooden statue of the saint was in the hereditary keepership of the O'Herlihy family. Since 1601, the year Clement VIII authorized the celebration of Gobnait's feast day in the parish church, Ballyvourney accords very special display to its much worn likeness of the saint on February 11. In the churchyard, discarded crutches and other mementoes at her grave bespeak continuing answers to prayer through Gobnait's intercession.

Tradition holds Gobnait was born in County Clare. She was in the Aran islands where a church is still named for her on Inisheer, when at the bidding of an angel she set out for "the place of her resurrection." Near Ballyvourney she recognized the spot by the nine white deer grazing there, the sign the angel had given her. Practical arrangements cooperated. St. Abban came into that rugged country anciently ruled by the O'Herlihys, was given a grant of land in their district and chose Gobnait to govern the convent he founded for women.

Famous among the miracles of Gobnait's prayer was the staying of a pestilence by marking off the parish as consecrated ground. Another tradition is that she routed an enemy by loosing her bees upon them. Down long centuries, Gobnait's beehive was a precious relic of the O'Herlihys. The Deborahs may claim February 11 as their name day: Gobnait in Gaelic is the equivalent of the Hebrew Deborah which means Honey Bee.

1959 *Capuchin Annual*; O'Hanlon, II: 462; Sullivan, 315; Neeson, 41; Benedictine Monks, 269.

Jarlath
June 6   c. 550

The prelates of Tuam wear a ring engraved with a broken chariot wheel, Jarlath's chariot wheel of 1400 years ago. Still further back, the saint's ancestry is traced to Fergus MacRoy, the warrior romanticized into Irish epic literature.

Patrick taught Benen and Benen taught Jarlath and placed him at Clonfuis. Jarlath's pupils there numbered Brendan the Navigator and Colman MacLenini, later of Cloyne. Brendan told Jarlath he was not to remain at Clonfuis but should go eastward and where his chariot wheel should break, there he was to build his church. It broke at Tuam.

Jarlath's school at Tuam, founded about 520, rivalled Clonmacnoise as a center of Celtic art in the 11th and 12th centuries. Tuam's High Cross in the market square ranks with the finest of such monuments remaining in Ireland.

On the site of Jarlath's original church, the now Protestant cathedral was rebuilt in the 19th century, "in an attempt" at the fine old Celtic workmanship of the cathedral built by King Turlough O'Conor in the 12th century, remnants of which survive.

Ryan, 107; Butler-Attwater, II: 489; Benedictine Monks, 317; Healy, 542; Benn, 196.

Colman (Dromore)
June 7   c. 550

There are more than 200 Colmans in the long roll of Irish saints. Colman (Mo-Cholmóg), the first abbot-bishop of Dromore, seems to have spent his entire life in County Down but nevertheless to have exerted wide influence through his disciples.

His teachers were Ailbhe of Emly and Coelan (otherwise called Mo-Choe) of Nendrum. He went to MacNisse for advice when he was founding his church at Dromore. At Nendrum, while still a student himself, Coelan gave him charge of the younger boys, among them Finian, the future abbot of Movilla.

Whether Colman ever made missionary expeditions into Scotland and Wales, or whether his many Dromore missionary monks carried his discipline and schooling with them, at least two churches were named for him: Inis mo-Cholmaig in Scotland and Llangolman in Wales. His name is entered in ancient Calendars of both Scotland and Ireland.

The medieval Cathedral of St. Colman, burned down in 1641 in the religious troubles of the period, had stood on the site of the ancient monastery of St. Colman. Today the Protestant Cathedral of Christ the King occupies the site and contains an old gravestone to which tradition assigns the name "St. Colman's pillow," thus recalling Tommasini's remark "The Irish monks rivalled the solitaries of the desert in the asceticism of their lives and the rigor of their discipline."

Ryan; Butler-Attwater, II: 493; Healy, 143; Tommasini, 53; Neeson, 109; Benn, 115.

Ninnidh
January 18   Sixth century

Ninnidh, afterwards revered as one of the apostles of Ireland, is first heard of on the Curragh at Kildare, late for classes and in such a hurry he didn't have time to talk to Brigid — he was running to heaven, he said, and the gates might be closed against him if he didn't hurry. But Brigid made him stop and kneel with her to pray that she might get to heaven too. When Brigid was dying she sent for Ninnidh to give the last Sacraments to her.

Another story has come down from Ninnidh's seminary days under Finian at Clonard. When they were learning the Gospel of St. Matthew, Ninnidh borrowed the text from his fellow student, Kieran of Clonmacnoise, with the result at class time Kieran knew only the first half of the Gospel. The boys called him Kieran Half-Matthew. Finian, however, said "Not Kieran Half-Matthew, but Kieran Half-Ireland, for he will have half of Ireland while the rest of us share the other half."

Ninnidh's island retreat of Inishmacsaint in Lough Erne in Fermanagh has ruins of a church, an ancient cross 13 feet high, and other remains of earthworks and foundations that point to a monastic settlement of considerable extent and importance. It is believed to have continued until the 12th century. Eleven miles south of Enniskillen lies Knockninny (the Hill of Ninnidh), a little over 600 feet in height, with a holy well dedicated to the saint. This hill was the seat of the powerful McGuire family, one of whom, the layman Conor McGuire, Baron of Inniskillen, was executed for the faith at Tyburn in 1645.

Ryan, 118; Benedictine Monks, 435; O'Hanlon, January 18; Neeson, 25.

Sinell, Cleenish
November 12   Sixth century

The monastery and hospice Sinell founded on Cleenish Island in Lough Erne in Fermanagh survived until the 12th century. He was one of that group of holy men (Ireland called them her twelve apostles) who handed on, with so great a harvest, the sanctity and learning acquired under Finian at Clonard.

Even in that period of asceticism, Cleenish was unparalleled for the severity of its rule and for the more frugal and more unpalatable than usual fare for the brethren, rigors which in no way discouraged applicants. Before he enrolled at Bangor, Columban came first to learn of Sinell at Cleenish.

Ryan, 175; Healy, 372; Neeson, 199; McManus, 238.

Phelim (Felim)
August 9   c. 560

Dubthach, the chief poet of Ireland and the first of the druids to rise to honor Patrick at Tara, was the great grandfather of Phelim, one of six brothers, all in religion. Colmcille schooled him for the church.

Kilmore grew up around Phelim's hermitage. He is designated a bishop although Kilmore was not a see until 1454. Phelim's original church, rebuilt at that time and known as St. Phelim's Cathedral was later taken over by the Protestants and is now used as a hall. In front of it, in 1858, the present edifice, used as the Protestant Cathedral of Kilmore, was built, incorporating in it a fine old 13th century Romanesque doorway brought from the Abbey of Trinity Island in Lough Oughter. The historian, Aubrey Gwynn, S.J., believes that this doorway came from an earlier establishment somewhere near Lough Oughter. The present Kilmore Catholic Cathedral of SS. Patrick and Phelim was opened in 1942, in Cavan town, five miles from Kilmore.

Kilmore diocese, about the year 680, gave Kilian to Franconia (now in Bavaria). During the Penal years, a Catholic bishop of Kilmore, Andrew Campbell, was a skilled bagpipe performer, and he used that subterfuge to go about administering to his people. His portrait, done in oils and now hanging in the dining room of the diocesan college at Cavan, shows the bishop in kilt and tartan with his bagpipes.

O'Hanlon Aug. 9; *Catholic Encyclopedia VIII*: 643; Butler, VIII: 343; Benn, 59.

Senan
March 8   c. 560

Of some 22 Seanans listed in the Irish calendars, the most celebrated was Senan of Inis Cathaigh, or Scattery Island.

Archaeologists say that Senan should be named in the same company as Ibar, Brigid, Ailbhe, perhaps MacCartan. Senan took under Christian auspices the water of the great river Sinaan, now the Shannon. In pagan days Senan was a river god with his sanctuary on Inis Cathaigh, so named from the dragon-like creature the pagan Senan had expelled. It is believed that in Christian times, the Christian saint who was afterwards called Senan, and who was the founder of the church of Inis Cathaigh, turned Inis Cathaigh from a pagan to a Christian shrine, but in doing so he fell heir to the name of the god he overthrew.

Senan's school on Inis Cathaigh was highly regarded. Old records say that, in the year 563, there arrived in Ireland from the Continent a company of 50 students and seminarians who, separating into bands of ten, enrolled at the monasteries of Finian, Brendan of Clonfert, Finbarr, Kieran and Senan. Another ancient entry tells that Kieran of Clonmacnoise sent a monastic habit as a gift to Senan at Inis Cathaigh.

The Abbot-Bishop Senan died and was buried at his Inis Cathaigh monastery which continued to be the seat of a bishop until 1189. There were once as many as eleven churches on the island and the Keanes of County Clare were the hereditary keepers of the Clogán Óir, or Golden Bell of St. Senan, now in the National Museum. The island is now known for its fine ruins and its impressive round tower.

. Ryan; Kenney, 364; Moran, 178; *Catholic Encyclopedia* XIII: 713; Fitzpatrick, I: 53, 220; Stokes, 52; Benn, 13.

Molaise (Devenish)
August 12   c. 563

One of Ireland's holy places is Devenish Island, a green dot in Lough Erne in Fermanagh. Standing guard there is its round tower, one of the finest in all Ireland, described by de Blacam "as sturdy as if the saints built it yesterday, its stones shaped with flawless curves that are a marvel still." Mingling with the island soil is the blood of martyrs in earth Molaise brought to it from the Colosseum in Rome. He ruled his church and school on Devenish from about 530. It flourished until the Anglo-Normans.

Molaise of Devenish gives his name to the oldest of Ireland's surviving cumdachs, the book shrine made to enclose manuscript Gospels. An inscription which runs around the bottom of the box dates it between the years 1001–1025. On the face of the jewel-studded casket with its handsome clasp, are representations of the four evangelical figures, the names of three of which, Leo, Aquila, Homo, can still be deciphered along with Mark, Johan, Math. Over the centuries the shrine containing the manuscript of Molaise of Devenish was in the keepership of successive generations of the O'Meehans. Since 1859 it has been in the National Museum, Dublin.

In Irish catalogues there are 16 saints named Laserian, or Molaise, with the prefix Mo, a term of endearment used as a prefix in many saints' names.

Ryan, 123, 175; de Blacam, 64; Porter, 41; Stokes, 74; Benn, 153; *Catholic Encyclopedia*, VIII: 643; MacLysaght, 225.

Ita (Deirdre)
January 15   570

A beautiful legend claims that the Infant Jesus appeared to Ita and that the old Irish poem attributed to her is a lullaby she sang for Jesukin, her name for the Divine Child. Two translations of the Gaelic poem are given in Hoagland's *1000 Years of Irish Poetry*.

Confidence in Ita's intercession was unbounded. Cornwall dedicated churches and chapels to her. Ancient litanies on the Continent invoked her name. It appears in Alcuin's poem on the Irish saints.

Foster Mother of the Saints of Erin, the Brigid of Munster, Ita (said to denote Thirst for Divine Love), all are titles given Deirdre, the Irish girl of royal blood of Waterford, afterwards the holy abbess of Killeedy (Cell of Ita) in County Limerick.

This foster mother of the saints enrolled very young boys in her convent and many of them were afterwards saints, among them Brendan the Navigator. A beautiful window in the St. Brendan Cathedral in Loughrea pictures a gentle stately Ita with the baby Brendan and an angel playing at her feet.

Unlike Brigid's and Attracta's convents that continued for centuries, Ita's convent at Killeedy when next heard of after her death, was a monastery for men. A well and the ruins of a Romanesque church in Killeedy occupy the presumed site of her monastery. In the ruins lies Ita's grave which, even today, is frequently decorated with flowers. A few miles away is Boolaveeda (St. Ita's milking place), an ancient enclosure.

Kenney, 389; O'Hanlon, I: 201; II: 719; Ryan, 138; Mould, 196; Butler-Attwater, I: 96.

Brendan (Birr)
November 29   c. 571

Brendan of Birr, like Brendan of Clonfert, came of the race of Fergus MacRoy which was said to have produced more heroes and more saints than any other of the Celtic septs.

Kenney mentions, from an incomplete ancient text, that a wonderful flower from the Land of Promise was seen by the twelve apostles of Ireland who were then together at Finian's school at Clonard. Brendan of Birr was chosen by lot to go in search of that land but, as he was old, Brendan of Clonfert went in his place.

The little that is known of the founder of Birr assigns him a high place among his contemporaries. Mention of him occurs especially in connection with Colmcille. And when Brendan of Birr died, Colmcille in a vision saw the soul of his friend carried by angels to heaven. He said a special Mass of requiem for Brendan at Iona.

The School of Birr was still in operation in the 9th century as is known from the Irish book now in the Bodleian library, the *Gospels of MacRegal* (scribe and bishop, abbot of Birr, who died in 822). The manuscript of the four gospels, in the Irish type of text and described as a wonderfully rich and beautiful example of illumination, is of very elaborate ornamentation of purely Irish character.

Ryan; Kenney, 417, 641; Healy, 522; New Catholic Encyclopedia, 8: 641.

Finian (Moville)
September 10   C. 575

Nendrum Abbey on Mahee Island (the modern form of Mochaoi, former abbot of the abbey) in County Down was Finian's first school and his teacher was an older seminarian, Colman, later of Dromore. It happened that the abbot of Rosnat in North Britain came on a visit to Mochaoi and when he departed Finian went with him. He was in Scotland some 20 years, first as a student, afterwards as a missionary.

The Scottish historian Simpson traces Finian's wide-ranging activity along the east coast of Scotland into Pictland as far north as Dornoch. He notes dedications in Finian's name in Ayreshire, in Angus, and in Caithness. Before returning to Ireland, Finian made a pilgrimage to Rome. In about 540, he founded Moville in County Down in an area dotted with religious communities. Bangor was only five miles away. And scarcely less distinguished than Comgall of Bangor was Finian of Moville.

Finian had procured precious biblical manuscripts in Rome, and the Martyrology of Aengus records that Finian was the first to bring the Mosaic Law to Ireland. It was in his monastery at Dromin that his former pupil, Colmcille, transcribed that "preciously conceived" manuscript, the *Psalter* now in the Irish Academy, Dublin. More generally known as the *Cathach of the O'Donnells*, it is one of the great treasures of ancient Irish Christian art.

Moville was long one of Ireland's most flourishing schools. An 11th century alumnus, Marianus Scotus, became the famous incluse of Fulda and Mainz (Germany) where he penned his *Chronicle of the World*. Finian's still extant penetential *Code*, made up of 53 canons for his monks, and important as one of the earliest records of the primitive Irish church, was published in 1851 from manuscripts found in the libraries of St. Gall, Paris, and Vienna. Monastic ruins at Moville are of interest for the several fine 10th to 13th century grave-slabs with foliated crosses which have been built into the north wall.

Finian has been identified with Fridian of Lucca but it is Irish tradition that he "sleeps among miracles in his own city of Moville."

Kenney, 390; Simpson, 65; Ryan, 106, 125; Healy, 245; Butler-Attwater, III: 531; *Benn*, 114.

Brendan (Clonfert)
May 16   C. 583

Brendan's ancestry went back to Fergus MacRoy, the king whose prowess was embellished into Irish mythology. The story of Brendan's own exploits, handed down in the *Navigatio Brendani*, was widely circulated and read in the whole of Europe throughout the middle ages. It is at least possible that Brendan landed in America long before either Christopher Columbus or Leif Erickson. Cartographers relinquished his Isle of the Blest only in the 15th century.

Bishop Erc claimed Brendan as his special charge and when he was only a year old, saw to it he was handed over to the young nun Ita, afterwards famous for the number of young boys she started on the way to sainthood. Erc himself tutored Brendan from the age of six until he was ready for the priesthood and the customary round of other great abbots, Jarlath of Tuam, Finian of Clonard, Enda of Aran. Erc blessed his going but admonished him "Come back to me that you may receive priestly Orders from my hands before I die." In due time Erc ordained Brendan at Tralee. Erc and Ita are remembered in connection with the monastery Brendan founded in Tobernamolt, a few miles from Ardfert in County Kerry. A holy well there is attributed to Ita's prayer and it was with water from that well that Erc baptized Brendan.

The saint's foundation at Clonfert became one of Ireland's great monastic schools. The convent he founded at Annaghdown for his sister Briga was the origin of an important religious center and the Annaghdown Cathedral which was long the chief church of the O'Flaherty Country. One of Brendan's monks was the first to contrive a cell on Skellig Michael with its Way of the Cross and 600 steps at the edge of the stone cliff. To the saint's foundation on the island of Inchiquin came Fursey whose visions would rival Brendan's travels. There was also a Brendan church on Inisglora (County Mayo, near Belmullet), the burial place of the Children of Lir, immortals of Irish mythology. One of the finest existing monuments to Ireland's past is the magnificent Irish Romanesque doorway of the Clonfert Cathedral, the successor to the church Brendan founded there in 558.

A mirage that is still supposed to be seen at intervals out in the western ocean from Ireland was from the most ancient times believed to mirror a fabulous, beautiful Island of Paradise called Hy-Brasil. A wonderful flower from that Land of Promise is said to have been seen by the twelve apostles of Ireland then together at Clonard, and Brendan was chosen to go in search of that heaven on earth. He was not at first successful. But, back in Ireland a crew of 60 men made ready again with sturdy boats and 40 days of fasting and prayer for another voyage, the account of which became the prime travelogue of the middle ages. It traces them in the Orkneys, in Wales, in the Scottish Isles. And to a land luxuriant with fruit and flowers the description of which convinces students of the Brendan legend that he actually sailed down the east coast of America to Florida, a feat not at all impossible in light of the Kon-Tiki and other voyages of our time. Thirty-five years before the Norwegians in the year 860 "discovered" Iceland and found Irish books, bells and staffs there, Dungal wrote of conversations with Irish monks who had spent the summer months there. And in 1966, William Verity of Fort Lauderdale made a solo voyage from Florida to Ireland in a 12 foot wooden sloop. His purpose was "to show that ancient man was capable of making a voyage from America to Europe and to put the Brendan legend in working order." Verity repeated this feat in reverse, Ireland to America, in 1969.

The epic *Navigatio Brendani* — "the Odyssey of the old Irish Church" — was translated into French, English, German, Flemish, Spanish and Italian and is to be found in all the great libraries of Europe. The oldest copies are one in Latin from the 11th or 12th century and one in French dated 1125. Old maps all showed Brendan's island — "The Fortunate Isle," "Hy-Brasil," "Land of Promise of the Saints," "San Brendan." In 1375 the Catalonian Chart located it southwest of Ireland. The Herford Chart placed it among the Canary Islands. The Pizzigani Map of 1367, the Wiemer Chart of 1424, the Chart of Beccario in 1435, substituted it for the Island of Madeira. Martin Behaim moved it back to the west of Ireland.

Christopher Columbus was educated at the University of Pavia, the precursor of which was the flourishing liberal arts school founded by the Emperor Lothaire "under the superintendance" of the Irish Dungal about 825. And in 1492 Columbus sailed to Galway to search out traditions and records of Brendan — a fact of record in the National Archives of Madrid, according to George Little, together with the names of Irishmen on the roster of the Santa Maria on the voyage to America.

Some 3000 monks in Brendan's communities looked to him as their head. Moinenn (March 1), companion in all the projects, was the disciple chosen by the saint to rule Clonfert, his final effort and his crowning glory. One of his converts was Colman MacLenini, the royal bard of Cashel, who became the bishop-founder of Cloyne. Another was one Crossan, a man of irreligious life, won by Brendan to a blessed peace at the last. Crossan asked wonderingly "What of good have I ever done to have earned this death?"

Brendan died at Annaghdown and was buried in his Clonfert Cathedral (now Protestant). The present Catholic St. Brendan's Cathedral at Loughrea is a treasury of Irish art with a mosaic ship in the floor of the sanctuary and 32 pictures sculptured in stone to tell the story of Brendan's life.

Daniel-Rops, 7, 11; Kenney, 408, 415; Little, 191; Healy, 210; Benedictine Monks, 114; Graham, 178.

Ruadhan (Rúán)
April 15   c. 584

Ruadhan was one of the great men Finian of Clonard trained and one of the disciples commemorated by posterity as the "twelve apostles of Ireland." Thirteenth century ruins at Lorrha in north Tipperary mark the site of his abbey which flourished down to the advent of the Anglo-Normans. In its time it was one of the greatest monasteries in Munster and great wonders came to be attributed to it.

Within Lorrha's walls in the 9th century was compiled the manuscript known as the *Stowe Missal*, one of the most valued of surviving great books of ancient Ireland. It received its misnomer from its centuries later sojourn in the Duke of Buckingham's Stowe library.

The "Stowe" missal offers wide ranging study: illumination for the artist, history for the antiquarian, paleography for the student of that science and, for liturgy scholars, the question whether it represents the ancient Patrician liturgy or the later Mass from Candida Casa. The Cumdach, or book shrine, for the Lorrha Missal dates from sometime between the years 1023–1052. It was commissioned by Donagh, son of Brian Boru, and is the work of Dunchad, a silversmith "of the family of Cluain," as is known from its inscription.

Just how the old Missal survived the dissolution of the Lorrha monastery is not known nor are its subsequent travels clear. One account says it was found in the wall of the ruins of the O'Kennedy Castle at Lackeen a few miles away about 1735. Another itinerary takes it to the Irish monastery at Ratisbon in Austria; in 1784 into the possession of John Grace, an Irish officer in the Austrian army; from the Grace family to the Duke of Buckingham for his library and eventually back home to Ireland, to the Royal Irish Academy.

Many modern writers on Irish history perpetuate the romantic story of Ruadhan's cursing of Tara and its subsequent desertion. The tale relates that Aed Guaire, a king of Connacht, decapitated an emissary of the High King Diarmuid and then fled to Ruadhan for sanctuary. Notwithstanding the protection of sanctuary, Diarmuid dragged Aed Guaire forth and the whole of the saints of Ireland converged upon Tara to join with Ruadhan in maledictions upon Diarmuid and upon Tara. The most intriguing incident of all is attributed to St. Brendan. We are told Brendan negotiated with Diarmuid for the release of Aed Guaire in exchange for fifty horses with blue eyes and golden bridles. But the horses were in reality seals metamorphosed for the occasion by Brendan, seals that a year and a half later resumed their former shape in the middle of a horse race.

Writers such as Father John Ryan, S.J., Eoin MacNeill, former Professor of Ancient History in the National University of Ireland, and others cite the many anachronisms and other features which should suffice to warn any reader from taking the story of the cursing of Tara for serious history. Aed Guaire is unknown to history. Some of the saints named were dead at the time and others still in their childhood. The High King is pictured as a god-king of sacred person, protected by the magic of the druids still present at Tara. The archaeologist Macalister would assess the half-pagan extravaganza as a parable of the despairing rage of the ancient gods at the usurpation of their thrones by the teachers of a new Faith. With the advent of Christianity, it followed that the pagan prestige of Tara gradually declined; after Diarmuid the great druidic assemblies were discontinued. Ruadhan died in 584. Tara continued to be a royal residence. Both a son and grandson of Diarmuid came to the throne of Tara and, concludes Macalister "the name 'king of Tara' appears in the Annals of Ulster in 670, 737, 764; enough to show the futility of the curses fathered upon Ruadhan."

Ryan, 123; MacNeill, 233; Macalister, 35, 171, 188; Healy, 218; Stokes, 19, 60.

Fachtna
August 14   c. 588

Fachtna was the first of a distinguished line of prelates at Rosscarbery in Cork, 27 bishops of his own lineage, of the same ancestry that produced Kieran of Saigher. He had an earlier foundation near Youghal where Brendan came to teach with him, his friend since their childhood days with Ita, the "foster mother of saints." But his great achievement was the school of Ross.

Ross flourished for 300 years, until the coming of the Norsemen. Thereafter, instead of abbots or bishops, "airchenechs" appear in the records. As a consequence of the disorders caused by repeated invasions, there came about a lay succession of secular owners of church property, "airchenechs," in full possession of all revenues who were, however, obligated to provide for the support of the clergy and the maintenance of religious services out of such revenues.

Manuscripts and textbooks continued to be turned out, even to be newly compiled. The death of Fergus, a scribe and anchorite of Ross, is noted for the year 866. The 10th century *Manual of Geography*, 136 lines in verse in the Irish language extant in the *Book of Leinster*, was written by the professor MacCosse in times so unpropitious he was taken prisoner by the Norsemen, although later ransomed by Brian Boru.

About 1168, when the Anglo-Normans laid waste all the surrounding country, Fachtna's school disappeared.

Graham, 98; Ryan, 131, 174; MacNeill, 351; Healy, 490; O'Hanlon; Butler-Attwater, III: 329.

Dallan Forghaill
January 29   c. 598

In ancient Ireland the poet, as has been said earlier, was of highly privileged status. And Dallan Forghaill, the chief poet of Ireland in 575, exemplified the finest of the bardic class. But there were others who grossly abused the old Irish unwritten law of hospitality, descending on whom they would, staying as long as they pleased. Among the hosts groaning under their avarice and insolence, Aedh MacAinmire, king of Ireland, called upon the Assembly of Drumceat to dissolve the Order and take away their privileges. Then Colmcille, a graduate of the bardic school himself, rose to the defence of the ancient guild. Who would then preserve the records of the nation, celebrate the great deeds of its kings and warriors, or chant a dirge for the noble dead? Let the bards be corrected, let them be punished, but why destroy the Order itself?

Dallan Forghaill celebrated Colmcille's victory in behalf of the bards with the famous panegyric, the ''Amra Colmcille,'' which, legend relates, Colmcille permitted only on the condition it be incomprehensible to the men of Erin. The ''Amra Senain'' (Eulogy of Senan) ascribed to Dallan Forghaill, is written in similar language of intentional difficulty and obscurity. The poet-saint is named a martyr, having been murdered by sea rovers who broke into and rifled the island monastery of Inniskeel, Donegal, where he is buried.

Dallan Forghaill's real contribution to Irish literature was the reorganization and reform of the bardic Order. He initiated a strictly supervised bardic school system that continued and encouraged the cultivation of the Gaelic language and general literature outside the monastic schools. To Dallan Forghaill is largely credited the preservation of ancient chronicles and the immense mass of literature in the Gaelic language now available to modern Gaelic scholars.

The bards were a part of every great Irish celebration until the end of the 17th century. In 1738 died Turlough O'Carolan, the last of the great Irish bards, who went about Ireland travelling in the grand manner with an attendant to carry his harp, a celebrity gladly received by the elite wherever he went. He repaid his host by composing and singing, impromptu, verses in his honor. Tourist guides for Ireland list the town of Keadue (Roscommon) as the last home of O'Carolan "the last of the Irish bards and [it is said] the composer of the tune of the 'Star Spangled Banner.'"

Kenney, 366, 427; Healy, 323, 616; Montalembert, II: 63; Hoagland, 177; *Benn*, 67.

Bronach
April 2   Sixth century

For 50 years, fireside reminiscing kept alive the memory of the mysterious former ringing of an invisible bell in Kilbroney churchyard. Scoffers called it a ghost story. Then in 1885, a storm felled a great oak there and workmen chopping up the old tree found in the fork of two branches a very ancient bronze bell which is ascribed to 6th century craftsmanship. The ring holding the tongue of the bell had worn away and so the mystery of the ringing and of the silence was cleared up. It was Bronach's lost bell, one more holy relic that was hidden away in the Reformation and finally recovered.

About a mile from Rostrevor in County Down is the ancient church of Kilbroney, so named for the saintly Bronach registered in the martyrologies of Tallaght and Donegal as the virgin of Glenshesk and of Kilbroney of which she is the patroness. In the Rostrevor churchyard may be seen Bronach's Cross and in use in the parish church there is Bronach's own bronze bell.

Neeson, 71; *Benn*, 121; Benedictine Monks, 116; *Irish Digest*, July, 1951.

Colman (Cloyne)
November 24   c. 600

Colman, Mac (that is son of) Lenini, was the royal bard of Munster and chief chronicler and genealogist to the king of Cashel. Interestingly enough, his becoming a Christian was the result of a robbery.

The shrine of St. Ailbhe had been stolen and the robbers drowned while taking it across a lake. At the time of its recovery, MacLenini helped to lift the shrine from the water. Brendan of Clonfert, when he heard about it, said to the royal bard that hands that had been hallowed by the touch of that sacred relic should not remain the hands of a pagan.

MacLenini forthwith became the disciple of Brendan who baptized him, gave him the name Colman, took him to Jarlath at Clonfuis and, for counseling, to Brendan's own foster-mother, Ita. Colman became the bishop-founder of Cloyne in County Cork.

Five of Colman's sisters, "The Daughters of Lenin," made up a small community at Killiney Hill, Co. Dublin, so named from their church *Cill Inghean Léinín.''* Killiney Old Church there is now a national monument.

Carty, 75; Benedictine Monks, 148; *Benn*, 46; Butler-Attwater, IV: 419.

Comgall
May 10   c. 603

    Comgall was the founder of Bangor which has given the largest number of great names to Irish religious history — Columban, Gall, Moluag, Maelrubha, Dungal, Malachy, to name a few of them. De Blacam in *The Black North* says that Columban was not daunted by Romans or Gauls: what he had learned at Bangor-by-the-Sea gave him confidence against the world.

    The future great abbot spent many years in the highly regarded Clonenagh under Fintan (whose rule was so extreme even fellow ascetics protested its rigor). Later, Colmcille, Cainnech, and Kieran of Clonmacnoise were his friends and companions at Glasnevin. About 555 he founded Bangor in his native Ulster, thirteen miles from Belfast, on the southern shore of Belfast Lough. It was a cluster of wooden buildings — saints and scholars, not buildings, were its glory. Friars in seven choirs chanted unendingly the praise of God. They lived a life so severe there were some who said Comgall's hard discipline brought upon him the punishment of God in the combination of terrible diseases that afflicted his last years. Nevertheless, the figures given for the large enrollment he attracted to Bangor in those far off days are almost unbelievable. There, says the *Martyrology of Donegal*, he "kindled in the hearts of men an unquenchable fire of the love of God."

    The saint trained Columban and gave him the twelve picked companions with whom he accomplished "the second conversion of Gaul." Comgall visited Scottish Dalriada and Pictish eastern Scotland. He planted a monastery at Tiree where he "dwelt for a while." He brought over the very notable disciple Moluag who with other Bangor monks radiated out of Scottish Lismore. Along with Cainnech of Aghaboe he sponsored Colmcille on the occasion of his successful interview with the Pictish King Brude. During Comgall's lifetime two of his monks, Meadhren or Mirran, and Toman founded a monastery at Paisley. A century later Maelrubha came from Bangor to Applecross. Historians note that throughout three centuries, until the incursions of the Norsemen, Bangor exercised a profound influence upon Christianity in Scotland.

    Comgall died at Bangor. His monastery, like his casket adorned with gold and precious stones, became the spoil of the sea pirates who on one occasion, we are told, murdered 900 of the brethren. Malachy restored the ruined abbey in 1125. After the coming of Henry II the statutes of Kilkenny excluded "mere Irish" from Bangor. (The annalist observes it did not profit thereby.) In 1469 the Franciscans came, a century later the Augustinians. In 1617 Bangor fell in the seizure of the O'Neill estates by England.

A celebrated monument to Comgall survives, the *Antiphonary of Bangor*, a liturgical manuscript which was compiled in his monastery in the 7th century. It was one of the considerable gift of books the scholar Dungal made to Bobbio (the Irish monastery in northern Italy) when he fled the Vikings in 824. In 1606 Cardinal Borromeo acquired it for his Ambrosian Library at Milan where it is today. It contains the anthem "Sancti Venite," said to be the oldest Eucharistic hymn in Europe. The Bangor College Song and other hymns in the Antiphonary in honor of Comgall testify to the love of the men of Bangor for their Alma Mater and to the honor accorded Comgall in his own monastery.

Kenney, 395; Ryan; Simpson; Mould; Benedictine Monks, 149; Fitzpatrick, II, 105; de Blacam, 155.

Fintan (Clonenagh)
February 17   c. 603

Fintan, abbot-founder of Clonenagh in Leinster, surpassed his teacher, Colman of Terryglass, and all the other abbots of his time in the austerity of his life and Rule. So much so, Cainnech and other neighboring ascetics felt it their duty to remonstrate and together they proceeded to Clonenagh. But, forewarned by an angel, Fintan received them with all cordiality, had a bountiful meal and friendly conversation for community and guests as long as they stayed. At their departure, Clonenagh was put back exactly as before. In spite of all, or perhaps because of it, Fintan's monastery was crowded with youth from all over Ireland, devoted to him and his bidding. Fintan taught Comgall, who taught Columban, who in turn founded the monasteries of Luxeuil and Bobbio. Another famous later alumnus of Fintan's school was Aengus the Culdee.

The holy well at Clonenagh was long held in reverence. In passing, men doffed their hats and women curtsied in memory of Fintan. In Elizabeth's time, the Protestant owner diverted the water to the roadside to rid himself of "undesirable visitors" to the well.

Clonenagh had its scribes. It had its great Book. In the 17th century Father Keating quoted from it in the history he compiled in hiding from the priest hunters. The *Book of Clonenagh* is believed to have passed into the hands of a Crosbie family, to one of whom Elizabeth granted the large estage of Ballyfin and knighthood as Sir Patrick Crosbie. Until the early 19th century, Fintan's Book was at Ballyfin House. Its whereabouts now is unknown. Ballyfin House is now a college of the Patrician Fathers.

Ryan, 127; Kenney, 386; Benedictine Monks, 235; Healy, 402; *Benn*, 204.

Eugene (Eoghain)
August 23   618

A comparison of the Anglicized, Latinized, Eugenius with the saint's actual Gaelic name, Eoghain (pronounced Owen), explains how many Irish missionaries' names became lost under Continental equivalents. Eoghain was the first bishop of Tyrone, the county named for the O'Neill prince, Eoghain (Tir-Eoghain, land of Eoghain).

In his youth, raiders carried Eoghain off to Wales where he was rescued by the abbot of Rosnat, or perhaps of Whithern in Galloway. One account tells that he labored as a missionary in Britain and on the Continent. With him were two other Irish boys, Tighernach, afterwards of Clones, and Coirpre of Coleraine. Before he founded his church at Ardstraw and before his appointment as bishop of Tyrone, Eoghain had a monastery and school at Kilnamanagh in Wicklow. His nephew, Kevin of Glendalough, was one of his pupils there.

Ryan, 106, 123; Healy, 415; Neeson, 152; Benedictine Monks, 210.

Kevin
June 3   618

In Kevin's lovely Glendalough valley, two of the many notable reminders of past glory have very special association with the saint: St. Kevin's Church, his little private oratory, and the Church of Our Lady, his final resting place. Kevin (Coemghen in Irish: of gentle birth) came of a family of saints of the royal house of Leinster. He was one of Ireland's many great Irish abbots who chose never to be elevated above priestly dignity. Their authority was supreme in their communities and the bishop was one of the brethren who performed episcopal functions and who, like the abbot, lived the Rule.

Following ordination, Kevin became a contemplative in the Glendalough valley. His shelter, originally a prehistoric tomb cut in a rock, was accessible only by boat and a steep climb 30 feet above the water. But disciples found him out and a community formed around him. One by one rose the several churches and the monastery of Glendalough. Its repute was of the highest.

Kevin continued his periods of prayer and solitude, some of them in

Scotland where memory of the saint of Glendalough lived on, principally in Argyll, down to the Reformation. His Rule for his monks was in verse, and in the O'Longain Manuscripts in the Irish Academy, a poem by a St. Comgan is attributed to Kevin. Music was another of his talents. His harp was one of Glendalough's great treasures down to the 12th century.

In that same troubled century another high born Leinster youth, Laurence O'Toole, came to Glendalough, modelled his life on that of the holy founder and brought fresh fame to the 500 year-old monastery. The name O'Toole is met with again in 1714, in an account of Kevin's feast day. During the Penal days, when the English offered five pounds for the head of a priest or a wolf, and ten pounds for the head of a bishop, the sheriff of Wicklow recorded putting down a ''riotous assembly'' on June 3, at Glendalough. The ''disturbance'' was a little band of the faithful who came to kneel and pray according to their custom at Kevin's shrine on his feast day. English soldiers had ridden forth in the night in order to reach the scene at four o'clock in the morning when they immediately dispersed the ''rioters.'' Their foray netted them ''one Toole, a popish schoolmaster.''

The writings of Gerald Cambrensis make mention of a famous willow at Glendalough, growing with other similar trees having willow-like leaves and form, yet bearing apples each year. Another 12th century notice of the fruit called Saint Kevin's apples states they were in great demand even to the most distant parts of Ireland. Legend as well as history has its account of the willow at Glendalough: a little boy in Kevin's care in that valley of ascetic men asked for an apple, and ''the servant of God blessed one of the willows and immediately through his prayer sweet apples grew thereon.'' A second beloved tree at Glendalough was the yew that Kevin himself planted near the portals of the Cathedral. About 1835, when a neighboring landed proprietor had it cut down to make it into furniture, people gathered up even the fragments to keep as precious mementoes of the saint.

Kevin's city flourished until the 11th century, a sanctuary of highest prestige and importance. Seven kings are entombed in its former church, the Reefert, or Sepulchre of Kings. Glendalough knew little peace from the time of the Anglo-Normans and came to final destruction in the 16th century.

Ryan, 130, 186; Butler-Attwater, II: 463; Moran, 178; O'Hanlon, June 3; Healy, 414.

Finbarr
September 25   c. 623

Basically a pastoral saint, Finbarr comes through as a great church builder before founding the church and monastery in the corcaigh, or marshy place, on the river Lee that were the beginning of the city of Cork. He became its first bishop and the patron saint of all the wide territories of the entire sept of the tribal prince Tighernach for whom his father was master metalworker.

Not very far from Cork is Garranes, once an ancient fort which has been identified with Rath Raithleann, the birthplace of Finbarr. Tying in with this are the interesting findings of excavating done at Garranes in 1941 — an enamelled disk now in the Museum at Cork, 5th and 6th century smith and glaziers' stone and clay molds for casting of bronze objects, fragments of glass, of enamel, of unfinished pins and rings for brooches, the remains of an apparently secular industrial activity. It may well be Garranes was his father's workshop and that the little boy Finbarr used to play there, turning out art work of his own.

Finbarr's *Book of Gospels*, which was afterwards enshrined in gold and gems, has disappeared for long centuries past. The Protestant Episcopal Cathedral occupies the site of his church in Cork City. Gougane Barra, Finbarr's little island solitude in a mountain lake a good distance west of the city, is changeless and grand still, with ''its thousand wild descending fountains streaming down the perpindicular cliffs'' — with its ''indescribable air of sanctity.'' It is a place of annual pilgrimage in honor of the saint, especially on ''Gougane Sunday,'' the first Sunday after Finbarr's feast day.

Ryan, 114, 169; Benedictine Monks, 87; Moran, 179; Healy, 475; Butler-Attwater, III: 634; *Benn*, 265; Neeson, 171; Henry, vol. I.

Cronan (Roscrea)
April 28   626

Clonmacnoise-educated Cronan was of the sept and the territory of Ely O'Carroll, the same O'Carrolls that long centuries later produced John Carroll, the first bishop of the United States. Cronan abandoned his first monastery in a remote, inaccessible spot, to move closer to the main road in order to be more easily reached by the poor and those in need. In 1826, workers, digging for the foundations of a new church at Roscrea, uncovered a memorial from ages past, an ancient stone having the simple inscription ''Cronan.''

From Cronan and Roscrea comes the 7th century *Book of Dimma*. When Cronan asked Dimma to transcribe the Gospels for him, Dimma said he could give only one day's time to the work, from sunrise to sunset. Cronan bade him write. He did, ''never stopping for forty days and forty nights'' until he finished the 74-page manuscript. The scribe's autograph at the end of the Gospel of St. Matthew asks ''A prayer for Dimma, who wrote it for God, and a blessing.'' In 1150 Tatheus O'Carroll had this O'Carroll treasure enshrined in a handsome silver casket, brass plated with silver and studded with lapis lazuli.

At the suppression of the monasteries by the English, Dimma's *Book* disappeared, shrine and all, carefully hidden away by the monks. In 1789, two boys hunting rabbits found the *Book* and its case, safe and sound, in a crevice in a Tipperary mountainside. It passed to lay hands and finally to Trinity College, Dublin.

The *Book of Dimma* has been out of Ireland twice. In 1819, it was shown in London in a lecture describing it for the Society of Antiquarians. In 1961, it was taken to London for the exhibit of Irish art treasures arranged by Trinity College in its fund-raising campaign for the new Library.

Kenney, 460; Stokes, 20; Neeson, 85; Bulfin, 8; O'Hanlon, IV: 519.

Aidan (Ferns)
January 31   c. 632

Connacht-born Aidan was educated by David of Menevia (Wales) where he remained for so many years as pupil, teacher and, finally, abbot, Wales came to regard him a native and the Triads recorded him with a genealogy from Welsh nobility. Cardinal Moran states that David of Menevia was born of an Irish mother, baptized by Ailbhe of Emly, and that he died in the arms of a loved Irish disciple. That disciple was Aidan. In after years, the religious of Menevia put forward a claim of jurisdiction over the clergy of Ferns in Ireland on the grounds that one of their first abbots of Menevia was the founder, first abbot and chief patron of Ferns.

Following Menevia, Aidan returned to Ireland and to Ferns, the first of about 30 churches, among them Drumlane, credited to him in his native land. Brandubh, the King of Leinster, bestowed upon him the royal seat of Fearna with its banquet halls, champions' quarters, woods, hunting grounds and all. Subsequently, Aidan's church and Ferns displaced Sletty of Fiach as the bishop's seat with Aidan the Metropolitan of Leinster.

Maedoc-Edan, Moedoc, Mogue, all are names for Aidan of Ferns. Accordingly, among the saint's personal belongings which survive are the Bell of St. Mogue (now in the Armagh Library, formerly in the hereditary keepership of the MacGoverns in Templeport, County Cavan) and one of the most remarkable of Irish reliquaries, the Breac Moedoc, the stamped leather satchel and the superb shrine made to encase relics which Laserian of Leighlin brought from Rome to his friend Moedoc, then abbot of Ferns. The shrine, preserved for centuries in the Catholic church of Drumlane, was stolen from that parish in the early decades of the present century. It is now in the National Museum, Dublin.

Kenney, 448; Moran, 29; Stokes, 52, 86; Porter, 42; Neeson, 32; *Capuchin Annual*, 1960.

Colman (Kilmacduagh)
October 29   c. 632

The story that angels intervened to bring Colman to the attention of his kinsman, Guaire, King of Connacht, is one of the cherished fantasies the Irish people have told and retold, generation after generation. Colman, son of Duac, born about 550 in Kiltartan in Galway and educated in Enda's monastery in Aran, was a contemplative given to a life of prayer and prolonged fastings, first in one of Aran's walled-in bee-hive cells, afterwards blessedly lost to the world in the Burren in County Clare.

There came an Easter Sunday when Colman was without food after a rigorous Lenten fast. Several miles away King Guaire was sitting down to a festive meal when angels whisked his dinner away before his very eyes. The startled king and his attendants took chase. Today there is a pathway formation in the rock terrain surrounding Burren that tourist guides point out as the "road of the dishes" that led Guaire to Colman's door.

The king and the saint co-founded Kilmacduagh, the church of the son of Duac, and Colman became the first bishop of all the territory subsequently to be the diocese of Kilmacduagh in Galway.

Down the centuries the O'Heynes of the barony of Kiltartan (descendants of Guaire) and their kinsmen, the O'Shaughnessys, were custodians of Colman's crozier which is now in the National Museum, Dublin. As in the case of other sacred relics, it was long used by contending parties to prove the innocence or guilt of any accused whose oath with hand upon the crozier was acceptable to all.

Among the very interesting Kilmacduagh ruins, the little oratory of St. John may go back to Colman's own time. There are 10th–13th century O'Heyne Abbey Church ruins, notably the Irish Romanesque piers of the chancel arch and the two-light east windows; the 16th–18th century O'Shaughnessy tombs. Dominating all is Ireland's "leaning tower," almost twice as old as the leaning tower of Pisa, a magnificent specimen of Irish round towers, 112 feet high and 2 feet out of plumb when restored in 1880.

Stokes, 81; *Benn*, 241; Carty, I: 69; Benedictine Monks, 148; Butler-Attwater, IV: 218; MacLysaght, 180, 265.

Carthage (Cuda, Mochuda)
May 14   637

Twelve-year old Cuda, while tending his father's sheep, chanced to wander close to the monastery ruled by Carthage at the foot of Slemish mountain where he heard the brethren chanting the sacred psalmody. He listened enthralled. Next day, accompanied by his parents, he presented himself for admittance to the community. Eventually there were two saints named Carthage, the abbot and the disciple he called Mochuda (his name plus the term of endearment Mo) who was so devoted to the master he took the name Carthage for himself. After ordination, Carthage Mochuda made the customary round of other great abbots, Comgall of Bangor, Molua of Clonfert and Colman Elo at Lynally on whose advice he settled at nearby Rahan in Offaly where there are interesting remains of the old abbey.

Rahan grew and flourished during his 40 years there. But Carthage was an outlander and he was asked to depart. He was from what is the modern Kerry and local ecclesiastical and racial jealousy were responsible for his expulsion. At Easter time in 635, Prince Blathmac took Carthage by the hand and led him forth.

When the homeless old saint reached his native Munster, the prince of the Decies of Waterford knelt for his blessing and offered him the tract on which he founded the famous "holy city" of Lismore in the beautiful valley through which the Blackwater flows. Carthage lived only two years longer, but long enough to see his community take up almost without interruption in the new location. Rich endowments flowed to Lismore and many holy men from every part of Ireland, from England and from abroad enrolled in it. Carthage's Rule survives, 135 four-line stanzas in verse in Gaelic.

Lismore became a place of pilgrimage and of retirement for many Irish kings and princes, the first of whom was 7th century Turlough, King of Thomond and father of Flannan of Killaloe. Another was Murtagh O'Brien, grandson of Brian Boru. Cormac MacCullinan, King of Cashel, bequeathed to Lismore a gold and silver Chalice and a set of vestments. Celsus, primate of Armagh, was buried in Lismore.

In the 12th century, Strongbow's son plundered and burned Lismore and under English forces, the church, the abbey, the convent for women, the leper hospital, all were destroyed.

In 1185, Prince John, son of Henry II, built the first castle of Lismore on the site of the old abbey, which, retaken by the native princes, was given to the bishops of Lismore. After the Reformation, Sir Walter Raleigh acquired Lismore. Finally it passed to the Duke of Devonshire. (In our own time, Lismore was one of the homes of President Kennedy's sister Kathleen who married the oldest son of the Duke of Devonshire.) In 1814, in the course of extensive additions and repairs to the castle, workmen discovered behind a walled-up doorway an old hand-written vellum book and a superb crozier with an oaken core that is believed to have belonged to Carthage. It is supposed the custodians of the manuscript and the crozier hid them behind masonry walls to save them from destruction at the hands of the English.

The manuscript is the *Book of Lismore*, a treasury of valuable history and romance tracts, made in the 15th century from the now lost *Book of Monasterboice*. Although chewed about the edges and damaged from damp, it is still fairly legible. In 1839, the Gaelic scholar O'Curry reproduced as exact a copy as painstaking skill could turn out, the facsimile transcript of the *Book of Lismore* now in the Irish Academy.

The Lismore crozier, which is a masterpiece of 11th–12th century Irish art and one of the two finest Irish croziers in existence, is executed in pale bronze, ornamental gilt and lapis lazuli. The inscription asks prayers for Nial, son of Aeducain, who was bishop of Lismore 1090–1113 and for the artist Nechtan who made it. In 1949, the Marquis of Hartington, in a transaction of importance in art circles duly noted in American papers, handed over Carthage's crozier on permanent loan to the National Museum, Dublin.

Kenney, 260, 451; Ryan; Healy, 447; Benedictine Monks, 129; Stokes, 840.

Laserian, Leighlin
April 18   c. 639

At the national synod of 630, Cummian of Clonfert, Laserian of Leighlin, and others advocated the change-over from the prevailing Irish method of reckoning Easter to the Roman way of calculating the Feast. There were dissenters, however, and to satisfy them it was decided a delegation should go to Rome to investigate the question more fully. Laserian headed the group and as a result of their report, all of Ireland, except the monasteries of Colmcille, adopted the new Easter reckoning in 633.

Laserian (affectionately, Molaise) was of Ulster nobility, a grandson of Aidan, the Irish king in Scotland, and a nephew of St. Blane. He made his studies at Iona and in Rome, was ordained by Gregory the Great, and succeeded Goban in the abbacy of Leighlin in Carlow. Pope Honorius in 633 consecrated Laserian the first bishop of Leighlin and appointed him legate to Ireland. In the penal times, owing to the ''extreme tenuity'' of the combined annual revenue of a total of about 30 pounds for the two dioceses of Leighlin and Kildare, Laserian's see, in 1678, became a part of Kildare.

One of the precious relics of early Irish Christian art is the shrine made in the 11th century for the relics Laserian brought from Rome for Aidan of Ferns. The shrine and its satchel of stamped leather are now in the National Museum, Dublin. Stokes calles attention to the intricacies of the metal-work, the coloring of the pale to darker bronze gilt, the blue glass insets, the blue, red, and white enamel on gold, and especially, the details of the figures. Of an original 21 saints arranged in three rows, 11 figures and three pairs of feet survive. Three nuns are in uniform habits with their hair hanging in long curls. Eight male figures are in varied dress and various postures, one with a sword, one "standing in sorrow, his cheek resting in his hand." Porter's book has photographs of both the satchel and the casket. He comments "This shrine is of exquisite quality."

Kenney, 451; Porter, 42; Stokes, 86; Catholic Encyclopedia, VIII: 636; Benn, 14; Benedictine Monks, 360.

Caimin
March 23   653

A hundred years before Caimin, a saint who was honored as one of the "twelve apostles of Ireland," Colm of Terryglass, had a monastery on Iniscaltra in Lough Derg in the Shannon. But Caimin is the reason the people called Iniscaltra "Holy Island." He was of high-born Leinster lineage. Guaire, King of Connacht, and Cummian of Clonfert were his half brothers. Caimin was a distinguished scholar: a fragment of his Commentary on the 119th Psalm, written in his own hand is extant. St. Caimin's Psalter, an illuminated Manuscript now in the Franciscan library, Killiney, County Dublin, is later than the time of the saint, but is believed to have originated in his monastery.

The Shannon was the highway of the Danish pirate ships and Iniscaltra lay in the direct pathway of their plunderings and burnings. It functioned nevertheless: the last abbot of record died in 1010. It was first plundered by Turgesius in about 836. In 898 the anchorite, Cosgraich, who dwelt in the round tower there, died. In 922, the Danes "drowned its shrines and its relics and its books." About 1009, Brian Boru restored Iniscaltra and repaired and rebuilt Caimin's great church. Iniscaltra was the great school of Brian Boru's own hereditary kingdom and only a few miles from his palace at Kincora.

Now, the round tower eighty feet tall, early grave slabs in the "Saints Graveyard," ivy covered ruins of four churches, an elaborate Romanesque doorway, are eloquent reminders of Iniscaltra's past. No one knows where, among those ruins, Caimin's body rests.

Healy, 516; Benedictine Monks, 121; Neeson, 66; *Benn*, 248.

Cummian
November 12   c. 662

Donegal-born Cummian of Clonfert figured prominently in Ireland's change-over to the revised Easter date. He had gone into every angle of the question before the national synod in 630 and was largely responsible for the decree to celebrate Easter, thenceforth, with the universal church. However, in order to satisfy dissenters, delegates were sent to Rome, a journey of three years. They brought back the report that Greeks, Hebrews Scythians, Egyptions, all celebrated Easter on the same day, a date which that year differed a whole month from the Irish Easter. From about the year 633, then, all of Ireland, the communities of Colmcille alone excepted, conformed to the Roman Easter.

The same year that Iona received the request from the English King Oswald for Irish monks to teach Christianity to his people, Iona also received a letter from Cummian urging acceptance of the new Easter reckoning. Iona was adamant then and adamant thirty years later when Colman departed from England rather than deviate from the traditions of Colmcille.

Cummian's "Paschal Epistle" survives, valuable not only as evidence of Cummian's own scholarship but of the high order of the schools of his native land in which he was educated. In his enumeration of the various Easter cycles, one is "that which Patrick our father brought." It is one of the earliest, if not the earliest, allusion to Patrick extant, and is the only definite testimony that the apostle's paschal system differed from that of the later Celtic church. The oldest extant copy of Cummian's letter is in a 9th century Irish manuscript now in St. Gall, Switzerland. Migne reproduced the Epistle in his Patrologia. Healy has a detailed digest of it in *Ireland's Ancient Schools and Scholars*.

Kenney, 220; Healy, 228; Skene, II: 159; Benedictine Monks, 159.

Fechin (Vigean)
January 20   c. 664

Old Scottish calendars gave a high place to Connacht born, Achonry-educated, Fechin. The Dunkeld Litany invoked him under the name Vigean. Ecclefechin and St. Vigean's near Arbroath also perpetuate his memory.

At Fore, in Ireland, Fechin ruled a community of 300 monks. Fore was important for its manuscript books. It was better remembered and more revered for the water mill the saint was said to have made miraculously in the side of a rock with his own hands. Cambrensis wrote in the 12th century that

Fechin's mill at Fore was held in as much reverence as were any of the churches dedicated to him.

Ruins mark the site of the church Fechin founded at his birthplace, Ballysodare. His church and abbey at Cong were sumptuously rebuilt in the 12th century for the Irish Augustinians by Turlough O'Connor who brought there from Tuam the beautiful jewel-studded processional Cross he had made to enshrine a particle of the True Cross. Cong Abbey was later the refuge of the last High King of Ireland, Roderick O'Connor. The Cross of Cong which had been hidden away in an old oaken chest in the village, is now in the National Museum, Dublin.

Kenney, 458; Stokes, 88; Moran, 180; Benedictine Monks, 225; Neeson, 27; *Benn*, 14.

Colman Mac Ui Cluasigh
? May 6   Seventh century

One of Ireland's some 120 saints named Colman was Colman Mac Ui Cluasaigh, a professor at Cork. About 664 he composed in verse a prayer for protection against the yellow plague that was devastating Ireland, leaving only one man in every three alive. It was then the belief that pestilence never extended more than nine waves from the shore. So Colman took his boys and setting out in boats for an island in the ocean, they chanted the prayer verse by verse in turn as they want. One of the school asked Colman what was the blessing wherein it had befallen them to take to the sea. "What blessing is it" the saint replied "but God's blessing?" Colman's "Lorica," or prayer, is said to be the only piece of writing that survives from Finbarr's school at Cork. It is given in *1000 Years of Irish Poetry*, edited by Kathleen Hoaglund.

Healy, 487; Hoagland, 15.

Lua (Killaloe)
? May 11   Early Seventh century

Irish Calendars list some 37 saints by the name of Lua or Molua. The saint of Killaloe was said to have been of noble parentage of midwest Limerick, and to have been educated at Bangor and Clonard. Among his pupils at his school and church on the Shannon was the future Bishop Flannan to whom he transferred his abbacy. But as the city would be renowned, Lua said, he asked for the sake of mutual love that it be associated by name with him. And so, Killaloe, or Church of Lua, it is.

Lua had a little stone oratory on a green dot called Friar's Island just off the

Tipperary shore, a sanctuary that continued to be a place of pilgrimage until 1929. When the power dam raised the level of the Shannon in that year, Friar's Island sank from view. But preserved intact, with every stone numbered for reassembly, Lua's stone chapel had been removed, not to the original St. Flannan's Cathedral churchyard, now in Protestant ownership, but to the hilltop square of the present day Catholic church on the site of Brian Boru's palace overlooking the Shannon.

Gone with submerged Friar's Island is the big flat rock with its hoof marks and its wondrous legend of St. Patrick, the story that in days gone by thrilled every small boy that ever swam in the Shannon at Killaloe. The apostle, pursued wickedly by the pagans, came at break-neck speed to the opposite shore and had no choice but to make the leap, about an eighth of a mile wide at the spot. His charger rose to the occasion and landed to safety on Friar's Island, but with such force his hoof prints sank deep into the rock. And that, any small boy could tell you, is how those hoof prints got there.

Flannan
December 18   Seventh century

Flannan, Prince of Thomond, was born in the fortress castle of his father, King Turlough, on Craig Liath, about two miles from the place afterwards called Killaloe. He was schooled for the church in the nearby monastery of St. Lua, became abbot there, went on pilgrimage to Rome and was consecrated first bishop of Killaloe by Pope John IV. He preached the gospel along the route of his travels, especially in the Hebrides where his name survives in the Flannan Islands.

The saint's father, Turlough, is believed to be the first of many native princes to retire to penance and peace in the monastic life. He donned the religious habit under Colman at Lismore and observed the austere rule of a monk there until his death. Flannan brought Turlough home for burial in the Killaloe church he had so generously endowed.

Brian Boru made Killaloe the principal church of his kingdom. After Brian, son of Cinnéide (Kennedy), the royal line descended in the O'Briens and the O'Kennedys. One of them, King Donal O'Brien, built, about 1180, a new cathedral, remnants of which are incorporated in the present 13th century, now Protestant, St. Flannan's Cathedral, which was restored in 1887. Luxuriant with ivy, Gothic in style, with a massive bell tower rising from the center of the building, its elaborate, richly carved Romanesque doorway, dated about 1180, is one of the masterpieces of pre-Norman Irish architecture. Built into the stone wall surrounding the cathedral grounds is another antiquity, a fragment of a bilingual stone cross inscribed with runes and oghams from about the year 1000.

Loveliest of all is the little ivy-bedecked St. Flannan's Oratory with its steep-pitched stone roof. It is now a national monument. Tradition has it that it was once the parish church of Brian Boru. Its chancel is gone but its Romanesque doorway survives, as does its stone roof which is supported by the walls of the loft above the vault of the interior. Brian Boru died in 1014. Some antiquarians would assign the Oratory to a somewhat later date. Siding with the older tradition, however, would seem to be the name by which the Oratory is also known, "Brian Boru's Vault."

Kenney, 404; Butler-Attwater, IV: 582; Moran, 184; Leask; Harbison; *Benn*, 247.

Moling
June 17   c. 697

As Aidan's express choice, Moling was called to succeed that saint as bishop of Ferns, the ecclesiastical capital of Leinster. He very reluctantly left his beloved foundation at Techmolin (from Teach Moling, House of Moling.) He was a classical writer in Latin and in Irish, and on one occasion, so universal was the recognition of a poet's high status in ancient Ireland, brigands into whose hands Moling had fallen, released him when they discovered he was a poet. More ancient poems in the Gaelic language, several of them still extant, are ascribed to Moling than to any other saint except Colmcille.

In 693, Moling obtained remission of the heavy tribute of oxen which the high kings had claimed from Leinster, reportedly, since the year 106, and all Leinster held him in high honor. After a time he resigned the see of Ferns to return to his own monastery of Techmolin, now St. Mullins in Carlow. His church there continued even to recent times to be an important religious center and place of pilgrimage.

Twelfth century Gerald Cambrensis mentioned Moling's book in the Irish language, extant in his time. Father Keating in his history, 1626–40, made extensive use of the saint's now lost manuscript, the *Yellow Book of Moling*. Gougaud found Moling's invocation of Brigid, patroness of travellers, in a 15th century German *Reisesegen*, or blessing before a trip. Named for Moling, but later than the saint, is the illuminated Gospel manuscript, the *Book of Mulling*, which takes its place among those works dated prior to the year 800 in the remains of ancient Irish monastic libraries. Francoise Henry includes a page (portrait of an Evangelist) from the *Book of Mulling* in the picture section of volume I of her work on Irish art.

Kenney, 461; Gougaud, 111; Benedictine Monks, 429; Healy, 426; O'Hanlon, Introduction; Henry, I: plate 111.

Tirechan
July 3   Seventh century

Tirechan is important for his "Breviarium," or Memoir, of Patrick, written about 670–700, and preserved in the *Book of Armagh*. He came from Mayo and was a cleric in Meath, a disciple of Ultan of Ardbraccan (who died in 657) from whom he had his notes on Patrick. Although Tirechan is more than a century removed from the time of Patrick, he is one of the earliest biographers of the saint. He hands down the tradition that Patrick journeyed to Gaul, Italy, and the Tyrrhenian Sea, and especially to Auxerre and Lerins. His memoir is valuable also for a great deal of information concerning 7th century Ireland.
Needham; Binchy; Ryan, 60; O'Hanlon, Introduction.

Muirchu
June 8   Seventh century

Muirchu, writer of *Lives of Patrick and Brigid*, is believed to have been an Armagh man attached to the church of Sletty. His *Life of Patrick* was written "at the dictation," or order, of Bishop Aed of Sletty. The introduction states that Muirchu considered his information uncertain and unsatisfactory and his oar unskilled in that deep and dangerous gulf of sacred narrative. His works are valuable for their information concerning Ireland in the 7th century.

Needham; Binchy; Kenney; O'Hanlon, Introduction.

Cogitosus
April 18   Seventh century

Cogitosus was a monk of Kildare and one of Ireland's earliest historical writers. He is important for his *Life of Brigid*, a work which offers little of genuine biographical material and much of legend and the miraculous, but which is, nevertheless, of special interest for the light it throws on Brigid's monastery, the personnel, the succession of abbesses and abbots. The most valued portion of the work is the description of the great Kildare church, its elaborate ornamentation, the tombs of Brigid and Conleth and the provision made in the church for separate accommodation for the monks and nuns, a description of the church as it was in the time of Cogitosus, it is believed, rather than as it was in Brigid's time. The original manuscript of the *Life of Brigid* by Cogitosus is in the Dominican Convent in Eichstadt in Bavaria.

Kenney; O'Hanlon, Introduction; Stokes, 33; Tommasini, 47; Benedictine Monks, 147.

Samthann
December 19   739

One tradition claims the convent at Clonbroney, near Granard in County Longford, was founded by Patrick for the two daughters of his former master, Milchu. Another says it was founded by disciples of Brigid. In later times, Samthann, one of the great women saints of Ireland, was honored as its foundress. Clonbroney ranked with Kildare and the convent of 6th century Cairech Dergan at Cloonburren, Roscommon, as one of three Irish foundations for women that remained places of importance through the centuries. Clonbroney's last abbess of record died in 1160. Irish missionaries took word of Samthann to Europe. An ancient litany at Salzburg, Austria, invokes the saints Ita, Brigid, and Samthann.

Kenney, 253, 464; Ryan, 140; Benedictine Monks, 524; Pochin Mould, 283, 156.

Blathmac MacConbreton
                                                                            c. 750

In 1954 there came to light in a bundle of old manuscripts in the National Library, Dublin, four poems written in Gaelic of great antiquity. One is a narrative poem of about 50 stanzas on the boyhood of Christ. The other three are in praise of the Blessed Mother. One of these is a work of 150 stanzas. A companion piece, or continuation, is incomplete, the end being missing. These two poems are the work of 8th century Blathmac MacConbreton writing about the year 750.

A short anonymous poem to the Blessed Mother is written in Gaelic more ancient than the others. It is assigned to the 7th century. Heretofore, listed as probably the earliest writer in the west in praise of the Blessed Virgin was the Anglo-Saxon Cynewulf. The *New Catholic Encyclopedia* says of Cynewulf's four old English poems, "the runic spellings indicate a 9th century date."

The 7th and 8th century Gaelic poems to the Blessed Virgin are described as lyrical in quality and full of deep religious feeling. The discovery of these poems is one of extraordinary interest. Poetry from such an early period is almost unknown. These lines to Our Lady may be the earliest in any of the vernacular languages of Europe. They are the discovery of James Carney of the Dublin Institute for Advanced Studies.

Brogan (Clonsast)

c. 750

Brogan of Clonsast was the composer of the old Gaelic litany of the Blessed Virgin Mary. It is to be gathered he was attached to a monastic school since his great work is thought to have been inspired by a Latin composition of the Spanish Ildephonsus. However that may be, about 750 he composed for the Irish laity in their native language that "unfading glory of the early Irish church" the first and oldest Marian litany, a pious *laus*, extant in the 14th century *Leabhar Breac* in the Irish Academy, Dublin. Mrs. Concannon gives the complete text in *The Queen of Ireland:*

> O Great Mary
> O Mary, greatest of Marys
> O Greatest of Women
> O Queen of the Angels
> O Lady of the Heavens
> O Woman full and replete with the
> Grace of the Holy Spirit
> O Blessed and Most Blessed
> O Mother of Eternal Glory
> O Mother of the Heavenly
> and Earthly Church
> O Mother of Fondness
> and Forgiveness
> O Mother of the Golden Light
> O Honor of the Sky
> O Sign of Tranquillity
> O Gate of Heaven
> O Golden Casket
> O Couch of Love and Mercy
> O Temple of the Divinity
> O Beauty of the Virgins
> O Lady of the Kindreds
> O Fountain of the Gardens
> O Cleansing of the Sins
> O Washing of the Souls

O Mother of the Orphans
O Breast of the Infants
O Solace of the Wretched
O Star of the Sea
O Handmaid of God
O Mother of Christ
O Spouse of the Lord
O Shapely live a Dove
O Serene like the Moon
O Resplendent like the Sun
O Cancelling of Eve's Disgrace
O Renewal of Life
O Beauty of Women
O Chief of the Maidens
O Enclosed Garden
O Pure locked-up Fountain
O Mother of God
O Eternal Maiden
O Holy Maiden
O Prudent Maiden
O Serene Maiden
O Chaste Maiden
O Temple of the Living God
O Throne of the Eternal King
O Sanctuary of the Holy Spirit
O Virgin of the Root of Jesse
O Cedar of Mount Lebanon
O Cypress of Mount Zion
O Purple Rose of the Land of Jacob
O Flowering like a Palm
O Fruitful like the Olive Tree
O Glorious Son Bearer
O Light of Nazareth
O Glory of Jerusalem
O Beauty of the World
O Noblest born of the Christian Flock
O Queen of the World
O Ladder of Heaven

Hear the prayer of the poor. Despise not the sobs and the sighs of the wretched. Let our longing and our groans be born by thee before the Creator for through our ill deservingness we ourselves are unworthy to be heard. O mighty Lady of Heaven and Earth, abolish our crimes and our sins, destroy our wickedness and our corruptions. Uplift the fallings of the feeble and the fettered. Loose the enslaved. Repair through thyself the transgressions of our evil ways and our vices. Grant to us through thee the blossoms and ornaments of the good deeds and the virtues. Appease for us the Judge with thy prayers and with thy intercessions. Let us not for mercy sake be carried off from thee in a foray before our enemies. Nor let our souls be enslaved. And take us to thyself forever under thy protection. We beseech and pray thee further, O Holy Mary, through thy great intercession with thy only Son, ever Jesus Christ, Son of the Living God, that God may protect us from all straits and temptations. And ask for us from the God of the elements that we may obtain from Him forgiveness and pardon of all our sins and crimes, and that we may obtain from Him moreover through thy intercession the lasting habitation of the heavenly Kingdom forever and ever in the presence of the saints and holy virgins of the world. May we deserve it, may we inhabit it in saecula saeculorum. Amen.

Maelruain
July 7   792

Tallaght, where Maelruain is buried, has been a favorite home of religious men from his time to the present. Still thriving there is the famous wide-spreading walnut tree which tradition says he planted in the garden of what is now a Dominican monastery. The name Maelruain, "devotee of Ruadhan," suggests he came from Lorrha or its neighborhood. He founded Tallaght about 755.

Tallaght is considered the mother foundation of the Culdee movement and through it Maelruain's impact on the religious circles of his time was far reaching. The very rigorous canons of discipline he laid down for his own monks came to be the general rule of all the religious known as Culdees, holy men who lived in solitude and lived by the labor of their hands. There were Culdees at Armagh, at Clonmacnoise, and at many other Irish monasteries. The Rule stressed the intellectual as well as the ascetic: "The kingdom of heaven is granted to him who directs study, who studies, and who supports students."

The "Martyrology of Tallaght," produced before 792, by Maelruain and Aengus together, is the oldest of all compilations of the saints of Erin, a prose catalogue of the Irish saints, their festival days, brief notices of their parentage and their churches. The oldest extant copy of this Martyrology is in the *Book of Leinster*. Another copy, made by Brother Michael O'Cleary of the Four

Masters, is now in the Burgundian Library at Brussels. It was borrowed from the Belgium government and copied in 1847 by Eugene O'Curry. In the same year, the same text was translated and published by Matthew Kelly of Maynooth.

Kenney, 469; O'Hanlon, July 7; Healy, 407; Neeson, 130.

Colgu (Colgan)
February 20   c. 796

Colgu was the head lecturer in scripture and theology at Clonmacnoise. So versed was he in the Epistles of St. Paul, legend said, the apostle himself used to counsel and instruct him.

Colgu of Clonmacnoise is believed to be the Colgu, teacher of England's scholar, Alcuin, who became head of the palace school of Charlemagne. There is extant a letter Alcuin addressed to "Colgu, Professor in Ireland, the blessed master and pious Father of Albinus" (the more usual name given Alcuin in France by Charlemagne and his Court.) Alcuin complains that for some time past he was not deemed worthy to receive any of those letters "so precious in my sight from your Fatherhood" but he daily feels the benefit of his absent father's prayers. He adds he was sending a gift of fifty shekels of silver from King Charles to which he added fifty more of his own for the brotherhood and a quantity of olive oil for the Irish bishops for sacramental purposes.

It is possible Colgu of Clonmacnoise was a teacher at York in England. In tracing Irish art and its influence on the Continent, Francoise Henry names Tours among abbeys generously supplied with Irish models, tracing the Irish influence at Tours to Alcuin's abbacy and stating that Alcuin was brought up as the pupil of an Irishman at York.

The Irish Josephus Scotus, who accompanied Alcuin to France, is believed to have been another of Colgu's pupils and to have taught at York. From Charlemagne's court he addresses Colgu as his "blessed master and dear father." Irish schoolmen were a continuing influence at the palace school of Charlemagne. It is suggested that Colgu, through his pupils, gave as much impetus to the Carolingian revival as many of those whose names are more closely associated with it.

Daniel-Rops, 158; Kenney, 534; Fitzpatrick, II: 121; Healy, 272; Benedictine Monks, 147.

Diarmuid
June 21   823

Diarmuid founded his monastery in 818, only a few years before his death in 823. Apparently, however, he brought great prestige and importance to the foundation where his name is perpetuated at Castledermot in Kildare. The future king of Munster and bishop of Cashel, scholar and saint, Cormac MacCuileanain (August 17), came there to be educated and legend says that at Cormac's death in 908, the abbot of Castledermot led the procession that brought the bishop's body there for burial.

Castledermot relics number a round tower, a Romanesque doorway and two magnificent sculptured Crosses. Francoise Henry's *Early Irish Art* has eight full page views of those Crosses. In *Crosses and Culture of Ireland*, Yale's Arthur Kingsley Porter devotes no less than 17 cuts of the sculptured panels to the illustration of Castledermot's High Crosses.

Porter; Henry, II: 22–3, 53, 137; Neeson, 121, 149, 167; *Benn*, 86.

Aengus the Culdee
March 11   842

One day as Aengus was praying in a little wayside chapel, he saw angels hovering over a newly made grave in the churchyard there. On inquiry, the pastor told him that resting there was an old soldier who had every day of his life invoked the intercession of every saint he could call to mind. Ever after, Aengus devoted his studies and his writings to the saints. He is best known for his "Féilire," a Lives of the Saints, written in verse for easier remembering.

Aengus was born, educated by Fintan, lived and died, all at Clonenagh. After ordination he became an anchorite at nearby Disert Enos, so given to penance and prayer, the people called him the "Céile Dé," or Companion of God, anglicized, Culdee. They came to him in such crowds he slipped away to the monastery of Maelruain at Tallaght where he enrolled as the humblest lay monk ready to perform the most menial work. In the monastery barn one day he discovered and helped a young pupil weeping bitterly over lessons he could not get. When the poorest of all the students suddenly became the best of them, Maelruain went in search of an explanation and so was disclosed the true identity of the Clonenagh scholar.

Maelruain enlisted his collaboration and jointly they compiled the "Martyrology of Tallaght." After Maelruain's death, about 792, Aengus returned to Clonenagh. His "féilire," or Festology of the Saints, appeared about 800. Next came "Pedigrees of the Saints" which includes many topographical notes. One section of it, the "Book of Litanies," dates the invocation of the saints as a form of devotion in Ireland as early as the year 800. Aengus is thought to be the earliest of the writers on the Irish saints.

Kenney, 471, 479; Butler-Attwater I: 559; *Catholic Encyclopedia* I: 173, VII: 677; Healy, 404; Neeson, 57.

Buo

February 5   c. 900

When the Norwegians "discovered" Iceland in 860, they found Irish books, bells and staffs on the island. Brendan, perhaps, other monks in fact, were sailing to the Faroe Islands and to Iceland in the 7th and throughout the 8th century. In 825, the Irish geographer Dicuil, in his *De Mensura Orbis Terrae*, quotes, concerning the summer solstice, "certain clerics who remained on the Iceland Island from the first of February until the first of August." Irish place names mingle in the local topography of Iceland.

Norse settlers were Christianized by Irish missionaries, chief among whom were Buo and Ernulph. The Icelandic writer, Arngrim Jonas, tells us that in the 9th century, a Northman, Helgo, received an Irish exile Ernulph with his religious family and gave him welcome and permission to build a church dedicated to Colmcille in a village called Esinberg. He states that a holy Irishman by the name of Buo while yet a young man became a distinguished missionary in that same province.

O'Hanlon, II: 341; Fitzpatrick, II: 147; Little, 74, 96, 168, 223; Neeson, 37; Toynbee, II: 324.

II

Irish Saints in Scotland

In *Irish Monasticism* Father John Ryan, S.J., observes that a study of the calendar of the saints of Scotland makes it abundantly clear that Ireland is the mother church of that country. Until the advent and good offices of Irish missionaries from Scotia (as Ireland was then known), Alba, or Caledonia, was a Pictish nation. It came to be called Scotia Minor, then the Land of the Scots and finally Scotland.

Colmcille from Donegal is the apostle of Scotland. Out of his ministrations from Iona flowed religion, schooling, peace in the whole country. Moluag of Lismore in Alba, Donnan of Eigg, Cathan of Kingarth in Bute and, a century later, Maelrubha of Applecross were founders of other important missionary centers in Scotland. History records that the Irish colonized Scotland, gave it a name, a literature and a language, gave it Christianity and gave it sixty kings of the Irish race.

Iona was not only the repository of the most ancient Scottish records, it housed literary treasures that long through the middle ages were to be found there in spite of many destructive inroads. Samuel Johnson, the 18th century English writer, paid this tribute to Iona: "We are now treading that illustrious island which was once the luminary of the Caledonian regions, whence savage clans and roving barbarians derived the benefits of knowledge and the blessings of religion. . . . That man is little to be envied whose patriotism would not gain force upon the plain of Marathon, or whose piety would not grow warmer among the ruins of Iona."

The great feat of the Irish monks in Scotland after Iona itself was the conquest of the greater part of England for the faith. On the Iona outpost of Lindisfarne in Northumbria England bestowed the name Holy Island, as it appears on the map today.

71

Lua (Moluag, Murlach)
June 25   C. 592

Moluag of Lismore in Scotland is the Lua referred to by Bernard of Clairvaux when he says that Comgall of Bangor was the father of many thousands of monks whose schools filled both Ireland and Scotland, with one of that sacred family, Lua, alone the founder of a hundred monasteries. Moluag's Irish name, Lugaigh (pronounced Lua), plus the prefix Mo that denoted affection, became Molua.

Modern research credits Moluag no less than Colmcille with covering Scotland with centers of Christianity. Whereas Moluag's mission was directed to the Picts, Colmcille came to the Irish colony. When it happened that the Picts, their language and their culture were entirely absorbed by the Scots (Irish), Moluag's importance was obscured and his achievements were merged into the Iona legend.

A year before the arrival of Colmcille Moluag, accompanied by Comgall, came from Bangor to fix his headquarters on the pleasant grassy island of Lismore off the west coast of Scotland. From the first, the Pictish King Brude was cordial to Moluag and his work, Comgall, of the Pictish race himself and familiar with the language, having gone in person to obtain the royal sanction.

Moluag far outstripped Colmcille in eastern Scotland and among the Picts. His activities extended from Lismore into many neighboring islands, across Drumalban far into eastern Pictland, north and south inland into mountain passes and along river valleys, up and down the east coast line, each monastery a center for dependent churches. All of these stations looked to Lismore and, more remotely, to Bangor from which came a long continuing stream of workers to Scotland. A century of missionary labors stretches between the two great Bangor saints in Scotland, Moluag and Maelrubha.

Moluag was long remembered. King Malcolm II attributed his victory over the Vikings near Murlach to the intercession of Our Lady and St. Murlach. In thanksgiving, in 1010, he founded at Murlach, under their joint patronage, an abbey, a cathedral and an episcopal see. The latter, however, was subsequently transferred to Aberdeen. In the 13th century, Moluag's church at Lismore was the cathedral of the diocese of Argyll. Up until the Reformation, the saint's bell was in Argyll, and the Livingstone family of the village of Bacuil (crozier) were the hereditary custodians of his staff for long generations. Documents of the year 1544 tell of a transfer of lands that included the keeping of the great staff of St. Moluag as freely as the owners, father, grandfather, great-grandfather and other predecessors held the same. His blackthorn stick, now in the collection of the Duke of Argyll, is believed to have been covered originally with a gilded copper casing. In the days of clan warfare, it was carried at the head of the army of the men of Lorne.

Moluag died on June 25, 592, in eastern Scotland in Nairnshire, where a magnificently carved slab of sandstone commemorates him at his Rossmarkie church. Lismore claims he was brought back across Drumalban for burial in his churchyard there. Wherever he rests, his foot prints may be traced by the widespread Kilmoluags that dot the map of Scotland — the survival of Moluag's hundred monasteries.

Simpson; Daniel-Rops, 96; Mould, II; Skene, II: 133, 407; Moran 77; Butler-Attwater, II: 641.

Colmcille (Columba)
June 9   521–597

Colmcille was a Prince of Tirconnell (Donegal), a great, great grandson of Niall of the Nine Hostages, founder of the dynasty of Ulster kings that continued until 1610. On his mother's side were Leinster kings. Three of his cousins became monarchs of Ireland. Colmcille chose the austere life of a monk-priest, electing never to receive episcopal rank. His name, nevertheless, towers aloft in that distant age without equal in the annals of Ireland, Scotland, or England.

Apostle of Scotland, founder of the Scottish nation, bearer of culture and Christianity to Iona and Scotland (and indirectly to all of northern England), Colmcille remains one of the most impressive figures of the Middle Ages. From his own day to the present, historians have done him honor. Chambers in his *Caledonia* writes "Columba's name will always be remembered as the disinterested benefactor of Scotland." The Duke of Argyll speaks of Columba, a man of powerful character and splendid gifts — his monument the place he has secured in the memory of mankind. Others extol his standing in the people's hearts, his way with words and song, the Celtic charm that reaches across the centuries still.

From his infancy, Colmcille was place in the care of the holy priest whom he later commemorated in the church named for him Kilcronaghan in County Derry. He was schooled for the church by Finian of Moville, Finian of Clonard, Mobhi of Glasnevin. He studied music and poetry in the Leinster Bardic School of Gemman. A large number of his poems are preserved in manuscript collections in the Bodleian Library, Oxford, and in the Burgundian Library, Brussels.

In 545, Colmcille built his first church at Derry, ever after the spot on earth he loved the best. Durrow came next; then Kells which reached its real importance at the beginning of the 9th century when the monks of Iona, fleeing from the Vikings, made Kells the Columban headquarters: Swords, Drumcliff, Tory, some thirty-seven monastic churches in his native land. To this period also belongs that art treasure for the ages, the manuscript Psalms, written in Colmcille's own hand and known as the Cathach. But his great title to glory was his island monastery at Iona.

Colmcille, at the age of forty-two, "wishing to be an exile for Christ," set out with twelve companions on his life-long pilgrimage exile from Ireland. Writers in general like to repeat, one after the other, the story of a penetential exile as given in the collection of legends brought out by Manus O'Donnell in 1532, a compilation more readable than historical. Skene in *Celtic Scotland* deplores the O'Donnell work as "the grand repertory of all the late and loose traditions overlying the real biography."

Two of these stories attempt to "explain" Colmcille's exile. A well-known tradition is "the copyright dispute." Allegedly Colmcille transcribed against the abbot's express prohibition, the copy of the Psalter which Finian of Moville had recently brought from Rome, and Finian claimed the copy for his own. The matter, allegedly again, was carried to the High King Diarmuid who ruled against Colmcille "to every cow its calf, to every book its copy." In another, the Cul Dremne legend, Colmcille's connection had to do with a violation of sanctuary. During a game of hurling, Curnan, son of the King of . Connacht, struck and killed the son of Diarmuid's chief steward. Curnan fled to Colmcille but Diarmuid seized the youth and had him put to death. The King of Connacht, joined by two princes of the north (first cousins of Colmcille, Fergus and Domhnaill with grievances of their own) marched against Diarmuid, vanquishing him at Cul Dremne but with a loss of 3000 dead on the field. At a synod of "many venerable seniors" assembled to deal with Colmcille's complicity, the saint appeared before them. Brendan of Birr saw holy angels accompanying him. Finian of Moville likewise testified to his own reverence for his former pupil. A confessor, whose name is not agreed upon, supposedly pronounced upon Colmcille the penance of exile from Ireland forever. He often, in fact, returned to look to his various communities.

Butler-Attwater *Lives of the Saints* cautions us it must be admitted that missionary zeal and love of Christ are the only motives ascribed to Colmcille by his earliest biographers and by Adamnan. Bede had the simple record "There came from Ireland into Britain a famous priest and abbot, a monk by habit and life whose name was Columba to preach the Word of God."

Not until two years after the battle of Cul Dremne did Colmcille land on the island of Iona, off the coast of Irish-occupied territory, the kingdom of Argyll (the eastern Gael), in the west of Scotland. It was already holy ground. Odhrain of Latteragh, who died in 549, had founded churches on Iona, Mull, and Tiree. In the Iona cemetery, Reilag Odhrain, were buried the Irish kings of Scottish Dalriada down to King Gabhrain, whose death in the battle with the Picts in 560 had reduced the fortunes of the Irish colonists to very low ebb.

Then came Colmcille "not to destroy, but to save, not to conquer but to civilize" in the words of Chambers in his *Caledonia*. The long history of Gaelic Scotland had begun.

Colmcille's mission was primarily to the Irish colony in Scotland but indispensible to that mission was sanction from the Pictish King Brude. Colmcille's first overtures were a failure. Then, Comgall of Bangor and Cainnech of Aghaboe, Pictish speakers, both of them, arranged a meeting for all three with the king. At that meeting, Brude became Colmcille's life-long friend. Most amiably he granted him the island of Iona already held under the rival King Conall. Especially worthy of note is the fact there is no record of any battle between the Irish colony and Brude after this meeting.

The first Christian inauguration of a sovereign of record in history and the precedent for the coronation ceremonies of Westminster Abbey, is Colmcille's consecration of Aidan, King of the Irish colony in Scotland. Thus auspiciously he launched the king from whose line came Kenneth MacAlpine, crowned at Scone the first Irish king of all Scotland; Malcolm Canmore who in 1093, laid the foundations of the Cathedral of Durham as it now stands; Alexander III, 1249–1286, the last Irish king of Scotland. Concerning the latter, Moray McLaren comments "The rich seed of his kingly line had died unfruitful within him."

In 575 at the Convention of Drumceat in Ireland, Colmcille obtained freedom for Aidan's kingdom from all tribute to Ireland, another important step in peaceable relations between the Irish and the Picts. He pleaded the cause of the Irish bards, now fallen into disrepute and threatened with extinction. Under his direction the guild which had merited such high honor in the past was reorganized into a national bardic school system.

Colmcille's austerity, fasting and vigils passed credibility. His bed was a stone, as was his pillow. For his monks, however, there was a pallet, probably of straw, and a pillow. And always there was tender consideration for the poor and the afficted. During his thirty-four year mission, he studded Scotland with Christian churches and schools. He staffed them with the stream of Irish disciples who came to him at Iona. And to every church he founded he gave a Book of Gospels. In that day of laboriously hand written books, "three hundred splendid lasting copies" of the Gospels are said to have come from his pen alone.

One of Colmcille's poems is addressed in affectionate envy to a sea gull which came flying from the west, in envy that it so recently had seen Ireland. He never got over his nostalgic love of home, never lost his great pride of race. He preferred, he said, the Gaels to all other men of the world and his own kindred of Conall to the other Gaels and the kindred of Lugaidh to the rest of the kindred of Conall. His love and solicitude centered especially in his monastic families. Angels of heaven, he declared, crowded every leaf of the oaks at Derry when his holy monks there chanted the praises of God. At Iona every evening as the brethren returned wearily from the day's labors, he would lay down his pen to ask God's blessing upon them. One day Baithin asked, were the others also sensible of something unusual as they approached the monastery? The oldest of the monks spoke up. Every day at that place and at that hour he breathed a fragrance as of all the flowers of the world and he felt a sudden joy of heart so incomparable, all trouble and fatigue, even the heavy sheaves he carried, were forgotten.

Colmcille died at Iona on June 9, 597, without illness as he had foretold. He had made a last fond circuit to inspect and bless the island in every part and, returning to the monastery, he took up his constant occupation, the transcription of the Bible. Having written ''But they that seek the Lord shall lack no good thing,'' he laid down his pen and said ''Let Baithin write what follows.'' Baithin and a line of eleven other abbots of Colmcille's own race of Conal Gulban ruled at Iona. Forty-nine Irish abbots in all continued until 1202.

Within Reilag Odhrain, the Iona cemetery, lie great dead of many centuries. The prestige of Colmcille's name was without equal and the great of the land held it the final distinction to be buried near him. Some sixty Irish, Scottish and Norwegian kings took up their rest there, among them Duncan and MacBeth made famous by Shakespeare.

> *Ross.* ''Where is Duncan buried?''
> *MacDuff.* ''Carried to Colme-kill
> The sacred storehouse of his predecessors
> And guardian of their bones.''

During the 14th centenary of Colmcille's landing on Iona, in 1963, one of the many pilgrimages was a nine-day journey made in a row boat manned by thirteen members of the Church of Ireland who travelled the traditional course taken by Colmcille and his twelve companions when they sailed from Derry to land on Iona on Pentecost Sunday in 563.

When Ireland won Catholic Emancipation in 1829, Derry, the site of Colmcille's first foundation, received world-wide newspaper publicity. Ever since the Protestant Williamites defeated Catholic King James at Derry in 1688, a great statue of the leader of the Protestants, the Rev. Mr. Walker, stood guard on the walls of Derry. All through the Penal years, all through wintry storms and summer rains, Walker's effigy stood with sword uncompromisingly aloft. On the 13th day of April, 1829, the very day the royal signature was given to the Act of Emancipation, the sword fell with a prophetic crash on the ramparts of Derry and shattered into pieces.

''Colm's great Book,'' the Book of Kells, a work of almost miraculous perfection with no peer in the world of ancient caligraphy, is housed in Trinity College, Dublin. There may be counted in it in the space of a square inch no less than 158 interlacements of white ribbon edged in black in which even under a magnifying glass no flaw is discernable. The date of "the chief relic of the western world" is variously assigned — to Colmcille's own hand, with later illuminations and decorations, to a scribe, or scribes, of the ninth century. In 1006, it was stolen from Kells in County Meath and when it was found "twenty days and two months" later, its gemstudded cover was gone. In 1950, Urs GrafVerlag of Berne, Switzerland, brought out a reproduction of the Book a work of four years. One hundred twenty copies of the two-volume edition ($450.00 a set) were allotted to the United States, facsimilies that may be found in rare book collections and in the large libraries — New York, Los Angeles, Portland, the Newberry Library of Chicago, etc.

The earliest known Irish portraiture of the Blessed Mother and Child is to be found in the Book of Kells. The highly elaborate border, the glory around her head bearing three crosses, the angels and their sceptres, present symbolism of great interest to scholars. But probably the greatest interest in the picture is in the proof it affords of the veneration of the Virgin Mary in the early Irish Church.

The Book of Kells, insured for three million dollars, heavily guarded day and night, was shown in London, in 1961, in a fund-raising exhibit of Irish art treasures arranged by Trinity College, Dublin. The staging of the exhibit, in itself, was hailed as a triumph of art and photography. Flanking the Book of Kells were the Books of Durrow, Dimma, Armagh, and the Lindsifarne Gospels. *The Daily Telegraph* reported ". . . . There is much of interest in the exhibition . . . but inevitably one moves on to the last gallery where the early manuscripts are gathered together. Around the walls are large photographs of details from the Book of Kells and others of the Irish countryside. They conjure up something of the atmosphere and magic that produced some of the greatest of European works of art."

The Book of Durrow, also in Trinity College, Dublin, is a small illuminated manuscript described as an incomparable copy of the four Gospels. An entry in one of the folios asks "A remembrance of the scribe Columba who wrote this evangel in the space of twelve days." The first cumdach, or book shrine, of record, elaborately conceived and jewel studded, was made for the Book of Durrow. The cumdach has disappeared, but its inscription survives, "The prayer and benediction of Colmcille be on Flann, son of Malachy, King of Ireland (877–916) who caused this cover to be made." In 1961, the Swiss firm of Urs-Graf Verlag brought out a fac-simile edition of six hundred and sixty copies ($216 each) of the Book of Durrow. With the Book of Kells and the Book of Lindisfarne, it is the third such Irish book to be completed. Dublin

National Museum has another Durrow memorial — a crozier executed in the remarkable Celtic bronze work of the 11th century. It encloses a wooden stick treasured as a staff that Colmcille carried.

Still another famous book connected with the Saint is the Psaltair he is said to have copied in the monastery of Finian of Moville, the *Cathach* or Battle Book of the O'Donnells, so called from the ancient days when it was carried into battle by that family who claim Colmcille's same ancestry.

In his *Irish Illuminated Manuscripts* Sweeney describes the *Cathach* of Saint Columba: ''. . . . a preciously conceived book, the earliest surviving manuscript in Irish majuscule (in all probability, from the end of the sixth century) . . . . . . it already announces in its integrity, its clarity and the concreteness of its detail, the great works (more colourful if no less intense) to come after it.''

A hereditary keepership under the MacRobartaigh family was set up for the *Cathach* with generous lands for its maintenance. In the 11th century was executed the lovely old richly embossed, gem-studded cumdach or shrine which is inscribed "Pray for Cathbar O'Donnell for whom this casket was made . . . . and for Domnal McRobartaigh [Abbot] of Kells at whose house it was made." Daniel O'Donnell, Brigadier-general in the French service, took the Psaltair to the Continent in 1723 and a dated inscription states he had a new rim affixed. In 1814, the widow of Sir Neal O'Donnell brought suit against Sir W. Bethan to whom the shrine had been loaned, for his transgression of the age old tradition that the casket must never be opened. He, however, brought the relic out of hiding. Inside the rich shrine was a ravaged, much decayed wooden box and in it was Columcille's manuscript, reduced to a dark damp mass. It had folios damaged beyond salvage at the beginning and the end, but 58 pages, the 31st to the 106th psalms, have been saved. The last owner, Richard O'Donnell, turned the *Cathach* over to the Irish Academy, Dublin.

Kenney, 425, 630; Simpson; Pochin Mould; Porter; Skene; Montalembert; Fitzpatrick, I; Daniel-Rops, 47; Ryan, 125; McLaren, 29.

Riaghail (Regulus, Rule)
March 30   Sixth century

Regulus, Riaghail in Gaelic, was famous in the early Irish church as abbot of Muicinish in Lough Derg in the Shannon before becoming a missionary in Scotland in Cainnech's monastery at Rigmond, the ancient name of St. Andrews. He is believed to have died there.

In the fanciful legend of the origin of St. Andrews, a 4th century Greek monk is made to bring relics of St. Andrew to Scotland. In reality, those relics were acquired in the 8th century in the time of the Irish Abbot Tuathal, who died in 747. Skene in *Celtic Scotland* identifies the alleged 4th century Greek Regulus, or Rule, with Riaghail, the 6th century Irish monk.

Benedictine Monks, 505; Moran, 199; Skene, I: 299.

Cathan
May 11   Sixth century

Cathan, Bishop and Abbot-founder of an important center at Kingarth, was of the race of the Irish Picts and the contemporary and friend of Comgall and Cainnech. Blane of Dunblane was his nephew. The churches called Cillchattan commemorate Cathan and the extent of the Kingarth influence in the Irish mission territory of the southern Picts can be traced by the many churches dedicated to Cathan and to his successor, Blane.

Simpson, 81; Skene, II: 133, 138.

Blane
August 10   c. 590

Aidan, the Irish King in Scotland, was Blane's father, Cathan of his native Bute his uncle. He was educated in Ireland under Comgall of Bangor and Cainnech of Aghaboe and returned to Cathan at Kingarth whom he succeeded as bishop and whose missionary work he continued.

Blane's chief monastery was on the south side of Bute within the district of Kingarth, at the place named for him Dunblane. Churches commemorated him at Kilblane in Kirkmahoe, at Kilblain near Caerlaveroch, at Southend in Kintyre, at Kilblane in Glenshira near Inveray at a site on Loch Shiel, at Dunblane at Caibeal Bhlathain, Lochearnhead and at Kilblain near Old Meldrum and Petblane in Daviot, both in Aberdeenshire. In the southern part of the kingdom of Strathclyde beyond the Solway a group of churches bear Blane's name in Cumberland. He died about 590 and was buried in Kingarth in Bute. The monastery at Kingarth continued to flourish and the list of its rulers extends to 790. In 794, Irish Annals recorded "the devastation of all the islands of Britain by the heathen" meaning the Vikings.

The pre-Reformation cathedral built on the site of the saint's monastery at Dunblane continued an episcopal see until the change of religion. His bell is still preserved there. Dioceses that observed Blane's feast are St. Andrews, Dunkeld (which included the former see of Dunbland), and Argyll.

Simpson, 81; Skene, II: 138; O'Kelly; Benedictine Monks, 109.

Drostan

July 11   Sixth century

Various churches along the northeastern coast trace their origin to Colmcille's disciple, Drostan, who is venerated as one of the apostles of Scotland. He was of Irish royal blood, of the family of Cosgrach. The *Book of Deer* tells that Colmcille, on obtaining grant of a fort in the district of Buchan, blessed it and named Drostan first abbot of Deer Monastery. It flourished for a thousand years.

After Deer came a period of eremitical life and a church he built at Glenesk in Angus where he was famed for miracles and sanctity. The ancient *Breviary of Aberdeen* marks his festival at December 15 and adds that "his relics are preserved in a stone tomb at Aberdour where many sick persons find relief." Drostan's Fair was celebrated November 14. Aberdeen and Argyll kept his feast on July 11.

Cambridge University houses the Irish manuscript *Book of Deer* which is ascribed to an eighth century member of the community. It is one of the oldest monuments of Scottish literature. Distinguishing features are the minuscule lettering of Irish schoolmen, peculiarities common to Irish Bible editions, and the entries at the end which have the account of the foundation of the Abbey of Deer, written in the Irish language. A printing of the *Book of Deer* was made in 1869. It came to light in the library of Cambridge University in 1857 and is of special interest as the earliest Scottish Gaelic writing in existence.

Butler-Attwater, III: 71; Skene, II: 134; Simpson, 69; Moran, 75; Montalembert, II: 52.

Cainnech (Kenneth, Canice)

October 11   c. 517–600

Irish bards in Cainnech's time were men of power and prestige. Ulster-born Cainnech's father was a scholar-poet and, accordingly, the saint was of high social status. He studied under Finian of Clonard and was with Comgall of Bangor, Kieran of Clonmacnoise, and Columcille in Mobhi's school at Glasnevin.

His two most important foundations in Ireland were Aghaboe and Kilkenny, named from his Church of Cainnech (pronounced Kenny).

By race an Irish Pict and a speaker of the Pictish language, the saint spent much of his religious life as a missionary in Scotland, especially among the Pictish people. He accompanied both Comgall and Colmcille to obtain sanction for their bases at Lismore and Iona from the pagan Pictish King

Brude. He was often on missions with Colmcille out of Iona, which formerly had a Killchainnech.

He built churches in Scottish Dalriada, on the islands of Coll, Tiree, Mull, South Uist and in Cantyre. He was also the patron of Kennoway in Fife. Another dedication was Laggan-Kenny on the east end of Loch Laggan. Until the 16th century, ruins could be traced of the monastery maintained for centuries by the brethren of St. Kenneth at Maiden Castle.

Aengus records "Aghaboe was his principal church and he has a Recles (monastery) at Kill-Rigmonaig in Alba." The ancient name of St. Andrews in Scotland was Rigmond and the first mention of a church there was the 6th century Kil-Rigmond, a monastery of Irish monks under Cainnech. One of the brethren was the Irish Regulus (Riaghail in Gaelic) formerly abbot of a monastery in Lough Derg in the Shannon and commemorated at March 20.

With the change of religion and a different and more ancient origin being considered desirable, there appeared the fanciful legend that a 4th century Greek monk, Regulus, or Rule, by divine admonition carried relics of the apostle St. Andrew to Scotland and deposited them at Rigmond, thenceforth known as St. Andrews.

In sober fact, it was only in 736 that the Pictish monarch acquired those relics and changed the name to St. Andrews. At the time, the abbot of Rigmond was the Irish Tuathal who died in 747. Skene in *Celtic Scotland* identifies the alledged 4th century Greek monk with Regulus, the Irish Riaghail of the 6th century.

Simpson, 83; Mould, I: 102; Moran, 81, 199; Ryan; Skene, I: 296; II, 137; Montalembert, II: 83; Benedictine Monks, 505.

Kentigern (Mungo)
January 14   c. 603

Kentigern, resplendent in mitre and staff, is emblazoned on the coat of arms of the city of Glasgow. Displayed with him are the bell that announced his services and one of the "trees of St. Kentigern" that, as late as 1500, were a landmark in the title deeds of the city.

Ireland claims that Thenog, Kentigern's mother, was Irish. According to the legend, Thenog was cast adrift in disgrace in a little boat "made after the fashion of the Scots." She was carried in safety to a sandy beach in Fifeshire and there was born the boy destined to be the first bishop of Glasgow and one of the chief patrons of Scotland. St. Servan, or Serf, became the protector and instructor of mother and child and from him Kentigern received the term of affection, "Mungo."

Thenog was also to win a place in Scottish Calendars. St. Encoh's (Thenog's) Square in Glasgow was named from the church dedicated to her. It was demolished in the Reformation.

Kentigern is believed to have restored the church founded earlier by Ninian in Glasgow. It was there he built his cell around which disciples gathered and in St. Ninian's cemetery he planted the famous Glasgow trees. The king and clergy, seeing in the saint some one to build back the ruins of Ninian's work, "called a bishop from Ireland after the manner of the Britons and Scots of that period" and Kentigern was consecrated bishop. Disturbances later on sent him into exile. After a stay, as abbot perhaps, at St. Asaph's in north Wales and a visit to St. David's at Menevia, he returned to his missionary labors in southwestern Scotland with Glasgow his chief center. An episode of note was the exchange of croziers by Kentigern and Colmcille, a very formal pledge of friendship.

Skene, II: 39; 179; Simpson; Mould; Butler-Attwater, I: 83; Moran, 142.

Donnan
April 17   c. 616

Old records represent Donnan as having started out from Iona. Simpson points out that his churches follow the same missionary trail the earlier Ninian had travelled, at Kirkmaiden next door to Whithorn and on to the Kildonnans in Colmonell, Ayrshire, Sutherland among the many places before Eigg of his later days.

The *Martyrology of Aengus* records the martyrdom Colmcille is said to have foretold for him: "Donnan then went with his monastic family to the Western Isles and they took up their abode there in a place where the sheep of the queen of the country were kept. 'Let them all be killed,' said she. 'That would not be a religious act,' said her people. But they were murderously assailed. At this time the cleric was at Mass. 'Let us have respite till Mass is ended,' said Donnan. 'Thou shalt have it,' said they. And when it was over, they were slain, every one of them." The island of Eigg is believed to have been pasture land for flocks of sheep, and while the people would seem to have been favorable to the Christian colony, the rule was in the hands of a queen still pagan, who employed sea pirates to destroy the community. The names of Donnan's 52 martyr companions are preserved in copies of the *Martyrology of Tallaght* which was compiled about 792.

Eigg, afterwards restored, gave the names of at least four abbot successors of Donnan to Irish Calendars, and the saint's staff was cherished for long centuries at Husterless, until its destruction in the Reformation. On the island of Eigg, the Catholic faith survived all vicissitudes and Donnan continued to be venerated "as if by special blessing of these martyrs."

Skene, II: 134, 152, 169; Moran, 77; Montalemberg, II: 81; Butler-Attwater, II: 113; Simpson, 66.

Adamnan (Eunan)
September 23   624–704

Adamnan's abbey at Dull is termed the cradle of the University of St. Andrews by Montalembert.

Scotland's literature begins with Adamnan's *Life of Columcille*, "the most complete piece of such biography that all Europe can boast of . . . . throughout the whole of the middle ages." A copy made prior to 713 is the oldest manuscript in Switzerland, the emporium of old manuscripts.

Adamnan's "Holy Places of Palestine" is the only extant description of the Holy Land as it was about the year 700. It records information obtained from Arculf, a returned pilgrim from the Holy Land who was stormbound on the island of Iona. Bede incorporated the tract in his *Historia Ecclesiastica*; about a hundred copies remain of Bede's larger abridgement of the work. Important manuscripts of the unabridged narrative are preserved in Berne and Paris.

Donegal-born and of Colmcille's own high lineage, Adamnan made his studies for the church at Iona. From boyhood he was a special favorite of the southern prince, Finachta, later High King of Ireland, whose chaplain and confessor he became at Tara. Ancient Tara had many memorials of the saint. In 679, Adamnan was elected ninth abbot of Iona. It was a very important post. The successor of Colmcille was hardly equalled in influence by the primate of Armagh.

One of Adamnan's pupils was the English prince Aldfrid who because of his love of literature, "ob studium literarum exulabat," spent some twenty years in Ireland. Afterwards he was king of Northumbria and the first literary king of the Anglo-Saxon race. During his abbacy at Iona, Adamnan continued as Finachta's ambassador in matters of state. One of his missions took him to his former pupil, Aldfrid, to obtain the release of sixty Irish captives taken in an unprovoked attack in 684 by the English King Ecfrid, which act Bede said, brought down from heaven upon Ecfrid his death the following year.

Try as he might, Adamnan was never able to move the Iona brethren one iota from the tradition of Colmcille's calculation of the Easter date. Revision came to the Columban foundations, but not in Adamnan's lifetime.

Named with Adamnan as religious writers of the seventh century are Cogitosus, Tirechan, and Muirchu. Adamnan's works remain the chief record as well as the most important literary production to survive from the old Celtic church of Ireland, the most important of the four historical sources of real worth from the seventh century.

Healy tells us "In the year 1845, Dr. Ferdinand Keller was poking with a German's pertinacity through the shelves of the town library of Schaffhausen in Switzerland. In a corner of the room he found a high bookchest filled with all kinds of manuscripts without title or number of any kind and at the very bottom of the heap he came upon a dark brown parchment manuscript bound in moth-eaten beechwood, covered with calfskin carefully clasped in front and very neatly and curiously sewed at the back. It was a goodly quarto of sixty-eight leaves with double columns written on dark-colored goat skin parchment in large heavy drawn letters of the character known as minuscular. Everything about the manuscript showed great antiquity, the cover, the parchment, the lettering and the ornaments. Dr. Keller at first thought he had come upon a hitherto undiscovered treasure, but in this he was mistaken. He only rediscovered a lost treasure and procured its preservation for the learned world. On examination the manuscript turned out to be the oldest and most authentic copy of Adamnan's *Life of Columcille*, made in Iona during the lifetime of Adamnan himself, or certainly a few years after his death." The copy is the work of Dorbene, abbot of Iona who died in 713, and it is the identical manuscript formerly at Reichenau, copied by the Jesuit Stephen White. Father White's copy was used by John Colgan in his *Trias Thaumaturga* published in 1647, and was the one used by the Bollandists in 1698.

Macalister, 48; Kenney, 433; Fitzpatrick, I: 122; II: 154; Healy, 334; Moran, 108, 301; Butler-Attwater, III: 625; Montalembert.

Maelrubha
April 21   642–722

What Colmcille and Moluag accomplished in ancient Scotland in the sixth century, Maelrubha rivalled in the seventh with a final great flowering of the Celtic Church before the Vikings. Maelrubha was of princely Niall lineage on his father's side, and through his mother was of Comgall's race of Irish Picts. He went to the monastery Comgall had founded for his education to the priesthood. His mission base at Applecross, like Moluag's, was an offshoot of Bangor.

The saint's Applecross brethren ranged widely over both Pictland and Scottish Dalriada, and Maelrubha's name is recorded in place names scattered over the length and breadth of Scotland. He won great fresh extensions of the

Celtic territory, all of the rugged, almost inaccessible western seaboard between Loch Carron and Loch Broom, the south and west parts of the Island of Skye and eastern Ross. Twenty-one known parishes were dedicated to Maelrubha under such forms of his name as Maree, Mulruby, Mary, Murry, Summuruff, Summereve. For fifty years he tramped the high roads and the low roads with such a reputation for sanctity and miracles he was regarded as the patron saint throughout all of that territory.

To the north of Applecross in the long narrow scenic Loch Maree is Maelrubha's little island, Inis Maree, "the favored isle of the saint." On it besides his oratory and a cemetery was his holy well, a spring "of power unspeakable" in cases of insanity. It was famous until very recent times for the cures obtained there. He is still invoked for mental illness in Scotland.

Scottish legend makes Maelrubha a martyr at the hands of Norse pirates and the parish church at Urquhart is said to occupy the site of the chapel first built to mark the spot where he died. A mound outside Applecross, Cloadh Maree, is pointed out as his grave. Within a radius of six miles of this the area was accorded all the rights and privileges of sanctuary.

Irish abbots continued at Applecross for a while. In 737 died Failbhe, "Comharb of Maelrubha," who with twenty-two of his religious perished at sea. The Annals of Ulster enter the death of "MacOigi of Aporcrossan" in 801. Memory of Maelrubha seems to have survived a long time. In the time of clan warfare, when one of the MacDonald partisans in the feud with the MacKinsies in the seventeenth century was told it was a sacrilege to kill a MacKinsie within Maelrubha's sanctuary, MacDonald replied it was no sin to kill a MacKinsie wherever they might be found.

Skene, II: 169; Simpson; Mould; Moran, 187; Montalembert, II: 52; Attwater-Butler, II: 143.

Comghan (Coman)

October 13   Eighth century

Ceallach (Kelly), King of Leinster, was Comghan's father. Kentigerna, the saint of Loch Loman, was his sister; Fillan, famous in Scottish and Irish Calendars, his nephew. Comghan, his sister, her three sons, and seven other missionaries came into western Ross where he founded a monastery at Lochalsh. Two ancient churches there, Kilchoan and Killelan still preserve the names of Comghan and Fillan. Other church sites radiating out of Lochalsh trace Comghan's activities: in Islay at Loch Melfort, in Ardnamurchan, in Knoydart, in Skye and in North Uist. In eastern Ross he had a church at Kiltearn and at his more famous center at Turriff. Turriff, one of the most important Irish foundations between the Dee and the Spey, survived as a Celtic religious center until its disappearance in lay possession in the thirteenth century. Comghan's feast is observed in the diocese of Aberdeen.

Skene, II: 169, 380; Simpson, 84; Butler-Attwater, IV: 104.

Kentigerna
January 7   c. 734

Kentigerna, mother of saints and "Loch Lomond's Lady of Grace," was the daughter of Ceallach, King of Leinster, and the wife of Feredach. Irish Calendars set the feast-day of the Daughters of Feredach at March 23. Two sons are listed, Mundus Son of Feredach and the more famous Fillan of Scotland.

After Feredach's death, Kentigerna accompanied her brother Comghan and her son Fillan to Scotland. Skene includes her name with theirs as a founder of churches. She is remembered chiefly as a recluse on a little island in Loch Lomond variously called the Nun's Island, Inchelroide or Royal Island and, more generally, Tuch Cailleach. On it a famous parish church was named for her.

Skene, II: 169; Simpson, 84; O'Hanlon, I: 94; Butler-Attwater, I: 120.

Fillan (Foillan)
January 9   Eighth century

Fillan's name is famous in ancient Scottish and Irish Calendars. His grandfather was Ceallach, King of Leinster, his mother Loch Lomond's Lady of Grace. He received the monastic habit in Ireland in Fintan Munnu's monastery and is said to have spent some time in a hermitage cell near St. Andrews in Scotland. When Comghan, his mother's brother, established himself at Lochalsh, Fillan joined his community. He shared honors with Comghan there in two ancient churches named for them Kilchoan and Killelan.

Fillan's name, spelled many different ways, wanders over the map of Scotland in widespread commemorations: Killen in the uplands of Perthshire; a church Killphillane in Wigtown; two chapels named St. Phillane, one within the castle of Down, the other outside it on the banks of the river Teith; a fair at Srowan, Feile Fhaolain; Fillan's Fair on Fillan's Day in the parish of Killellan in Renfrewshire. Fillan's Cave at Pittenween in Fifeshire was a special objective in the seventeenth century demolitions. A local minister filled up

Fillan's Well at Killellan in Renfrewshire at the close of the eighteenth century to end the devotions there. At Strathfillan where he is buried, the church and monastery were named for him. Until the beginning of the nineteenth century, Fillan's Well or Holy Pool, there survived as a place of pilgrimage frequented for cures of the insane, brought there to be dipped in its water — and in many cases to be cured.

Robert Bruce had great veneration for Fillan, and on the eve of the battle of Bannockburn in 1314, having procured a relic of the saint to have with his army, he ". . . past the remanent of the nicht in his prayaris with gud esperance of victorie." Bruce attributed the amazing victory over Edward II to the intercession of Fillan, an explanation recorded by Hector Boece and other historians.

Fillan's crozier and bell are still in existence. The former, anciently called the Quigrich, or Coygerach, and now a national treasure, is executed in solid silver elaborately carved and fitted with a relic compartment under a white jewel. Interesting data traces its history. Long after its passing into secular hands, it was safeguarded by maintenance lands and a keeper. A letter of King James in 1487 mentions "ane relik of Sanct Fulane callit the Quegrith, in keping of us and of oure progenitouris sen the tyme of Robert the Bruys and of before." He charges all and sundry "to mak nane impediment letting nor distroblance in the passing of the relik throch the contre." Fillan's staff was taken from the highlands of Scotland to Canada by Father O'Donnell, the first bishop of Ontario, and was used in the consecration of Bishop Lynch in Toronto in 1859.

Fillan died on January 9. The diocese of Dunkeld names his festival at January 19.

Skene, II: 169, 175, 406; Moran, 190; Carty, 85; Butler-Attwater, I: 120.

Blaithmac
January 19   c. 825

A metrical Life of Blaithmac comes down from a contemporary, Walafrid Strabo, Benedictine Abbot of Reichenau, who died in 849. The 180-line poem tells that Blaithmac, heir to a throne in Ireland, entered a monastery, later to become its abbot. But from his earliest years he had wanted to preach the faith to pagan nations, to win a martyr's crown. Finally he obtained permission to serve among the brethren at Iona, long since a very perilous post in the path of the Norse marauders. One day in the absence of the Abbot Dermait, Blaithmac prophetically announced impending attacks. Hastily the monks buried the shrine containing Colmcille's relics, carefully replacing the sods above it. Blaithmac exhorted each one to choose whether to remain or to flee. The next morning as he was saying Mass the invaders rushed in and having put all the religious to death, offered to spare Blaithmac if he would tell them where to find the shrine. Steadfastly he denied all knowledge of its whereabouts, which, he said, he would not disclose if he knew. They hacked him to pieces on the steps of the altar. Returning brethren afterwards buried him where he had fallen.

The *Life of Blaithmac* by Strabo in Latin hexameter verse has often been reprinted, notably in Messingham's *Florilegium Insulae Sanctorum* and in Migne's *Patrologia*.

Moran, 195; Skene, II: 300; O'Hanlon, Jan. 19; Benedictine Monks, 108.

III

Irish Saints in England

There were Irish saints in Celtic Britain and Irish saints in Anglo-Saxon Britain. Before the close of the 4th century, Irish adventurers had begun to occupy territory all along the west coast of Scotland and England from north to south. Today many place names are reminders that Irish saints followed them, drawn either to dwell among their kindred in those Gaelic settlements or influenced perhaps by the Irish ideal of religious exile that became so powerful in the following centuries.

Roman-occupied Celtic Britain was Christian. The pagan Saxons, Angles, and Jutes began to arrive before 449 and such Christianity as survived was driven into the fastnesses of Wales and Cornwall. Despoiled and displaced by the newcomers, the antipathy of the Celtic Britons was implacable. They refused absolutely to have any hand in the conversion of the English. One hundred and fifty years were to pass before the faith was preached to the Anglo-Saxon invaders.

In 597 Gregory the Great sent the Benedictine Augustine and 40 companions to Britain. They landed in Kent. Augustine came reluctantly and they held Kent with difficulty. Thirty-eight years after the arrival of Augustine the spiritual conquest of England that was abandoned for a time by the Roman missionaries was taken up by the Celtic monks. What the sons of Benedict could only begin was to be completed by the sons of Colmcille, one of the greatest of whom was Aidan.

With Aidan began what Bede called the 30 year episcopate of the Scots (Irish). In 625 the Roman Paulinus had been sent to Northumbria but his mission failed in the north and receded to Kent. In its place the Iona mission out of Lindisfarne reached as far as the Thames. Irish bishops and monks spread out all over Mercia and East Anglia and as far as Glastonbury. Northumbria was their great conquest and its kings spoke Irish for a hundred years.

Lindisfarne, not Canterbury, became the most powerful center of religious influence in England. Foundations placed to its credit are Coldingham, Melrose and Lastingham in Northumbria; Ripon and Whitby in Yorkshire;

Burghcastle in Suffolk; Saint Bees in Lancashire; Malmsbury among the Saxons of Wessex; Bosham in Sussex and Glaston, perhaps, in Somerset.

Of all the kingdoms of the Anglo-Saxon confederation, that of Kent alone was exclusively won by the Roman monks whose attempts among the East Saxons and the Northumbrians ended in failure. Wessex and East Anglia were converted by the combined work of Continental missionaries and Celtic monks. As to the two Northumbrian kingdoms and those of Essex and Mercia, more than two-thirds of the territory occupied by the Anglo-Saxon conquerors, these four countries owed their final conversion exclusively to the missionary labors of the Celtic monks. The English historian Lightfoot declares "Augustine was the apostle of Kent but Aidan was the apostle of England."

Daniel-Rops, 47; Curtis, 15; Fitzpatrick, I: 194; Butler-Attwater, II: 407; Montalembert, IV: 125.

Brenach (Brynach)
April 7   Fifth century

Brenach, the first Irish saint of record to choose Wales as the place of his retreat, is expressly assigned the epithet "Brenach the Irishman" in the Welsh Triads. It is said of him that frequently he enjoyed the vision and conversation of angels and afterwards the mountain on which they came to him was called Carn-Engyli, Mountain of the Angels. At the foot of it stood his church, then and long after him the principal church of the district.

Moran, 6; Benedictine Monks, 118.

Ives (Hia, Iia)
February 3   Fifth century

St. Ives in Cornwall commemorates the Irish saint Iia or Hia who came into Cornwall in company with Fingar, Piala and others. She erected a cell near the mouth of the Hayle river and lived the life of prayer and austerities there that left her name to the promontory.

Moran, 20; Benedictine Monks, 302.

Fingar
December 14   Fifth century

Fingar, a prince of Connaught and one of Patrick's converts is described as a pilgrim saint who went first to Armorica (northwestern France) where he is commemorated at Vannes in Brittany. Soon after landing at the mouth of the Hayle in Cornwall, he and his sister Piala and a number of companions were put to death. They are named in the British Martyrology.

Benedictine Monks, 234; Moran, 19.

Breaca
June 4   Fifth–Sixth century

Breaca, said to have been with Brigid at Kildare, came into Cornwall in a large pilgrimage of Irish religious. Among her companions, two churches are named for St. Uni; Germocus, a royal prince, is remembered in the parish of Germo; and the parish of Gwinear preserves the name of Wynnerus. Breaca likewise is honored with parishes bearing her name.

Moran, 18; Benedictine Monks, 114.

Germanus
July 3   Fifth century

When Germanus of Auxerre visited Britain in the year 448 he met there an Irish colonist whose son became his disciple and chose to take the name of Germanus for himself. Subsequently a bishop with Patrick in Ireland, his name is met with in the Acts of Kieran and others of the early Irish saints. He evangelized many districts in Wales. Afterwards traced in Spain and Gaul, he was martyred in Normandy. He is honored as the apostle of the Isle of Man.

Moran, 10; Benedictine Monks, 263.

Buriana
June 4   Sixth century

All within a short distance of each other at the southwestern tip of England, three place names commemorate Irish saints. There is St. Ives for Hia near the mouth of the Hayle river. St. Warne's Bay in Scilly honors Warna who came over from Ireland in one of the little hide covered wicker boats of the time and landed at the bay afterwards named for him.

About five miles from Lands End, opposite the Scilly islands, is the town of St. Burian, where stood the oratory of the Irish Buriana, a king's daughter from Donegal, Bruinseach in the Irish Calendars. The church there was erected by King Athelstan who had prayed in Buriana's oratory at the time of his expedition against the Scilly Isles and promised if successful to erect a college of clergy at the spot called after the saint Eglos-Berrie. He gave the church the privileges of sanctuary and the kings of England continued to be its patrons until a very late period.

Benedictine Monks, 119; Moran, 17, 20.

Ruadan (Rumon, Ruan)
June 1   Sixth century

In the ancient Legenda preserved at Tavistock (Devonshire) where his relics were enshrined, Rumon, or Ruan, is styled ''an Irish Scot.'' He built himself an oratory in the nearby forest district out of which he labored. Three ancient churches in Cornwall bore his name. May 22 is a secondary feast day.

Benedictine Monks, 519; Moran, 20.

Tathai (Dathai)
December 26   Sixth century

In the early 6th century, Tathai and eight companions who set out from Ireland in a little coracle without sail or oar were carried to the Severn and to a landing in Gwent in the modern Glamorganshire. Caradoc, the king of the two Gwents, soon invited the saint and his monks to settle permanently in his kingdom, and Tathai founded the church since called Llandathan, ''Tathai's Church.''

Son of the Irish prince Tuathal, the saint was educated for the church and ordained in Ireland. His church and school at Llandathan attracted many scholars ''from all parts to be instructed in all the branches of science.'' When Ynyr, son and successor of Caradoc, built the monastery and school of Caerwent in Monmouthshire, he appointed Tathai the first abbot.

The most famous of Tathai's pupils was Cadoc, who was entrusted to him by Cadoc's parents ''in preference to all other teachers of Britain.'' After twelve years with Tathai, Cadoc studied for three more years in Ireland. During that time he formed the friendship with Finian of Clonard who is said to have visited Cadoc at the school he founded at Llancarvan.

Tathai's last days were spent in retirement at Llandathan. He died there and was buried in the church named for him.

Kenney, 182; O'Kelly, 23; Moran, 11; Butler-Attwater, III: 633.

Fursey (Fursa)
January 16   c. 648

Fursey, afterwards one of the most famous of the Irish saints on the Continent, was important in the conversion of England. The diocese of Northampton celebrates his feast day. Baronius assigns the chief merit for the conversion of East Anglia to him. Bede thought every one could read the story of Fursey's life with much profit.

Fursey was remarkable for his holiness, for his missionary zeal, and for his wondrous visions of the other world, which for centuries were religiously repeated and handed down in all the monasteries of the west. Born in the west of Ireland about 575, he was, according to Bede, of very noble Irish blood, but even more noble in mind than in birth. Brendan the Navigator was his uncle and on Brendan's island of Inchiquin he trained for the religious life under that Meldan who was later to appear in his visions among the souls of the just made perfect.

Bede tells he had his account of Fursey's visions from an old East Anglian monk as pious as he was truthful, who had heard the saint himself describe his trances. Their character was such that this wonderful man, though but poorly clothed in a thin garment during the rude winters of that English coast frozen by the east winds, was covered with perspiration at the bare recollection of the moving and frightful ordeals through which his spirit had passed. As long as he lived, recollections of what he had seen so ordered Fursey's thoughts and actions that an incomparable grace was said to pervade everything he did.

Fursey was a contemporary of Aidan but he was not connected with Lindisfarne. About 631, King Sigebert, who had been exiled to Gaul in his youth and was there fully instructed by Columban and his disciples, returned to England a Christian bringing with him the Burgundian Bishop Felix. Soon afterwards Fursey came into East Anglia accompanied by Foillan, Ultan, Gobain, Dicuil and others, all of whom, Bede writes, through grateful remembrance of his old Irish masters in the Burgundian monasteries, were joyfully welcomed and honorably received by King Sigebert.

The king gave Fursey a tract of land at Cnobbersburg, now Burgh-Castle near Yarmouth, on which he erected, Bede tells us, "a noble monastery," the center of his missionary operations in East Anglia. Cressy in his *Church History* names Cnobbersburg the monastery to which Sigebert retired when he abandoned his throne to become a humble monk, the more securely to provide for the life hereafter, the first example of an Anglo-Saxon sovereign, "not forced thereto by any calamity," who entered a cloister. For some twelve years, Fursey labored in East Anglia, beloved by all good men, feared by the wicked whose gifts he steadfastly refused to take. On his shoulder and cheek were scars which he said he had gotten when the demons of his visions hurled at him a lost soul of whose goods he had partaken in that soul's lifetime.

Some time after the year 640, Fursey placed his brother Foillan in charge at Cnobbersburg and set out on a pilgrimage to Rome that lengthened into a second missionary career in France. He never returned to England. He died at Mezeroles on the way to the coast on a projected journey back to East Anglia.

Kenney, 500; Gougaud; Tommasini; Fitzpatrick, I: II; Moran, 315; Benedictine Monks, 251.

Aidan (Lindisfarne)
August 31   651

"Blessed Aidan, Apostle of Northumbria, yes and of England."

Aidan came at the bidding of Oswald, the repatriated king of Northumbria, who had lived an exile in Ireland from childhood. While there he had become a fervent Christian, destined to be the first Anglo-Saxon prince venerated as a saint.

Augustine and 40 Roman missionaries, sent to England by Pope Gregory the Great, landed in Kent in 597. But with the death of the Saxon Ethelbert in 616 "it appeared as though much of the Kentish Christianity was buried in the king's grave." When the Northumbrian King Edwin, baptized in 627, died in 633 at the hands of the pagan kings Cadwallon and Penda, Paulinus, the Roman bishop of York, was driven from his See. He went back to Kent. Only the deacon Justus remained in the north.

Oswald returned to his native land in 634 and in December of that year having mustered a small army, took his stand against the superior forces of Cadwallon near Hexham at the place afterward called Heavenfield. The night before the battle in a vision all radiant with heavenly light, Colmcille of Iona appeared to Oswald and spreading his cloak protectively over the sleeping troops, told him to take the Cross for his standard and promised victory on the morrow. Next morning a cross was made and erected and Oswald had his soldiers kneel with him to pray to the One True God to be with them in their just cause against the superior forces of the powers of darkness. Cadwallon himself was slain in the battle and Oswald's victory was complete. As soon as he was established in his fortress castle at Bamborough, he applied to Iona for missionaries to bring the faith to his people.

The Irish monk first delegated to England was Corman, an austere religious of exemplary life, but he made no headway and in despair returned to Iona. Sitting in on the ensuing conference was a scholar monk who had trained in St. Senan's monastery on Scattery Island, Aidan, lately a bishop in Ireland, but now enrolled in the Iona mission. He spoke up: the Anglo-Saxons should first be given the milk of easy doctrine to nourish them until they should be capable of God's more sublime precepts. Without more ado, the seniors named Aidan the man to whom the arduous mission should be entrusted.

That same year there came to Iona another communication of great importance, one of which the abbot took no heed. Cummian of Clonfert wrote to inform him that all monasteries and churches of Ireland, except Iona and other of Colmcille's foundations, had conformed to the revised Roman Easter date.

In the year 635 Aidan fixed his See on Lindisfarne, a little island three miles long and half as wide, off the coast of northern England opposite Oswald's fortress castle at Bamborough. Aidan and his successors had only such buildings as were absolutely necessary for existence and for decency. They had neither money nor cattle. What the rich gave them they immediately distributed to the poor. Nor did they receive with spendor the lords and nobles who came to their monasteries. Even the kings were content with the ordinary fare of those apostles whose desire was to serve God and not the world, whose success was due as much to their example as to their preaching. Everywhere the white homespun wool garb of the Irish monks came to be held in the greatest respect.

Scholarship went hand in hand with the frugal life, the selfless devotion which the Irish monks brought to the cause of religion. According to Bede, every church and monastery founded by Aidan and his successors became immediately a school where the children of the English received from the Irish monks an education as complete as that to be had in any of the great monasteries of Ireland or the Continent. The distinctive Irish lettering of early English writing bears witness to the fact that England learned her writing from Irish teachers. The Irish handed on to the Saxons along with the faith the torch of learning.

Trained religious, arriving in a steady stream from Ireland and Iona, furnished Aidan with personnel to staff his ever wider spreading churches. Especially, he spared no pains to train a native clergy. It was his policy to select twelve likely Saxon youths, frequently from the many he ransomed from slavery, "to educate them in Christ." Montalembert writes of Aidan's seminary cloister "This outpost of Lindisfarne and Iona bore the name of Melrose, not the Cistercian Melrose . . . but a more ancient and more holy Melrose." The first abbot of Melrose was Eata, one of the first class of twelve young Saxons that Aidan educated. Today, landscaped and beautiful 14th-century monastic ruins are a monument as much to "old Melrose" as to the Melrose of later times.

Aidan professed Heiu who, Bede says, was regarded as the first nun of Northumbria and who has been identified with the Irish Begu of St. Bees Head. Heiu was placed by Aidan over the cloister he founded at Hartlepool, the mother convent of England. When Heiu departed inland, Aidan called the royal princess Hilda to succeed her at Hartlepool which later relocated at Whitby. Montalembert tells that Hilda had determined to become a religious on the Continent either at Chelles or in one of the convents on the shore of the Marne which sprang from the great Irish colony at Luxeuil and to which Saxon girls were already beginning to resort.

During Aidan's rule the problem of the different dates for the celebration of Easter was becoming progressively acute. Canterbury observed the revised Roman Easter; Lindisfarne adhered to the older computation handed down by Colmcille. But while Aidan lived "the confusion was patiently tolerated by all men, even those who thought and acted differently," including Honorius of Canterbury and Felix of East Anglia, because they esteemed Aidan as a holy and just man who could not be expected to keep Easter contrary to the usage of those who sent him.

Aidan labored out of Lindisfarne for 17 years, more than half of the 30-year episcopate of the Scots (Irish) which is regarded as the most fruitful period in English religious history. In Aidan's day, every native English bishop was of Irish ordination save one, and he was taught by Irishmen. From Lindisfarne tutelage came the northern England houses that reared the first English historian, the Venerable Bede, who records that the Irish monks gave Christianity and culture to the English.

Death came suddenly to Aidan at Bamborough. He expired leaning against an outside pillar of his church there. Bede tells that later on when pagan hordes destroyed the village of Bamborough it fell out in a wonderful manner that the post on which Aidan died could not be consumed by flames. It was afterwards revered as a relic in the rebuilt church.

The foremost authority on Aidan is Bede. It has been remarked that the chapters which he devotes to Aidan's piety and devoted zeal are unsurpassed for eloquence and earnestness by any other passages of his history. While he can scarcely find sufficient words of eulogy for the Irish monk, he has one complaint, Aidan's conflicting date for the celebration of Easter. Nevertheless, Bede's admiration for Irish religious traditions was such he had his own name inscribed in the roll of Lindisfarne brethren so that he might share equally in the prayers of the community. He was buried in the Durham cathedral, of whose bishops Aidan is first in line, the see of Lindisfarne having been relocated at Durham when abandoned because of the Vikings.

In 1951, on the 1300th anniversary of Aidan's death, Cardinal Griffin led the Catholic pilgrimage at Durham. The Anglican group went to Holy Island, as Lindisfarne is now called. On that occasion, Episcopal Bishop Hudson spoke the words "Blessed Aidan, apostle of Northumbria, yes and of England."

Together with religion and scholarship the Irish monks from Iona brought Celtic manuscript painting to their Saxon pupils at Lindisfarne. Their great surviving monument in England is the illuminated manuscript known as the

Book of Lindisfarne, sister to Trinity College Irish illuminated manuscripts, the Book of Kells, the Book of Durrow, etc.

Another example of Celtic craftsmanship from Northumbria has become famous since its discovery in the last century in a sacristy at Mortain in France, an old Irish Chrismale, or carrying case, for the Blessed Sacrament. It is a little box executed in beechwood and copper, inscribed "May God aid Eada, he made this Chrismale." Scholars term it "a great Christian document." Philology experts assign the runic lettering to Northumbria of the period 660–725, and through the Northumbrian runes, trace the relic to the Abbey of Iona and to Irish Christianity. It is assumed to have been a gift of the Norman conquerors to Mortain after the conquest of England when Normandy fell heir to many treasures. The name Eada may be an alternate spelling of Eata, who was one of the first and most beloved of the Anglo-Saxon youths educated by Aidan.

Daniel-Rops, 47, 164; Fitzpàtrick, I: 185, 222, 194; Montalembert, II: 225; O'Hanlon, VIII; Gougaud; Porter, 95; Moran; Benedictine Monks, 95, 292.

Dicuil

Seventh century

The Bayeux tapestry, which is credited to the wife of William the Conqueror, Matilda, and her needlewomen, and considered an origina source of historical information, pictures in its embroidery the pioneer Christian edifice of the Saxons of Sussex, Dicuil's church at Bosham.

Although the little strip of southern coast encompassed by sea and forest on which Dicuil and his Irish monks settled was next door to Kent, there is no trace of Roman missionaries ever attempting its conversion. Dicuil, a disciple of Fursey, came from East Anglia about 645 with five or six brethren and founded a small monastery at Bosham three miles from Chichester. Bede writes that the Irish monks served our Lord in poverty and humility, but few of the people cared either to follow their course of life or hear their preaching. However, one of Dicuil's disciples became bishop of Rochester in Kent in 656 and, in 661, the king of Sussex was baptized in Mercia which was administered by the Irish Bishop Jaruman.

The saint who accomplished the final conversion of Sussex was the Anglo-Saxon Wilfrid who began his religious life with three years under Aidan at Lindisfarne and was ordained by the French Bishop Agilebert who had studied for many years in Ireland, Wilfrid whose long stormy career began with his turning from his Celtic teachers in the Easter controversy. In 681, abandoned to his fate by the prelates of Roman Canterbury and ostracized by all the other kings of England, Wilfrid found refuge with the king of Sussex who gave him land at Selsey on which he built a monastery that was made into an episcopal see.

But Dicuil was first to preach the Gospel there and the episcopal see was afterwards removed to Chichester where the first religious center in Sussex had arisen, Dicuil's monastery.

O'Kelly, 26; Moran, 331; Fitzpatrick, I: 255.

Diuma
May 5   658

Diuma was the first bishop of Mercia, the Anglian kingdom in central England ruled by the young Prince Peada. At the time of his courtship and marriage to King Oswy's daughter about 653 and his baptism by Bishop Finan of Lindsifarne, Peada asked for missionaries to accompany him and his bride back to Mercia to bring Christianity to his people.

The priest chosen to head the four "learned and worthy" missionaries for the new field was Irish-born Diuma. His three companions were Anglo-Saxons trained by Aidan, Cedd, Adda and Bettin. They worked not only among the midland Saxons but into Mercia proper. At the request of Peada, Finan consecrated Diuma bishop of all the Mercians, the paucity of clergy, Bede remarks, making it necessary that one bishop rule over so vast a people.

Diuma's episcopate lasted little more than two years but "in a short time he won not a few to the Lord." His monastery dedicated to St. Peter, "the first resting place of Christianity in central England," was the origin of the present city of Peterborough.

Mercia's first five bishops were all Irish oriented: Diuma and Ceallach from Ireland; the Anglo-Saxon Trumhere trained by Irish monks and consecrated by Finan of Lindisfarne; Irish born Jaruman; Ceadda, or Chad, brother of the above Cedd, who had been educated at Lindisfarne and in Ireland.

Moran, 306; Benedictine Monks, 136, 134, 176.

Cealleach
October 6   c. 660

Cealleach, Irish bishop of Mercia or the Mid-Angles of England, is one of thirty-three Irish saints of that name. He was numbered a disciple of Colmcille, having come from Iona to Lindisfarne where Finan consecrated him and named him the second bishop of Mercia in succession to the Irish

Diuma. Cealleach was not long in England. After "some years of a too laborious episcopate" he returned to Iona and retired to die in his native land.

Benedictine Monks, 135; Fitzpatrick, I: 226; Montalembert, II: 298; Moran, 306.

Finan (Lindisfarne)
February 17   661

Finan succeeded Aidan at Lindisfarne, the Irish mission based on the northeast coast of England. Seventeen years earlier the Anglo-Saxon King Oswald had requested Irish missionaries from Iona to teach Christianity to his people and Aidan had gathered all of Northumbria to the faith. Beginning in 651, Bishop Finan carried forward into the other Anglo-Saxon kingdoms. The English historian Bede tells that the people flocked joyfully to hear the Word, that "the English great and small were by their Irish masters instructed in the rules and observances of regular discipline."

Lindisfarne was now an important see and one of Finan's first projects was a larger and more permanent structure to replace Aidan's church. He built it of hewn oak with a thatched roof "after the manner of the Scots." Men's hearts and the Word of God, not grandeur of buildings, were the concern of the Irish missionaries. Among the dignitaries present for the dedication of the new church was the Archbishop of Canterbury, Theodore of Tarsis. Lindisfarne-Canterbury relations were always and at all times most cordial, something never apparent between Canterbury and the Saxon Wilfrid who was increasingly hostile to all usages of the Irish church.

There were four areas of difference between Lindisfarne and Canterbury church discipline in England: the Tonsure of the Irish clergy; Lindisfarne adherence to the Iona computation of the Date of Easter; the Irish Baptismal rite; the use of Several Collects in the sacred liturgy. Words of Gregory the Great to Augustine of Canterbury contain no condemnation of Celtic church practices: "Where the faith is one, differences of custom do no harm to Holy Church."

Finan's king was Oswy, murderer of King Oswin, who otherwise proved to be so model a sovereign the people came to consider him a saint. Oswy built St. Mary's Church and Monastery at the mouth of the Tyne. His queen, Eanfleda, built a monastery at Gilling where Oswin had fallen, that prayers might be said there forever for the two kings, slayer and victim. Over Gilling as first abbot was Trumhere, an Anglo-Saxon trained by the Irish monks. As for the staffing of these new centers, "many of the Irish came daily into Britain" and many native Anglo-Saxon clergy were now trained for the church, either in Ireland or in the Lindisfarne foundations. Aidan had professed the royal princess Hilda. Finan received the vows of another Northumbrian princess, Ebba, sister of Oswy and Oswald, and established her in the double monastery at Coldingham.

Finan's baptism of the Mercian King Peada and all of his attendants at Oswy's royal village Admurum (At-the-Wall) where Newcastle now stands, was the beginning of the conversion of the English midlands. To accompany Peada back to Mercia, Finan consecrated Irish-born Diuma bishop and sent with him three Celtic educated Anglo-Saxon priests, Cedd, Adda and Betta.

At Oswy's same royal village, Finan baptized Sigebert, king of the East Saxons. It was thirty-six years since the Roman Mellitus had been expelled from his diocese of London and now idolatry prevailed in Essex. Sigebert asked Finan for Christian teachers to instruct his people and Cedd, the above companion of Diuma, was sent with another priest to the new field. Very soon, Finan consecrated Cedd bishop of all the territory of the East Saxons.

All of this time Easter was being celebrated twice each year in England, at different times even in the royal household. King Oswy, faithful disciple of the Irish bishops, observed Easter with Lindisfarne; his queen, with Canterbury. And although an Irish priest, Ronan, is on record as having tried strenuously to persuade Finan to change over to the universal date, even as the rest of Ireland had done, nothing could move Finan from the traditions of Colmcille. Commendable in every way, blameful in none, Finan died as he had lived, true in every smallest way to the traditions of Iona and the holy men from whom he proceeded. Aidan's regime won all of Northumbria. Under Finan, Celtic jurisdiction reached the Thames and the diocese of London where the Canterbury mission had failed.

Moran; Fitzpatrick, I; Butler-Attwater, I: 357; Montalembert.

Tuda

October 21   664

Irish born Tuda, a bishop from southern Ireland who enrolled in the Lindisfarne mission, was an advocate of the revised Roman Easter computation which was contrary to the Lindisfarne view, but in agreement with the practice, except in Columban monasteries, from long years past in Ireland. At Colman's resignation in 664, Tuda was appointed to succeed him as bishop of all Northumbria. All the rebels had not departed with Colman and it was expected of Tuda that he heal all discord and bring peace to the ranks. In this same year Tuda's name appears as one of the signers of the deed of dedication of the great new St. Peter's Monastery in Mercia of which Celtic born Jaruman was bishop. Tuda's episcopate was of short duration, only a few months. He died of the plague of 664 in a monastery in Durham and was buried in the church there.

After the death of Tuda, Aidan's favorite of all the first twelve Anglo-Saxon youths he trained for the church, Eata, was called from the novitiate he governed at Melrose to take over the see of Lindisfarne. Eata was succeeded by the Irish Cuthbert.

Moran, 268; O'Kelly, 31; Benedictine Monks, 582; Montalembert, II: 330.

Jaruman

669

Bishop Finan consecrated Irish born Jaruman the 4th bishop of Mercia, an offshoot of Lindisfarne. Little is known of his Mercian episcopate but he is credited by Bede with the final conversion of the neighboring kingdom of the East Saxons.

In the checkered religious history of Essex, Mellitus, the abbot sent from Rome in 601 by Pope Gregory the Great, had been forced to flee from London. After a long pagan interval, the East Saxon King Sigebert was baptized in Northumbria by Finan of Lindisfarne who named the Anglo-Saxon Cedd, schooled in Lindisfarne and in Ireland, to evangelize Sigebert's people. In 664, the plague that carried away Cedd and all of his priests except one, carried away all Christianity with them. Once more the East Saxons went back to their pagan temples, their pagan charms, and the worship of their former idols.

The person chosen to stem this second apostacy was Jaruman and zealously and successfully did he fulfil his mission. Bede gives the account of Jaruman's labors on the authority of one of his priest fellow-workers who accompanied him as he went about throughout the whole kingdom recalling the wanderers to the right path "so that they abandoned or destroyed their fanes and altars, reopened the churches and once more gladly acknowledged the name of Christ."

Jaruman afterwards returned to his own flock in Mercia where he served until 669.

Moran, 311

Maildulf

May 17   c. 673

Malmsbury in southern England originated with Maildulf, one of the workers for the faith in Wessex. It happened that "there came into Wessex out of Ireland, a certain bishop called Agilbert, by birth a Frenchman, who had then lived a long time in Ireland for the purpose of reading the Scriptures." He had, moreover, studied at Jouarre in France, an offshoot of the Irish Luxeuil. Maildulf came on a visit to Bishop Agilbert and stayed to erect the cell in the woods of Ingleborne that grew into the flourishing monastery of Maildulf's burg, now Malmsbury.

In the words of Bede, Maildulf was a philosopher skilled in all the learning of his age. William of Malmsbury writes of him that he was constant in prayer, that when he prayed he seemed to hear the voice of God addressing him. Bright states that Maildulf had brought with him all the culture for which Irish scholars were then famous. Equally enthusiastic mention of his Irish teachers is found in Aldhelm's writings. In a letter to Willibrord (the English missionary who studied for twelve years in Ireland) Aldhelm wrote that countless as are the stars that sparkle in the firmament yet more numerous were the saints and learned men at that time adorning the church of Erin. As well as for scholarship, Maildulf was known for that rigorous penetential practice of the Irish saints, the recital of the Psalter, even during the icy cold of winter, immersed to the shoulders in the stream of water that flowed close to his cell.

Maildulf's pupil Aldhelm was the first Anglo-Saxon to be called a classical scholar. He succeeded Maildulf as abbot. A deed by Bishop Leutherius gave to Aldhelm the priest "that portion of land called Maidulesburg." Maildulf's Abbey became one of the most important Benedictine Houses. It is said to have had the first organ in England. Its 12th century carvings of the Twelve Apostles are one of the major works of medieval art surviving in Great Britain.

Moran, 334; O'Hanlon, April 18; Fitzpatrick, I: 250; Benedictine Monks, 387; Butler-Attwater, II: 391.

Colman (Lindisfarne)
February 18   676

Bede describes Colman as a man of simple and austere piety, of innate prudence, and tells that he was greatly beloved by King Oswy. He was the third bishop of Lindisfarne in England. Like his predecessors, Aidan and Finan, he was an Irish monk from Iona, raised to episcopal status for the Northumbrian mission. He was in England only three years.

Lindisfarne had prospered greatly. The religious in Britain at this time were predominantly native Irish or Irish-educated Anglo-Saxons. According to Bede, the whole English nation so esteemed the piety and learning of the Irish bishops and clergy that a stream of noble and middle class Anglo-Saxons was steadily pouring into Ireland's schools where "the Irish most willingly received them all and took care to supply them gratuitously with daily food as also to furnish them with books to read and with their teaching without making any charge." They enrolled at Clonard, Bangor, Glasnevin, Lismore, Clonmacnoise, Armagh and other monastic schools in Ireland. There were so many of the English at Armagh that one of its districts was known as the Saxon quarter.

Colman's tenure at Lindisfarne was troubled from first to last by the Easter controversy, a great storm in Colmcille's name. Soon after Colman's succession there returned from abroad the Anglo-Saxon Wilfrid. He had studied at Lindisfarne for three years before his travels to France and Rome. He returned to Northumbria immoderately inimical to those Irish practices which were contrary to Continental usage, even to the Celtic tonsure which was made into a great matter. Siding with Wilfrid for the Roman date for the celebration of Easter were Oswy's Queen Eanfleda and their son Alchfrid who shared Oswy's kingdom. They were supported by two Irish-oriented bishops, the French Agilbert, who had studied in Ireland for many years, and Bishop Tuda, who had been born in the south of Ireland where the universal Easter had been observed for some 30 years.

Nowhere in evidence in the dispute were either prelates or clergy of Kent even though their Irish colleagues had carried the Lindisfarne apostolate, including the Iona Easter date, to the very doorstep of Canterbury.

On Colman's side, King Oswy and his Court observed the Celtic Easter as also did Cedd, one of Aidan's first Anglo-Saxon boys to be trained at Lindisfarne. He had gone to Ireland for further study and was now bishop of the territory from which Mellitus, the Roman bishop of London, had been expelled. Cedd acted as interpreter in the Easter Controversy. Princess Abbess Saint Hilda "one of the greatest Englishwomen of all time," was Celtic in her training, her affections, her sympathies, her loyalties and thus she remained. After the Council, held at her monastery at Whitby, Hilda changed over in obedience to the universal Easter, but Wilfrid, who spearheaded the opposition, was never personally admitted to her friendship.

King Oswy, in all this discord over the celebration of Easter which divided even his own household, called the Council of Whitby to determine once and for all upon a uniform system for the whole of his kingdom. The Abbess Hilda presided. Colman was called first to present his case. Wilfrid, stating erroneously that St. Peter had established the custom now followed in Rome then concluded his arguments by quoting the words ". . . and I will give unto thee the keys of the kingdom of heaven," which Colman agreed Our Lord had spoken to St. Peter. King Oswy, in spite of his love and loyalty to

Colman, finally chose St. Peter above St. Colmcille having, he said, no wish to oppose the keeper of the keys of heaven. Actually, Colman's touted Easter was the Popes' own Paschal cycle, long cherished as having come down to them from St. Peter, while Wilfrid's vaunted Catholic Easter was a foreign Alexandrian calculation repudiated by Rome for the best of three centuries.

Colman was ready to abide by Oswy's jurisdiction in all temporal affairs but he could not accept his authority in spiritual matters. Until Rome expressly prohibited the usage he upheld. Colman considered it his duty to follow the traditions of his fathers. Rather than be the cause of any discord he resigned the see of Lindisfarne and departed sadly and forever.

Irish monks who did not care to remain and some thirty Anglo-Saxons accompanied Colman. He proceeded to Iona but eventually settled his community on the island of Inisbofin. Later on in Mayo he founded a second, separate monastery for the English brethren over which he placed Gerald, the son of an Anglo-Saxon king. This English cloister became very flourishing and was known for centuries as Mayo of the Saxons. As late as 1579 it was still in operation: James O'Healy, a bishop of Mayo of the Saxons, was put to death for the faith in that year.

Colman died in his island monastery of Inisbofin. Some traces of his church may still be seen.

In the time of Cromwell, Inisbofin was a penal colony for Irish bishops. One of the prisoners, Bishop Lynch of Clonfert, Co. Galway, escaped to the Continent and to Gyor in Hungary, carrying with him the Clonfert treasure that is now called the Weeping Madonna, or the Irish Madonna. On March 17, 1697, at the height of religious persecution in Ireland, the Clonfert picture of the Blessed Mother in the Cathedral of Gyor shed tears of blood. The phenomenon which began at six o'clock Mass that morning lasted for three hours, the tears continuing even when the picture was taken from the wall. Eye witness accounts signed by the city mayor, the military commandant, the governor, the town's Calvinist and Lutheran ministers and Jewish Rabbi, are still preserved at Gyor. The picture hangs over the high altar of the Gyor Cathedral. It has always been, and continues to be, an object of great devotion. It is believed to be the work of the Flemish painter Peter Pourbus of Bruges.

Moran, 251; Fitzpatrick, I: 230; Butler-Attwater, I: 389; O'Kelly, 148.

Adamnan
January 31   c. 680

At Coldingham on the Berwick coast there was a double monastery, one for both men and women, that had been founded by the royal Princess Ebba who received the veil from Finan of Lindisfarne. Among her monks was an Irish priest, Adamnan, remarkable for fasts more severe and vigils more prolonged than even those of the Irish tradition. He learned in a vision that Coldingham would be destroyed by fire because of "senseless gossip and other frivolities" of the monks and nuns, contrary to religious life. But he reassured the troubled abbess this would not happen in her liftime. Although of great personal sanctity, Ebba was not an administrator. In spite of her renewed efforts, after her death community ardor declined again. And as Adamnan had prophecied, the monastery was destroyed by fire. His festival was confirmed by Leo XIII in 1897.

Benedictine Monks, 8; Butler-Attwater, I: 215, III: 402; Montalembert, II: 269.

Bee (Begha, Begu)
October 31   Seventh century

St. Bees Head in Cumberland commemorates the holy Irish nun Begha, or Bee. Legend relates she was the daughter of an Irish king, already promised in marriage by her father, bur resolved nevertheless upon the religious life for herself. In her dilemma, an angel appeared to her, gave her a bracelet engraved with a cross and in the night before her wedding day, she slipped away, across the Irish sea to the northwest coast of England. After a time there, given to prayer and the care of the sick poor and needy, she abandoned her life as a recluse to present herself to Aidan, the Irish bishop of Lindisfarne, who received her religious vows.

Some writers identify Bee with the contemporary Heiu (also professed by Aidan) who had abdicated Hartlepool in favor of the royal princess Hilda. Bede connects Begu with the event of Hilda's death. In another cloister where she had charge of postulants, Begu who had been a nun for thirty years, saw the beloved Hilda, surrounded by glorious light, ascend to heaven to the tolling of bells such as called the nuns to prayer. The community gathered in the chapel to pray for Hilda whose death messengers confirmed the next morning.

The monastery Bee founded on the promontory that bears her name flourished for nine hundred years, the recipient of rich grants from King Oswald, King Oswin, and others. There are 12th century records of Bee's famous bracelet, a precious relic upon which any statement sworn to was acceptable to all without further question.

Moran, 159; Fitzpatrick, I: 185, 222; Butler-Attwater, III: 498, IV: 369; Benedictine Monks, 95, 292.

Cuthbert
March 20   687

Bede is silent as to Cuthbert's birthplace. He introduces him as a boy of eight living in the neighborhood of Melrose in northern England, in the care of a pious widow Kenswith.

The Scottish historian Skene writes "It is certainly remarkable that Bede gives no indication of Cuthbert's nationality. He must surely have known whether he was of Irish descent or not. He is himself far too candid and honest a historian not to have stated the fact if it were so, and it is difficult to avoid the suspicion that this part of his narrative was one of the portions which he had expunged at the instance of the critics to whom he had submitted his manuscript."

Cardinal Moran cites the records of the Cathedral of Durham. Down to the Reformation, the cathedral altar screen with the figure of Cuthbert bore the inscription "St. Cuthbert, Patron of Church, City and Liberty of Durham, an Irishman by birth of royal parentage who was led by God's Providence to England." In that same cathedral, a series of stained glass windows depicting Cuthbert's life began with "the birth of the Saint at Kells." Although these windows were demolished in the time of Edward VI, they had been registered. Moran also refers to Alban Butler's 1845 Dublin edition of his *Lives of the Saints* in which he quotes a manuscript *Life* in the Cottonian Library that holds with the Irish tradition that Cuthbert was born at Kells in Meath; that his mother was the Irish princess Saba, the granddaughter of Muircerthach, King of Ireland. In *Ancient Rites of Durham* it tells that the child was baptized "Mulloche in the Irish tongue, the which is in English as much as to say Cuthbert." Domestic conflicts having brought Saba to misfortune and ruin, she set out on a pilgrimage to Rome taking her small son with her. In North Britain in the neighborhood of Aidan and Lindisfarne she gave Cuthbert into the keeping of Kenswith and continued on her way. She died in Rome.

On an August night in 651 as he was tending sheep Cuthbert had a vision of hosts of angels in streaming light ascending to heaven with a soul of exceeding brightness. The next day he learned that Aidan of Lindisfarne had died at that very hour. Sometime afterwards he presented himself at Melrose, the seminary founded by Aidan, then guided by two of the first Saxon youths he had "educated in Christ," Abbot Eata and Prior Boisel. Cuthbert arrived on horse back, lance in hand, and a squire in attendance, after the manner of royalty.

From the first he was a prime favorite. In 661, when Finan founded Ripon and named Eata abbot, Cuthbert accompanied him as guest steward. Before long, however, when the young King Alcfrid, donor of the Ripon monastery, required of the Lindisfarne monks that they abandon all Celtic traditions and practices, the brethren to a man returned to Melrose.

And now began Cuthbert's missionary travels. Not a village do distant, not a mountain so steep, not a cottage so poor that it escaped his zeal. About this time Boisel succumbed to the plague. As he lay dying he sent for Cuthbert to read with him for a last time the Gospel of St. John, dividing it up so as to finish before he died. Six centuries afterward that copy of the Scriptures was still laid on the altar at Durham on Cuthbert's feast day. Cuthbert succeeded to the office of prior only to be brought to the point of death by the same epidemic. But when he heard that the brethren had prayed the night through for his recovery, he demanded his staff and his shoes and arose from his bed. He was never again, however, to know his former robust health.

The adoption of the new Easter date for all of England brought the departure of Bishop Colman from Lindisfarne. He could not be unfaithful to the traditions of Colmcille, he would not be a party to religious discord. The Irish Tuda succeeded him as bishop of Lindisfarne, Eata was named abbot, Cuthbert, prior. Theirs was the task of bringing peace to the ranks, for the English Wilfrid's immoderation had engendered bitterness even among the Saxons. Cuthbert's way, ever to heal rather than vanquish, often meant the end of all discussion to be resumed later.

In 676, Cuthbert left Lindisfarne for the solitude of one of the small lonely Farne islands, a short distance to the south, a period not less productive than when he was actively engaged in missionary work. Eight tranquil years were his there, years far removed from the strife between King Ecfrid and Wilfrid that rocked England. His little patch of barley was so inadequate it was believed the angels of Paradise provided him with bread. "Cuthbert's beads", the little sea shells found no where else on that coast, which he blessed and gave to the people, were said by the fishermen to have been made by the saint himself. All the while pilgrims came to him from all parts and he was so uncommonly skilled in healing human woes they called him the wonderworker of Britain.

Reluctantly he had to leave his island retreat in obedience to a joint summons from Theodore, the Archbishop of Canterbury, King Ecfrid and the Princess-Abbess Alfleda, to administer the absent Wilfrid's See of Hexham. He obtained, however, an exchange with Eata for Lindisfarne instead, and was consecrated by Theodore with six bishops in attendance at York on Easter Sunday 685. Only his status was changed. His visitations continued the searching out of pathless mountain regions that gave his monastic career the character of a mission indefinitely prolonged. At Dull in Scotland he was the first to have an oratory with a large stone cross before it and a little cell for himself. Another Irish monk, Dabius came after him there, where still a third, Adamnan, founded the monastery said to have been the cradle of the University of St. Andrews.

After Christmas in 686, moved by presentiments of death, Cuthbert resigned Lindisfarne to return to Farne to prepare for the end he rightly judged was not far off. On the night of March 20, 687, one of the brethren attending him climbed the summit of the rock to wave two lighted torches, the prearranged signal to tell Lindisfarne their bishop was dead.

In 875, the monks of Lindisfarne fleeing the Danes, carried with them their ' Gospels and the body of Cuthbert, the beginning of more than a hundred years of wandering. An entire volume has been written on the travels of Cuthbert's bones. The journey came to an end at Durham and from that moment Cuthbert's name and his memory made it, after Toledo in Spain, the richest benefice in Christendom. By degrees its bishops came to possess all the attributes of royalty. And any criminal, or innocent, had only to reach and grasp the great ring of sculptured bronze in the door of the cathedral to have sanctuary from all accusers.

Cuthbert after his death became the patron saint of all things to all people. No other saint of the English people, it was pointed out, neither Queen Etheldreda, nor the martyred King Edmond, nor Thomas of Canterbury himself, was so much listened to before the throne of heaven. It was still told by seamen late in the 12th century that in the midst of a violent storm at sea, Cuthbert appeared to some sailors with his mitre on his head and in his hand his crozier which he used sometimes an an oar, sometimes as helm to save them from shipwreck. It occurred to no one to doubt the apparition or the intervention of God through the prayer of the kindly bishop. Another time, in one of the battles between Scotland and England, the people of Hexham had taken refuge in St. Wilfrid's church. One of the priests had a prophetic dream that reassured them all. In it with the unpredictable Wilfrid enlisting Cuthbert's aid, the priest saw two bishops on horseback arrive at a gallop from the south. One of them said "I am Wilfrid and this is Cuthbert whom I brought with me from Durham. We are come to deliver you."

King Alfred, in hiding at Glastonbury in the most critical moment of his struggle with the Norsemen, was encouraged to victory by a vision of Cuthbert. Canute the Dane went barefoot to the tomb of Cuthbert, the most venerated saint of the people he had subdued, to ask his protection. William the Conqueror, when he went to Durham to avenge the deaths of those Normans whom the inhabitants had slain, experienced such a supernatural impression before the tomb of Cuthbert he was moved to respect the immunities claimed in honor of the saint. Up to the time of Henry VIII soldiers marched under a sacred standard containing the corporal Cuthbert had used to cover the chalice at Mass. Sir Walter Scott in *Marmion* wrote of Cuthbert at his anvil making the little sea shells he blessed for the people. Wadsworth penned lines to Cuthbert's friendship with the hermit-saint Herbert.

Celtic influence lived on in Northumbria. The illuminated manuscript, Cuthbert's Gospels, transcribed by two bishops of Lindisfarne about 700, is classified as truly a work of Irish art as are the other great manuscript Bibles transcribed and illuminated in Ireland. Alfrid, prince and afterwards King of Northumbria, who had prolonged an exile in Ireland and at Iona because of his love of study, brought Celtic impetus to the English schools which Bede attests the Irish monks of Northumbria founded everywhere with their churches. Bede wrote two lives of Cuthbert and he records in glowing terms the contribution made by the Irish monks in England. The English Willibrord who inaugurated Anglo-Saxon missionary work on the Continent was a Northumbrian who went from Ripon in 678 to train for twelve years in Ireland and left from Ireland in 690 for Friesland. (Boniface did not arrive in Germany until 716.) The English historian Bright affirms that "The history of the Church in Northumbria during the greater part of the 7th century is conspicuously the backbone of the history of the Church of England."

Cuthbert rests somewhere in the Cathedral of Durham, the corner stone of which was laid by the Irish King of Scotland, Malcolm Ceanmore (also known as Malcolm III) in 1093.

Skene II: 205; Moran, 268; Butler-Attwater, I: 637; Fitzpatrick, I: 271; Montalembert, II: 456; Butler, XII: 339.

Modwena (Moninna) (Whitby)
July 6   c. 695

One of the several Irish saints named Modwena flourished in the second half of the seventh century. She was an abbess in Ireland when the English king Aldfrid (who had studied for twenty years in Ireland) called her to be the second abbess of Whitby at the death of Hilda about 680. The king gave his sister Elfleda into Modwena's care to be trained to the religious rule and to monastic administration. In due time Modwena, her mission accomplished, returned to Ireland and Elfleda succeeded her as abbess of Whitby.

Benedictine Monks, 429, 194.

Indract
February 5   c. 854

"Glastonbury of the Gael," the monastery which, alone in all England survived through the centuries, under British, Saxon and Anglo-Norman rule, is believed to be one of the places occupied by the Irish in the fourth century when they were making settlements in western Britain. While the influence was still Irish, at least at a very early date, a Celtic monastery was founded at Glastonbury. Legend links the Saints Patrick, Brigid and Benignus with Glastonbury. Its first church was dedicated to Blessed Mary and St. Patrick. A parish was called "Beokery, otherwise Little Ireland." The lives of many Irish saints were collected or written at Glastonbury, supposedly the source of John of Tynemouth's section devoted to Irish Saints in his Sanctilogium. Tenth century St. Dunstan was educated and became a monk at Glastonbury with Irish scholars as his teachers and Irish books for his studies.

Indract, an Irish prince and the 21st abbot of Iona, was matyred near Glastonbury. He had come to Iona about 832 in a time of constant danger from Norse pirates. Blathmac had been murdered on the altar steps. Already the "minda," sacred articles connected with Colmcille, had been moved back and forth to Ireland several times. Kenneth McAlpin had removed relics of Colmcille to Dunkeld and made it the chief church of Scotland and the Iona brethren transferred the Columban headquarters to Kells in Ireland.

Sometime before 854, Indract, his sister Drusa and other religious made a pilgrimage to Rome, setting out, perhaps, from one of the places in Cornwall or Somerset with which tradition connects their names. On the return they were murdered near Glastonbury by pagan Saxons. And in that place fostered, if not founded, by the Irish, were enshrined the relics of Indract and his companions.

Kenney, 308, 446, 607; Fitzpatrick, 184; Moran, 126; Butler-Attwater, I: 258; O'Kelly, 22.

Modwena (Polsworth)
July 5   Ninth century

Ninth century Modwena was perhaps the most famous of the Irish saints of that name. O'Hanlon quotes Holingshed's account of her: "In this season one Modwena, a virgin in Ireland, was greatly renowned in the world unto whom King Ethelwolfe (reigned 837–857) sent his son to be cured of a disease that was thought incurable; but by her means he recovered health and therefore when her monastrie was destroyed in Ireland [probably in the Norse invasions] Modwena came over into England unto whom King Ethelwolfe gave leave to build two abbies and also delivered unto her his sister Edith to be a professed nun." Holingshed also observes "manie monastries she builded both in England and in Scotland . . . and in Ireland." The monastery

Ethelwolfe built for Modwena was at Polsworth in Warwickshire. Edith was educated there and in widowhood became a nun and second abbess.

Modwena lived for some years a solitary on the island of Andresey which received its name from her little oratory on it dedicated to St. Andrew. The most important of Modwena's foundations in Scotland was in Chilnecase in Galloway where for centuries "a flourishing community of nuns perpetuated her virtues." Her body was interred at Andresey, as she foretold. Matthew of Westminster stated about 1201 that in his time Modwena's tomb was the scene of frequent miracles.

At Polsworth today, an impressive monument from bygone centuries is the sculptured effigy of an abbess — of Polsworth's first Abbess, Modwena, perhaps?

O'Hanlon VII: 52, 59; Benedictine Monks, 429; Butler, July 5.

IV

Irish Saints on the Continent

Dom Louis Gougaud tells us "For close upon four hundred years Irish saints, filled with burning missionary zeal labored incessantly to spread the Christian faith and monastic discipline in Gaul, Belgium, Alsace, in Alemania, Franconia, in Italy, along the course of the Danube and down the valley of the Rhine."

Religion and scholarship went hand in hand with the Irish missionaries. Heinrich Zimmer may be quoted: "The Irish were the instructors in every branch of science and learning of the time, possessors and bearers of a higher culture than was at that time to be found anywhere on the Continent and can surely claim to have been the pioneers — to have laid the cornerstone of western culture on the Continent."

There was only one library in all of Europe that would compare with that of the Irish Bobbio, either for extent, or for the value of its manuscripts and that was the library of St. Gall in Switzerland.

The distinctive Irish script traces the widespread influence of Irish scholars. In such centers as Luxeuil in France, St. Gall in Switzerland, Würzburg in Germany and Bobbio in Italy, Irish writing flourished and manuscripts in the Irish hand multiplied. Individual Irish monks were welcome everywhere for their admirable script and industry in that age of laboriously handwritten textbooks as well as the Scriptures. Irish monks performed still another service, the maintenance of countless "Hospitalia Scottorum" all over Europe for Irish and other pilgrims to holy places.

To keep the early Irish missionary record straight it is necessary to remember that the term Scot in all instances refers to a native of Scotia, as Ireland was then called. There was Fursey's Peronna Scottorum, Peronne of the Irish, from the 7th century. As late as the 11th century Marianus Scotus from Donegal was the originator of some 12 monasteries in southern Germany, a congregation governed out of St. James of the Scots in Ratisbon.

Gougaud; Graham; Butler-Attwater, I: 290; Zimmer, 130; Tommasini, 69; Montalembert; Porter.

Gibrian
May 8   Sixth century

Remigius, Archbishop of Rheims who died in 533, was very friendly to Irish pilgrims and legends have come down regarding a number of religious who labored in his diocese. Among them were the priest Gibrian and his six brothers and three sisters: Tressan, Helan, Germanus, Veron, Abramus, Petron and Franchia, Promptia, Possena. Remigius provided them with suitable retreats out of which they worked to spread the faith at Rheims and in the forest land near the Marne. In Bretagne there is a parish St. Helan; a parish St. Vran; a parish and other places dedicated to Abraham; the Strand of Petron and a grotto named for him in Trezilide. After Gibrian's death a chapel was built over his tomb from which the village of St. Gibrian takes its name. Flodoard, tenth century canon of the cathedral of Rheims, recounts in his *History of the Church of Rheims* the translation in his own time of the relics of Gibrian to the Abbey Basilica of St. Remigius. He has also a story of recovery of sight in answer to prayers to Gibrian and Veron.

Tressan, commemorated February 7, was almost as renowned as Gibrian. Ordained by Remigius, he taught, preached and died in the territory of Rheims and was buried at Avenay. A thousand years later an abbess there, with the sanction of Clement VIII and Archbishop Phillip of Rheims, procured the printing of an Office for the saint. Of Avenay's patrons, Tressan took precedence.

Kenney, 184; O'Hanlon, II: 376, 383; Benedictine Monks, 266, 580; Fitzpatrick, I: 17; Butler, V: 273; Butler-Attwater, II: 251.

Berthold and Amandus
June 16   Sixth century

In the late 5th century Berthold and Amandus came from Ireland into northeast France to Remigius, Bishop of Rheims.

The more celebrated Berthold settled in the solitude that is now the city of Chaumont, built an oratory and later governed for many years the community of religious that gathered about him there. After his death, miracles and wonders perpetuated his memory and in 1045 a monastery and church named for him was built on the site of his oratory, the origin of the town of Chaumont. Chaumont had an Office of six lessons for the feast day of the saint and a litany compiled in his honor was formerly recited. A breviary of the church of Rheims, printed in 1630, contained at June 16 an Office for Berthold, Confessor Abbot. Indulgences for visits to his shrine were granted by cardinals and popes, among them Pope Nicholas VI in 1451 and Pope Paul II in 1466.

Amandus, also commemorated on June 16, labored as a solitary around Beaumont where he died and where Remigius presided over his last rites. Afterwards his remains were removed to Chaumont to rest beside those of Berthold.

Kenney, 184; O'Hanlon, VI: 676; Benedictine Monks, 37, 105.

Ursus (Aosta)
February 1   Sixth century

Four saints of the name Ursus are venerated in Italy. One of them, Ursus of Aosta, was an Irish saint. His time was in the 6th century when Arianism was rampant in Italy.

Ursus was noted for his stand against Arianism, first as a devoted archdeacon under Bishop Jucundus, later in his departure when Plocean, said to have been an Arian, succeeded as bishop. With a few canons of the cathedral, Ursus withdrew outside the city to the church of St. Peter, the beginning of what was afterwards the famous collegiate church of Saints Peter and Ursus. Tommasini states that Ursus exterminated Arianism forever in that locality, that in the 16th century Calvin made no headway there, that "the fidelity of this valley, originally evangelized by an Irishman, to the Church of Rome is remarkable."

Memorials to Ursus at Aosta are numerous, important and varied, such as the St. Ursus lime tree under which the council of the valley met for deliberations. Aosta's Church of Saints Peter and Ursus is a veritable art repository of missals and precious reliquaries of inestimable value, among them the great coffin containing the body of Ursus. Traces of the original church are still to be seen in the crypt which is called the Confession of St. Ursus.

Churches, chapels, hospitals dedicated to Ursus extend out on all sides of Aosta, into France, Switzerland and inland Italy. An altar with the saint pictured above it is dedicated to him in the cathedral at Turin.

Ivrea, not far from Aosta, is of special Irish interest. It once had a church dedicated to Ursus with Brigit of Kildare and Ursus the patrons of the city and in it their joint feast of February 1 was kept as of obligation. It was at Ivrea Blessed Thaddeus McCarthy died in 1492.

Tommasini, 265; O'Kelly, 106.

Fridian (Frediano)
March 18   c. 588

In 1652, in the fourth and last translation of his relics, the bones of sixth century Fridian were recomposed into a body which, vested in pontificals, rests in a glass coffin below the high altar of the Cathedral of San Frediano in Lucca in Italy. There it may be seen today.

The concordant testimony of al! texts, according to Tommasini, is that Fridian came from Ireland. He is said to have been the son of a king of Ulster and to have been educated and raised to the priesthood in Ireland. On a pilgrimage to Italy Fridian came to the hermitages in the fastnesses of Monte Pisano near Lucca and was so attracted to that renowned retreat of holy men he decided to live out his own days there. Word of his sanctity, his austere life, his many good works reached John III who called him to the bishopric of Lucca about 560.

Twenty-eight churches, either founded or restored, correspond to the 28 years of a ministry made arduous by the Lombard invasions and the Arianism they brought with them. One of the destroyed churches was Fridian's own cathedral (now San Frediano) which he rebuilt and dedicated to the Three Deacons, Vincent, Stephen and Laurence.

In his *Dialogues*, written before 604, Gregory the Great relates in detail Fridian's miraculous diversion of the river Auser to a new river bed to avert the damage it caused to fields and crops. "The man of God Frediano" was one of those Gregory held up as an ideal for the encouragement and edification of the faithful in the storms that swept the Church in the sixth century.

In connection with his cathedral at Lucca, Fridian founded a community of monks with whom he lived and whose austere discipline he shared. Two charters attest the existence of his monastery, one dated 685, signed by Bishop Felix; one dated 688, signed by King Cunibert. Lucca was a chosen stop-over for Irish pilgrims and all through the middle ages "St. Fridian's City" was an important center of Irish influence.

Special significance is attached to the Irish element in the famous institution, "the Canons Regular of St. Fridian" that in the 11th century arose beside Fridian's tomb. The personnel of the parish church of St. Fridian, living in communal life so distinguished themselves above all other clergy of Lucca, Alexander II, at the request of Peter Damian, called some canons from St. Fridian's as from a house of strict observance. Paschal II, in 1105, invited them to Rome for the reformation, according to their rule, of the clergy of the Lateran Church. The Order for a time had the name Lateran Canons of St. Fridian.

Gougaud finds it very strange, but nevertheless a fact, that Brigid and Patrick are reckoned members of the Canons Regular of the Lateran in Rome. Tommasini, who states that the cult of their canoness, St. Brigid, Virgin, was particularly promoted by the Lateran Order, goes to that former assembly of the Irish, Lucca of St. Fridian, for the explanation: the important part played among the Canons Regular of St. Fridian at Rome by those members of the Order who resided at St. Fridian's in Lucca.

Tommasini, 360; Butler-Attwater, I: 626; Fitzpatrick, II: 318; Gougaud, 111.

Fridolin
March 6   Sixth century

Fridolin's Irish nationality is a long tradition at Sachingen in Germany. Five centuries passed before the appearance of the main source of historical information, a work by Balther, a monk of Sachingen. Eleventh century Balther's *Life* was written, he tells, from memory with the help of others who like himself had read an older *Life* at a monastery named Helera, a document which formerly had been at Sachingen.

Balther represents Fridolin as an Irishman who came to Poitiers and under the protection of Clovis I, conqueror of that region in 507, restored the church of St. Hilary and collected his relics, who later travelled up the river Rhine, founding monasteries in honor of Hilary, and finally, the one at Sachingen on the Rhine near Basle. (Kenney would place Fridolin's time in Poitiers a century later. He considers it more probable Fridolin was at Poitiers during the reign of Clovis II, perhaps during the episcopacy of Dido.)

Fridolin's path along the Rhine was a favorite Irish route to Rome and his foundation at Chur, or Coire, in the Grisons became an Irish literary and artistic colony that continued through the middle ages. An Irish reliquary and some sculptured stones with designs of Irish origin are still preserved there.

Fridolin is venerated both in Germany and in Switzerland. Among other Irish overtones in Sachingen's celebration of the feast of its patron saint, Ireland's flag, along with the German, Swiss and Baden flags, decorates the houses.

Kenney, 496; Fitzpatrick, II: 90, 272; Tommasini, 75; O'Hanlon, III; Gougaud, 141.

Wendel
October 21   Sixth century

Official leaflets from the Bishop's House, Trier, Germany, 1957, state that in the United States, 17 villages, founded by emigrants from the St. Wendel area, are called St. Wendell, or Wendell, after the village that developed around the tomb of "St. Wendelin, one of those missionaries who came in the sixth century from Ireland to Gaul and the Rhine to preach the Gospel."

On the return from a pilgrimage to Rome, Wendel settled in west Germany in a solitary place near Trier. And, the German writer Ressel tells us, the land between the Rhine and the Moselle rejoiced in his labors. Around his cell grew the community that was in later times the Benedictine abbey of Tholey. In modern times, a thriving Society of the Divine Word Mission House of St. Wendel trains students for missionary work all around the world.

The saint was buried first at Tholey. Before long, visions and wonders, at the place to which he used to retire for prayer, prompted his re-interment in a church built at that spot. In 1320, when Wendel's intercession was credited with the checking of a pestilence, Archbishop Baldwin of Trier, one of the Luxemburg counts, rebuilt the saint's chapel. About 1332, the little village that had developed around the church was chartered by the German Emperor as the town of St. Wendel. The repute of the saint was so generally known in the late middle ages and his veneration so widespread "even the German Emperor Maximilian visited St. Wendel when he came to Trier for a reichstag."

A favorable destiny has been kind to Wendel's church, ancient portions of which survive: the 1370 stone sarcophagus which was first used as a table to hold the wooden shrine of the saint, and, dating from 1300, in a special niche, the oldest representation of Saint Wendelin. It shows him "not as a herdsman of the later legend, but as the Irish monk with staff and Gospel." The pulpit, dated 1462 by the escutcheon of Archbishop Johann II, is the 2nd oldest stone pulpit in Germany.

Lively remembrance of Wendel continues. Parish stationery has a medallion image of the saint. Observance of his feast day is traditional: Catholic weeklies in a recent year carried a picture, "Mounted Prelate," the bishop of Strasbourg in pontificals astride a white horse in the feast day procession.

St. Wendel Booklet; Kenney, 511; Fitzpatrick, II: 94; *Catholic Encyclopedia*, XV: 587.

Ronan (Renan)
June 1   Seventh century

It is Breton tradition that every Breton must perform Ronan's "Great Tromenie" at least once in a lifetime.

According to the *Quimper Breviary*, Ronan came from Ireland to Brittany sometime in the 6th or 7th century. Shadowy and legendary though he may be, his name lives on as an apostle of the area around Laon. There is a village St. Ronan in the diocese of Laon, a St. Ronan in Quimper, a Laurenan in the parish of Lan Renan in the diocese of St. Brieuc. Lacronan preserves relics of the saint.

The path Ronan used to travel fasting across the rocky countryside has been made into a way of penance, a devotion that is known as the Great *Tromenie*, Breton for Tour of Refuge. Every 6 years through the centuries, in a great formal pilgrimage, the shrine containing relics of the saint is born in an immense procession that winds for 10 miles, often over rough terrain, through 5 parishes. American reporters have brought back pictures that show the beautiful, very large processional banners and crosses, the picturesque native Breton costumes, the narrow, single file, circuitous line of march. Visitors in the thousands converge on Lacronan for the *Tromenie*. Mostly French of Breton origin, others from far off towns and lands, devout, in penance or in great necessity, all are come to pray the penetential march. Back in Lacronan a pageant that depicts the life of Ronan and a special Mass conclude the Great *Tromenie*.

Kenney, 182; Gougaud, 137; O'Hanlon, VI: 8; *Catholic Encyclopedia*, XII: 612.

Columban (Columbanus)
November 23   615

"St. Columban," Pope Pius XI said in 1923 "is to be reckoned among those distinguished and exceptional men whom Divine Providence is wont to raise up in the most difficult periods of human history to restore causes almost lost. This illustrious son of Ireland worked within no narrow confines. As scholarship throws an increasing light on the obscurity of the Middle Ages, the more clearly is it manifest that the renaissance of all Christian science in many parts of France, Germany, and Italy is due to the labor and zeal of Columban, a demonstration to the glory of the whole church and more particularly to Catholic Ireland."

When Columban appeared on the Continent, sometime before the year 575, continuous wars had resulted in an almost complete collapse of religion in post-Roman Europe. The Frankish kings, according to Montalembert, were often generous to the bishops, but from their biographies it is hard to believe that in embracing Christianity they gave up a single vice or adopted a single Christian virtue. Germany, overrun with Teutonic tribes, was almost totally pagan. Anglo-Saxon England would not receive the reluctant apostle

Augustine until 597. And Boniface, who would reap the field the Irish missionaries had sowed and is called the apostle of Germany, was not yet born and would not arrive on the Continent until 716. In Italy herself, overrun by Lombards and infiltrated with Arianism, Monte Casino was abandoned, not to be rebuilt until 717 by the Benedictines whose "modest beginnings and obscure progress escaped the notice of history." Ireland alone hummed with the vigor and fervor of her saints and scholars.

Leinster born Columban, "the most intrepid of the intrepid Irish saints" made early studies under Sinnel at Lough Erne, completed his education at Bangor with Comgall. From Bangor came men of sanctity and scholarship and these attributes Columban sought to a high degree of perfection. There followed his great decision to preach the Gospel in foreign lands wheresoever Providence might direct. Comgall provided 12 seasoned religious to accompany him.

They passed through England, landed near St. Malo and wandered across Gaul from west to east, attracting ever more favorable notice as they went. On the invitation of Sigibert, who died in 575, the saint settled in his territory, choosing the ruins of an old Roman fort, Annegray, situated in the borderland between Austrasia and Burgundy. From the first, miracles and wonders there, the severe rule and austerity of the Irish monks attracted wide interest in both kingdoms.

Novices, visitors, the sick, made larger quarters necessary and about 590, Luxeuil, the second and principal monastery was built, followed two years later by Fontaines, all three within a few miles. Franks and Burgundians brought their sons to Luxeuil, lavished gifts upon it, often asked admittance for themselves. Monks replaced monks in the Laus Perennis to chant unendingly the praise of God.

As time went on there were some who viewed with uneasiness the spectacular strength and influence of this abbot who could dispense with the powerful, who accepted the gifts of the kings but attacked their morals, who went directly to Rome, admitting neither the control nor the jurisdiction of the bishops. There is extant from about the year 600 a letter Columban wrote to Gregory the Great regarding the Celtic Easter date. He touched as well on the episcopate of Gaul and asked the attitude to be observed towards certain of its members. Extant also from about this same time is a letter Gregory wrote to Abbot Chonon of Lerins, urging on him a reform of observances and recommending to him "Our son Columbus the presbyter." It is known that Chonon visited Luxeuil, supposedly as a result of this letter. When the bishops summoned Columban to a synod on the pretext of his Celtic Easter, he excused himself "lest he contend in words." But he did not hesitate to call to their attention matters more urgent than a difference in liturgical procedure, among them the scandals of the young King Thierry, whose court they frequented. Columban's own refusal to condone Thierry's conduct brought upon him the enmity of the old queen, Brunehaut. Earlier she had instigated the murder of Desiderius, Bishop of Vienne. Now she set about through devious wiles to deal with Columban. He was banished from Thierry's kingdom in 610.

The entire community made ready to accompany Columban. But Luxeuil gave a very special prestige to Thierry's kingdom. Only Irish monks were permitted to leave. Armed royal guards escorted them to Nantes and aboard a ship for Ireland. As they set sail, a storm arose out of a clear sky to drive them back to land, high and dry aground for three days. The captain, blaming all of his troubles on the religious, finally unloaded them and all of their belongings and would have no more to do with them. He then departed without hindrance from the elements.

From Nanteș, Columban passed to the courts of the two other kings, Clothaire of Neustria and Theodebert of Austrasia. At Soissons, Clothaire asked the abbot's advice concerning the warring kings, Theodebert and Thierry, envoys of each having come seeking his support. Columban counselled him prophetically, "Remain neutral, within three years both of their kingdoms will be yours."

Gougaud writes, "In order to take stock of the progress of monasticism in Gaul in the 7th century one need only follow the footsteps of Columban." The old saint Deicuil dropped behind a few miles from Luxeuil, the origin of the celebrated Abbey of Lure. Potentin, another Irish companion, left his abbot to found a monastery at Coutances in Normandy.

A chance meeting, a blessing devoutly bestowed, and those who were once induced by Columban to lead a life of grace never wished to leave it. Near Meaux lived Chagneric, the father of Chagnoald, a monk at Luxeuil who would later become bishop of Laon. Columban blessed the younger children, Faron, later bishop of Meaux, and the little daughter, Fara, who would found the famous convent of Faremoutiers. Columban blessed the sons of another noble, Autharius: Ado, future founder of Jouarre; Dadon or Ouen, founder of Rebais and archbishop of Rouen; Radon, who remained in the world, founder and chief benefactor of the Abbey of Reuil. Besancon's future bishop and the founder of the Abbey of Besancon was Donatus, the son the Duke of Besancon gave to Columban at baptism.

At Metz, Theodebert embraced Columban as a blessing of Providence and urged him to settle in his kingdom. Waiting there to rejoin the saint were disciples who had been escaping daily from Luxeuil, among them two of outstanding merit, Athala and Eustace. Athala was a Burgundian of noble birth who had spent some time at Lerins, but "anxiously desiring some place where the way of perfection would be more secure . . . came to the blessed Columban at Luxeuil.'' Earlier, Columban in his letter from Nantes to his Luxeuil community — ''some of the finest and grandest words which Christian genius has ever produced'' — had named Athala his successor. Now Athala was in Metz desiring to accompany the master. Columban prevailed upon Eustace to return to govern Luxeuil. For himself, having decided to preach the faith among the still pagan nations bordering the Rhine, his entourage set out along the Mozelle and Rhine to the present Switzerland. On the way Ursicinus dropped out at Basle to seek out a hermitage that grew into the Monastery of Ursanne. Athala was with the saint to the last.

Two beginnings were short lived: Tuggen, because of the ferocity of the pagan idolators; Bregenz, after a year and a half, when word came that Theodebert and his kingdom had fallen to Thierry. Columban had earlier returned to entreat his benefactor Theodebert to put aside his pride, yield to Thierry and become a cleric, a suggestion that only elicited laughter. ''If you do not become a monk by choice, you will be one by force,'' Columban told him. Now Thierry had delivered Theodebert up to Brunehaut, who had his head shorn, robed him in religious garb and then put him to death. Columban could no longer remain in Bregenz. At this point Gall fell ill and with his cell originated the monastery and city of St. Gall. Another disciple, Sigisbert, took leave of Columban at Chur to settle in the spot where arose the Abbey of Dissentis.

Luxeuil prospered exceedingly in a spectacular monastic colonization of Gaul which radiated out of it during the whole of the 7th century. There were other workers for the faith, Montalembert observes, but not one of them approached Columban's stature, not one of them left Columban's tremendous impress which dominates the entire 7th century, of all centuries rated the most fertile and illustrious in the number and fervor of the monastic establishments which it produced. History records at least 63 disciples who became apostles of France, Germany, Switzerland and Italy under the rule and spirit of Columban, disciples who were the founders of more than a hundred monasteries before the year 700. Episcopal cities sought for their bishops men trained in the government of souls in this great monastery, religious whom they concluded beforehand to be saints. In the short space of 20 years, Luxeuil produced 21 men who after their deaths were honored by the church with public veneration.

When Columban passed from the Alps into Italy, he founded Bobbio, in the Appenines between Piacenza and Genoa. Nowhere did the Irish monks leave a deeper or more abiding impression. Bobbio became a center of culture second to none in Italy. It rocketed to high repute in that time of the Arian heresy, becoming a citadel of orthodoxy out of which religion and the monastic life spread over all of the northern provinces. Here, after 1300 years, there may still be counted 34 parishes dedicated to Columban. He was not long in Italy when Eustace of Luxeuil came with an escort of nobles to Bobbio. At the moment of triumph, Thierry had died suddenly, the lords of both Thierry and Theodebert leagued with Clothaire who was now, as the saint had foretold, sole ruler of the three kingdoms. Clothaire asked Columban's return to Luxeuil. The saint declined but he took the opportunity to write Clothaire a letter of practical exhortations and recommended to the king's care his beloved Luxeuil.

Columban died at Bobbio, November 23, 615, succeeded by Athala. In Italy and throughout Gaul Columban's rule continued to be widely propagated and was long retained by his numerous disciples and those who came after them, even in many monasteries where the milder rule of Benedict was adopted by its side.

Bobbio's glory was its library, literary treasures that are now scattered all over Europe. Turin has, among some 70 volumes, the copy of the Gospels Columban is said to have brought to Italy in a wallet hanging from his shoulders — the beginning of the famous storehouse of ancient literature whose subjects, recorded in a 10th century catalogue, covered every branch of knowledge, human and divine. Bobbio copyists preserved for modern times many of the classics. Precious additional manuscripts came from Irish pilgrims who came and went regularly, from Irish monks fleeing the Viking invasions, from private collections. The Irish Dungal in the 9th century brought a handsome gift of 40 volumes. Cardinal Borromeo in 1606 acquired 73 Bobbio books for the Ambrosian Library he founded at Milan, and to this gift from Bobbio, says Achille Ratti, afterwards Pope Pius XI, the Ambrosiana "is indebted for much of the prestige it enjoys among learned men and scholars, it would be no exaggeration to say, all over Europe." Pope Paul in 1618 added 28 of its classical antiquities to the Vatican collection. Naples, Vienna, Wolfenbuttel and the Escorial profited at Bobbio's expense. These Bobbio books can often be identified by a sort of book plate in 15th century writing, "Liber Sancti Columbani."

Columban's letters in prose are of singular value to Irish historians in that they are among Ireland's oldest surviving documents. One letter sets forth the Irish computation of the Easter date. Annotations in his writings from pagan authors of Rome as well as from the great Fathers of the west are first-hand evidence of the literary training to be had in the schools of 6th century Ireland. Of Columban's poetry Porter writes, "This man of iron . . . still at moments relapsed into lyrics which are not only exquisite but so full of humanistic feeling that were they not in an 8th century manuscript one might almost take them for a product of the Italian Renaissance."

This, then, was the Irish monk reckoned by Pope Pius XI "among those distinguished and exceptional men whom Divine Providence is wont to raise up in the most difficult periods of human history to restore causes almost lost." To him goes the credit of raising up a legion of saints, of recruiting and setting on the march the most considerable force in saving the faith in Europe.

Today, Columban's name and his spirit march anew. On his feast day, November 23, 1882, was born Edward J. Galvin, prime mover in the St. Columban Missionary Society of secular priests which he co-founded with Father John Blowick in 1916. Bishop Galvin's life as told by William E. Barrett in *The Red Lacquered Gate* is a story well worth the reading.

The Columban mission magazine outlines some of the activities of the Fathers now serving in seven nations of the Far East and Latin America: "They preach God's word in the jungles of Burma; they celebrate the Eucharist in bamboo chapels in the Philippines; they hear confessions undismayed by the noise of roaring traffic in Tokyo; they baptize infants in the slums of Lima, Peru; they comfort the sick in the thatched-roofed huts of Fiji. But they also might set up a credit union in Chile . . . or a Boys Town in Japan or a boat-building project for poor Korean fishermen . . . or a family service center in a Philippines seaport . . . or a school almost anywhere. Wherever in the world they go, they help their people help themselves build a better life."

Working side by side with the Columban Fathers since 1922, are the Missionary Sisters of St. Columban, an Order of nurses, teachers, social workers and doctors.

Jonas; Kenney; Daniel-Rops; Gougaud; Porter; Tommasini; Fitzpatrick, II; Montalembert.

Cathal (Cataldus)
May 10   Seventh century

Among Irish saints in Italy, not even Columban is so widely commemorated as is "San Cataldo." The cathedral of Taranto is named for him. So are monasteries, churches, crypts, novitiates, palaces, hospitals, towers, farmsteads, guilds, festivals, cemeteries, harbors, lighthouses, scattered all over Italy, in Sicily, Malta and into France. In the Basilica of the Nativity in Bethlehem, a Byzantine painting on the 8th pillar of the nave on the left has Cathal's name inscribed in Latin and in Greek.

Ireland locates Cathal at Lismore in Waterford, first as a student, then as a professor who went on pilgrimage to the Holy Land. On the return, supposedly, he was shipwrecked at Taranto.

Almost all that is really known about Cathal's apostolate in Italy is that the Tarantines buried him in their cathedral and buried with him a little gold Cross of 7th or 8th century Irish workmanship. It is inscribed "Cataldus Rachau." Rachau is now impossible of precise identification: Rath Cua perhaps, or Rathan. It is considered well worthy of note and of added weight that Irish nationality should be attributed to Cataldus in a region like Taranto, one so remote from Ireland and so far off the usual route of Irish pilgrims.

Taranto was destroyed in 927 by the Saracens. In 1071, on May 10th, when the cathedral was being rebuilt, the body of Cataldus was discovered and during the removal to a place of honor in the new cathedral, four extraordinary miraculous cures occurred. That was the beginning of the long history of many miracles and of the great veneration paid to Cataldus.

Tommasini, 399; Kenney, 185; Neeson, 55; Benedictine Monks, 131.

Desle (Deicuil)
January 18   c. 625

The lonely mountain cell of the Irish Desle was the beginning of the city of Lure in northeastern France, the origin of the great, enduring Lure monastery, the abbots of which, 11 centuries later, were named princes of the Holy Roman Empire.

The Bangor scholar-monk Desle, Deicuil in his native land, was one of Columban's companions on the great pilgrimage into foreign lands. He labored beside the saint all through Annagrey and Luxeuil days. But only a few miles along the road of exile from Luxeuil, Desle succumbed to fatigue and Columban could only bless him in farewell. As Desle wandered about alone in the forest region, tormented with thirst, he knelt to pray. And before him, beneath the stick on which he was leaning, a little spring of water gushed out. There he built his cell. At the end of the 19th century children's clothes could still be seen hanging on the branches of the trees that shaded that spring, the water of which was reputed to cure childish illnesses.

Nearby was a little chapel dedicated to St. Martin to which, every evening after night had fallen, Desle would go to pray. The pastor objected to the stranger for whom doors "opened without keys." His complaints, however, served only to call attention to the kindly religious. Disciples soon were flocking to him, attracted by his preaching, his learning and his miracles. Generous patronage came to him from Columban's friend King Clothaire who came upon his cell on a hunting trip and the monastery that arose about the saint grew and became famous. Towards the end of his days, Desle turned over the care of the foundation to his disciple-successor Columban, believed also to have been Irish. Down to the present day, memory of Desle's sanctity and devotion to him continue in France and especially around Lure.

Daniel-Rops, 65; Dubois, 94; Gougaud, 134; Montalembert, II: 597; Butler-Attwater, I: 116; Benedictine Monks, 169.

Ursinus (Ursin)
December 20   c. 625

The town of St. Ursanne in Switzerland takes its name from the monastery of the Irish monk Ursinus who accompanied Columban from Luxeuil and into exile as far as the wild mountain gorges above the river Doubs, a wilderness populated only by bears. A bell, treasured as having belonged to him, is of Irish design. Whatever his real name, Ursinus is thought to have attached itself to him from the bears that were said to do his bidding.

When disciples came to join him, he moved down to the more accessible valley for his cloister and the hospice for the needy and the sick poor whom he brought to it with baggage cattle kept for that purpose.

Memories of his holiness and miracles gave an aura of sanctity to the scene of labors. It is recorded of Wandrille, founder of the monastery of Fontenelle, ''the remembrances of Columban haunted the mind of Wandrille.'' When he was preparing for the religious life he spent a considerable period as a solitary devoted to the practices of prayer and austerity of the Irish monks. The place he chose was near to the tomb of Ursinus.

Dubois, 96, 120; Gougaud, 13; Tommasini, 75; McCarthy, 97; Benedictine Monks, 586.

Sigisbert
July 11   c. 625

In 1914 the monastery of Dissentis in Switzerland celebrated its thirteenth century. Yet another offshoot of Luxeuil, it was founded under the Columban rule by Sigisbert. He was Columban's disciple at Luxeuil, was with him at Bregenz and in the setting out for northern Italy. At Chur in the Swiss Alps, Sigisbert left the group and in the Grison mountain wilderness he built the cell and the oratory that were the origin of Dissentis. He is regarded the apostle of the Grisons in Switzerland.

Luxeuil-trained Sigisbert from centuries past has been held to have been of Irish origin. Rightly so, perhaps. Or again, perhaps because in Merovingian Gaul, so usual a thing was it for a man of special sanctity to be an Irishman, that Sigisbert was thought to be Irish, too.

Dubois, 65, 97, 88; Tommasini, 75, 476; McCarthy; Fitzpatrick, II: 46, 70.

Gall
October 16   c. 640

St. Gall in Switzerland gets its name from the Bangor educated Irish monk who planted a cross in the wilderness there in the year 612. He had been the companion closest to Columban in the spectacular success of Luxeuil, in the sometimes difficult, always fruitful, journeying after the exile from Burgundy. Finally, with their cordial reception at the court of Theodebert, King of Austrasia, new mission fields were opened up to the Irish monks. Columban had the idea of leaving some disciples with the Alemans and to go on himself as far as Italy.

Now they were at Bregenz on Lake Constance. Not far from them at Arbon was a holy priest Willimar who had welcomed them with the words, ''Blessed are those who come in the name of the Lord.'' In the business of establishing themselves at Bregenz, Gall's work, with his facility for native dialects, was preaching and instructing.

All was going well until, in the war between the two kings Theodebert and Thierry, Theodebert was vanquished and put to death. Columban, having no wish for further encounter with Thierry, determined to push on over the Alps into Italy. At this point Gall fell ill with a fever, too ill to travel. It was the parting of the ways for Columban and Gall. But great things lay ahead. Columban's Bobbio and Gall's Abbey in Switzerland, two of the foremost monasteries of Christendom.

Gall returned to Willimar who nursed him back to health. Once on his feet again, Gall departed to find the solitude in which he erected a cell and an oratory, and where disciples soon gathered about him. One Sunday in November in 615 Gall announced it had been revealed to him that Columban had died in the night and he wished to offer the Holy Sacrifice for the repose of his soul. Gall sent his deacon Magnoald to Bobbio to inquire about the abbot's last moments and when Magnoald returned he brought with him Columban's staff which he had bequeathed to Gall. Records tell that this staff hung over the altar in the St. Gall church in the 9th century. Bavaria still preserves two fragments of it encased in silver croziers, one at Kempten and one in the monastery Magnoald founded at Fussen.

Honors came to Gall. Gunzo, the Duke of Alemania, offered him the bishopric of Constance. About 627, six monks came from Luxeuil to ask him to be their abbot. He chose to continue to the last his life of preaching and instructing, chiefly among the most abandoned souls in the mountainous parts of the country. He was at Arbon of his old friend Willimar to preach on the feast of St. Michael the Archangel when death came to him.

From the first, many pilgrim Gaels who were scholars and teachers took up residence of varying duration at St. Gall. Records of those early days call a benefactor, Talto, the "Protector Hibernorum." Copies exist of deeds recording gifts made to the Monastery of St. Gall to which the dates 670 and 680 have been assigned. Jodicus Metzler mentions illustrious Irish men residing at St. Gall in the year 720 when Charles Martel in what is considered the official charter of St. Gall appointed the priest Otmar to guard the relics of the saintly founder.

The Irish Moengal, or Marcellus, raised the monastery to its highest fame, foremost among all the other schools of its time in the 9th century. He trained up famous names in that period, among them Tuotilo believed by many writers to have been Tuathal from Ireland. St. Gall was especially distinguished as a school of music with its copyists providing all of Germany with Gregorian Chant in manuscripts often in themselves works of art. As late as 950 to the year 1000 outstanding Irish instructors were still to be found at St. Gall, among them Faelan and Clemens. The St. Gall necrology lists 20 Irish monks who died there.

Immense properties accrued to St. Gall, all served with pastorates from the monastery. Gougaud, citing such centers as Pfaffers, Einsiedeln, Bamberg, Hirshau, quotes the Swiss Stueckelberg that there are some sixty Swiss localities where Gall is, or was, venerated and more than a dozen German, Lorraine and Alsation churches that preserve his relics or have been named for him.

Tommasini traces widespread commemorations of the saint in Italy. He notes that a little hospice, close to the church of St. Gall in Florence, was the center to which St. Francis of Assisi in 1211 gathered the first Florentines to follow in his footsteps. Listed in the Italian official Roll of Nobility is the family of San Galli which took the title from holdings dedicated to the Irish Gall. The Italian surname San Gallo is traced back to about 1485 to Florence to one of the many dedications of chapels, churches, and place names honoring the saint in Italy.

The great baroque Cathedral of St. Gall and the St. Gall library, one of the finest, if not the finest rococo room in Europe, are a tourist attraction. The floor of the library, inlaid with rare woods of intricate pattern, is so precious visitors must don great felt slippers before inspecting its treasures. Accumulated there is a very large collection of Irish manuscripts dating from the 7th, 8th and 9th century, also an extant 9th century catalogue that lists them. There are rare early bibles and illuminated manuscripts, among them the Gospels which bear the number 51, illuminated in Ireland about the middle of the 8th century. From the same century is the Latin-German dictionary, recognized as almost the first monument of Teutonic speech, the work of an Irish hand.

Daniel-Rops, 79; Kenney, 594; Porter, 71; Fitzpatrick, II: 89, 282, 301; Gougaud, 123; Tommasini, 252; Butler-Attwater, IV: 126.

Potentin

Seventh century

Potentin was one of the monks especially named for his outstanding virtue in Columban's monastery of Fontaines. He had accompanied Columban from Bangor, he accompanied him again when the Irish abbot was dispossessed of Luxeuil. On the trip from Burgundy towards Ireland, when the almost destitute religious sent two of their number into the city of Orleans to beg, Potentin was one of them and their mission was successful. He was aboard the ship for Ireland that was driven high and dry aground until the captain unloaded the Irish missionaries and all their belongings. Finally, in Columban's subsequent wanderings through Gaul, Potentin parted from him at Soissons and founded a monastery near the city of Coutances. He was still alive when Jonas wrote in 643.

Wherever an Irish missionary settled, compatriots followed. Although no trace of Potentin's monastery remains, we are told that saints from Ireland and Gaul evangelized Brittany and that most of the ancient saints of the diocese of Coutances are of Irish origin.

Daniel-Rops, 165; Dubois, 95; Fitzpatrick, I: 15; Jonas.

Caidoc and Fricor

April 1   Seventh century

Caidoc and Fricor, two Irish missionaries in Picardy, landed in France about 622. Taking the Roman road, they preached as they went along. At Centule, now St. Riquier, their "intermeddling" met with violence, but a young nobleman, Riquier, came to their defence and invited them into his home. He became a very fervent convert. He cut his hair, discarded his silken robes and his jewel-studded girdle. Ultimately he took Orders. About 625 he founded the monastery of Centule, according to the Irish Rule of Columban. Relics of Columban, Caidoc and Fricor were preserved there as late as the 17th century.

Caidoc and Fricor lived out their lives in Riquier's community. They were buried in Riquier's church. And St. Riquier's named four feast days to commemorate them, January 24, April 1, March 31, May 30. About the year 1003, relics of the Irish Maugille, one-time monk of St. Riquier's, were brought there to rest beside those of Caidoc and Fricor.

McCarthy, 198, 220; Fitzpatrick, II: 72, 75; O'Hanlon, V: 615; Benedictine Monks, 121.

Monon
October 18   Seventh century

In 1920, when the bishops of Ireland appealed to Catholic Belgium, citing the atrocities of the English soldiery in Ireland, Cardinal Mercier in the reply from the hierarchy of Belgium, extols Monon among other Irish missionaries. The Belgian Prince of the Church said in part: "For long have the eyes of Belgian Catholics turned towards Ireland full of admiration and gratitude. Is it not to the first pioneers of Christian civilization that Belgium herself owes in large degree the grace, greatest of all graces, of belonging to Christ? The names of Irish missionaries who in the Merovingian epoch evangelized the north of France, St. Columban, St. Foillan, St. Monon and Eton, St. Lievan, the bishops St. Wirnon and St. Plechelm and their deacon St. Odger, St. Fredegand finally, and many other have remained popular among us. More than thirty Belgian churches are dedicated to saints from your island."

Monon, assigned to the first half of the 7th century, lived as a hermit in the Ardennes, going about preaching the Gospel. He was martyred at Nassogne in Belgian Luxemburg.

Kenney, 508; Benedictine Monks, 430; Fitzpatrick, II: 76.

Fursey (Furza)
January 16   c. 648

Fursey came to France on a pilgrimage to Rome from his mission in East Anglia. He was not destined ever to return to England.

In Gougaud's *Gaelic Pioneers* Fursey is named one of the great figures of the heroic age — A Columban, a Gall, a Furza — for whom Continental writers of those times cannot find sufficiently fitting expressions of praise. After Columban, Fursey was the most famous Irish saint on the Continent, famous on two counts: the long enduring apostolate he originated and his visions of heaven and hell that stirred all medieval Europe six centuries before Dante's *Divine Comedy*.

Soon after landing in France, Fursey's prayer restored to health the dying son of Count Haymon of Ponthieu who urged upon him a gift of his estate at Mazerolles. Continuing on his way, however, he came to Peronne where the nobleman Erchinoald, Mayor of the Palace, asked him to baptize his son. Fursey stopped there for sometime, praying often in the little church of Mont des Cygnes dedicated to the Saints Peter and Paul. In it before pushing on to Rome, he deposited his precious relics of Patrick and of Meldan and Beoeadh which he had brought from Ireland. He announced prophetically that there he too would repose in death.

His pilgrimage to Rome accomplished, Fursey returned to Peronne and, Erchinoald having offered him any site he might select for a monastery, he chose Lagny en Brie then in the diocese of Paris. Erchinoald's generosity, that of Clovis II and Queen Bathilde, and especially the good repute of Fursey's monks that spread over the whole of France made Lagny an important monastery. Bishop Autbert of Paris and after him St. Landry authorized the saint to establish religious centers throughout France, and Fursey's own untiring industry coupled with a great many wonders viewed as miracles prospered a great new harvest of souls. He built a church at Compans which when finished was consecrated by Bishop Autbert. Erchinoald built another monastery for the saint at Mt. St. Quentin in the neighborhood of Peronne that was dedicated by St. Eloy, Bishop of Noyon with Fursey's brother Ultan who had rejoined him from East Anglia installed there as first abbot. Erchinoald also began construction of a church at Mont des Cygnes to replace the oratory in which reposed Fursey's relics. In the meantime religious from Ireland were arriving at Lagny among them Aemilian, and Fursey, concerned to revisit his East Anglian community, placed Aemilian in charge at Lagny and started for England.

The saint died on the way to the coast at Mazerolles. Count Haymon would have wished to have him interred there, but Erchinoald came with a royal guard to conduct his body to Peronne where, pending completion of the new church, his remains awaited entombment in incorrupt state in a side portico. Four years later when they were placed in a shrine worked by the artisan-saint Eloy they were still found free from corruption. Bede tells that "concerning the incorruption of his body we have briefly taken notice that the sublime character of this man may be better known to the readers."

Peronne was long a living monument to Fursey. It had his figure in the city banner. It came to be called Perrona Scotorum, Peronne of the Irish, so many of them began their "wandering for heaven" at Fursey's tomb. Out of Peronne Irish missionary activity radiated all over Picardy and into Flanders. The abbots of the Peronne monastery, the first one on the Continent to be founded exclusively for the Irish, were all Irish from its inception until 774 which is as far as extant records go and perhaps until its destruction by the Norsemen in 884.

Six hundred years after Fursey's death, in 1256, Louis IX solemnized his return to France from the first crusade by a gift to the saint's church, a rich shrine for his relics with the saint-king himself placing his seal on the sepulchre. In January, 1853, the bishops of the Rheims province proceeded to Peronne and once more enshrined in a rich case the relics of its patron saint. Along with Peronne, Fursey is the patron of 7 other parishes in the diocese of Amiens. Several chapels and wells keep his memory alive in Picardy. His feast day is celebrated throughout Ireland and also in the diocese of Northhampton in England.

Kenney, 500; Gougaud; Tommasini; Fitzpatrick, I: II; Moran, 315; Montalembert; Butler-Attwater, I: 101.

Foillan
October 31   655

Every seven years, amid pageantry and a blaze of color, Fosses in Belgium commemorates its patron saint in the spectacular procession, the March, of Foillan. Joined by neighboring towns, each with relics of its own patron saint, mounted grenadiers, uniformed drum and fife corps, armed ''compagnies'' in uniforms of past wars — 2000 strong in 1970 — conduct Foillan's relics over a traditional course. At each station — there are seven — the compagnies fire a salute.

Bede tells that Fursey, a holy man of very noble birth, came into East Anglia accompanied by his brothers Foillan and Ultan and others; that King Sigebert built them a noble monastery at Burghcastle in Suffolk. Some 12 years later when Fursey set out on his pilgrimage to Rome, it fell to Foillan to govern the English mission; he did so until its destruction by the Mercians. With as many of their books and church valuables as they were able to carry the Irish monks fled to France.

By this time Fursey was dead and had been entombed at Peronne. Already hosts of pilgrims to his tomb, especially his own countrymen, were making Peronne a place of importance. They erected there the first monastery for the exclusive use of the Irish on the Continent. Foillan was its first abbot. But he was not long at Peronne. When Gertrude of Nivelles heard about Foilland and Ultan she invited them to Nivelles to instruct her monks and nuns in liturgy, Scripture, and sacred chant. The Breviary of Paris tells ''Rome at that time took care to have the relics of the saints and holy books brought to her (St. Gertrude). She sent to Ireland for learned men to expound to herself and to her people the canticles of the Holy Law which the Irish had almost by heart. The monastery of Vossuensis was built on the banks of the Sambre for receiving the Saints Fullane and Ultaneus, brothers of St. Furseus.''

Gertrude's mother, Blessed Itta, gave Foillan a tract of land for a monastery at Fosses over which he placed Ultan. His own labors were devoted to the missionary preaching which, furthered by Erchinoald and the family of Pepin of Landen, played an important part in the evangelization of Brabant and in Frankish ecclesiastical history. One of Foillan's missionary companions was the Irish Fredegand (July 17) who became abbot of Kerkelodor near Antwerp.

Foillan was in Nivelles to sing the vigil of the feast of St. Quentin, October 31. After it he resumed the missionary journey that ended in his martyrdom. Ultan read news of his death into a vision he had the night after Foillan's departure: a snow white dove, its wings dripping with blood, ascending to heaven. Two months later, on January 16, the mangled remains of Foillan were found in the forest of Seneffe. The day his body was brought to Nivelles the Mayor of the Palace, Grimoald, and Dado, Bishop of Poitiers, came there to assist in carrying it into the monastery.

Foillan's books and other mementoes became treasures in Gertrude's convent. Both Nivelles and Fosses were long continuing centers of Irish missionary activity. Fosses remained in Irish hands until its destruction in 880 by the Norsemen. Like Peronne it was known as the monastery of the Scots (Irish). A number of churches in Belgium and France do, or did, commemorate Foillan: Fosses on January 16, the date of the finding of his body; Namur on October 31, the date of Ultan's vision; Mechlin and Tournai, November 5. The March of Foillan is performed in September.

Daniel-Rops, 94; Kenney, 503; Tommasini, 79; Fitzpatrick, II: 73; Gougaud, 128; Butler-Attwater, IV: 230; Hennebert.

Eloquius
December 3   c. 665

Eloquius was one of Fursey's disciples who propagated the Gospel in Belgium and France. He succeeded Fursey as abbot of Lagny, died and was buried there. During the 10th century Norse disturbances, the relics of the saint were removed to the Abbey of Waulsort in Belgium, also of Irish origin.

Graham, 42; Kenney, 503; O'Hanlon, IV; Benedictine Monks, 197.

Gobain
June 30   c. 670

The town of St. Gobain in France, crystal called St. Gobain glass, the forest of St. Gobain, scene of heavy fighting in World War I, all get their name from 7th century Irish Gobain. He left Ireland with Fursey, was with him at Burghcastle in England and went with him to France where they were some time in the solitudes of the great forest near Oise. After many years of missionary preaching, Gobain was murdered by barbarian marauders at the place now called St. Gobain. Notice of the saint occurs in the writings of Bede.

Kenney, 506; Gougaud, 19, 134; Fitzpatrick, II: 74; Morgan, 329; Benedictine Monks, 269.

Fiacre
August 31   c. 670

One of the best known saints of ancient France was the Irish Fiacre, friend of the sick, the poor, of everyone who came to him. From his own time and all through the middle ages many blessings were attributed to his prayer; the fame of his miracles was prodigious. Anecdotes and other references to Fiacre in the personal histories of other saints, of English kings, of French kings and queens, make interesting reading concerning the place he held in the affections and esteem of the people. Paris called its horse drawn cabs fiacres: the first such vehicles ever to be let out for hire in Paris came from the Hotel St. Fiacre, an inn with a great picture of the saint over the door.

In his native land, a hermitage named for Fiacre south of Kilkenny was long a place of pilgrimage. Scotland invoked him in the Dunkeld Litany and placed churches under his protection, among them St. Fiacre's church and cemetery in the parish of Nigg adjoining St. Fickers Bay near Aberdeen. In about 626, the saint presented himself to Bishop Faron of Meaux in France, one of the future saints blessed in childhood by Columban. The bishop gave Fiacre a hermitage at Breuil in La Brie and he set about clearing the land at once and producing upon it most extraordinary vegetables and flowers. It was said he knew how to grow plants of every kind and that from them came healing as well as nourishment. But especially he was appealed to for his prayer.

Ancient France dedicated some 30 churches to him. Bede recorded that most of the breviaries of France had an office of 9 lessons in honor of Fiacre. Dramatists made the story of his life into a sacred mystery play to be enacted as a stimulus to piety. Meaux celebrated his festival with special pomp and extravagant floral decorations. The church of St. Ferdinand in Paris filled its chancel with flowers on his feast day. The number of churches that had relics of the saint was legion. Two villages were named for him: St. Fiacre in La Brie and another in the canton of Plouagat. Around another dedication in Brittany a pardon was held. In this century, Gougaud, writing in 1923, stated that the chapel of St. Fiacre at Radenac was the most frequented in all the Morbihan.

Twelfth century John of Matha, founder of the Trinitarian Order, had a special devotion to Fiacre. In the belief that ground sanctified by the saint would nourish his own soul, he erected for himself a hermitage as near as possible to Fiacre's shrine. In 1227, Philip, Bishop of Meaux, granted indulgences to pilgrims to Fiacre's chapel. About 1313, the sanctuary of the saint was made into a Benedictine priory with 9 choir monks and a prior, maintenance of whom was to be provided out of the offerings of the faithful who frequented the holy spot.

The English Edward, the Black Prince, in warring upon France, spared the sanctuary of Fiacre. But he took for himself a portion of the relics to carry home with him to England. On his way through Normandy, he deposited the relics on an altar at Montloup which had a chapel named for Fiacre. Legend avers that when he tried to take the relics with him again, no strength of man could remove them from the place. The death of the prince soon afterwards was regarded by the French as just punishment for his irreverence to their saint. Later on in the fifteenth century, during the projected conquest of France by Henry V of England, so many Irish fought on the side of the French, that Henry, because Fiacre was of the Irish race, allowed his soldiers to pillage the monastery at Meaux. When the king soon after fell ill of a fistula, which was called the malady of St. Fiacre, he said that not only did the Irish on earth favor the French, but those in heaven equally. By a strange coincidence, he died at a chateau near Paris on Fiacre's feast day in 1422.

There is extant from the year 1462 a receipt of payment to the artisan for decorations to Fiacre's shrine. In 1478, Louis XI had it redone in silver with fleur-de-lis and dolphins to represent the arms of the King of France. A 17th century record lists a bestowal of relics to the Grand Duke of Tuscany and to Cardinal Richelieu. A bishop of Meaux and a Count of Blois gave testimony of cures they had received. The great saint of the poor, Vincent de Paul, made a pilgrimage to the place in which Fiacre also had ministered to the poor. Other famous visitors to the shrine were James II and his Queen from their place of exile at St. Germain.

Louis XIII and his Queen, Anne of Austria, regarded Fiacre as one of the most powerful patrons of the kingdom of France. When the king fell ill at Lyons and doctors despaired of his life, he attributed his recovery to the prayer of Fiacre. When the queen, in thanksgiving in 1641, made a pilgrimage on foot from the village of Monceaux, she was careful to pray at the door of Fiacre's oratory: in respect to his memory, women never entered the precincts of his former cell nor the chapel in which he had been interred. The queen believed it was through Fiacre's prayer that she gave to France the future Louis XIV after 20 years of childless marriage. She presented to Fiacre's church in La Brie the royal layette which had been especially blessed by Pope Urban VIII whose gift it was. Each year thereafter the queen saw to it that some one should represent her as a pilgrim to the shrine. Louis XIII died clasping a medal of St. Fiacre in his hand and he left a magnificent legacy in his honor. In later years, in a time of grave illness of Louis XIV, Bishop Bossuet of Meaux went himself to the shrine of Fiacre to commence a novena made there for the king's recovery, a prayer completed by the priory religious.

A unique reminder of Fiacre was flashed across the country by Associated Press Wire Photo for a recent St. Patrick's day, a pretty colleen wearing a hat entered by a French designer in a New York benefit hat show, a "Cocher de Fiacre." It was a coachman's high hat made of green velvet and trimmed with a huge feathery flower they called a dandelion, as amazing a specimen, surely, as anything Fiacre himself ever grew.

He is the patron saint of gardeners. But statuary of the horticulturist saint is non-existent, a fact pointed up in a newspaper article by a tradition perfectionist who searched in vain for a statue of Fiacre for the 10th century monastic garden he entered in the Chicago flower show. He rightly thinks it is high time some statuary firm should make figures of Fiacre for gardens.

Daniel-Rops, 74; Dubois, 98; Gougaud, 135; Kenney, 493; Butler-Attwater, III: 460; Tommasini, 73; Moran, 314.

Kilian (Chillen)
November 13   Seventh century

On the return from a pilgimage to Rome, Kilian came to his kinsman, Fiacre of La Brie, near Meaux, and stayed on to become a missionary under Bishop Autbert of Cambrai-Arras. With Aubigny near Arras for his headquarters, he preached the Gospel zealously all through Artois until his death. Artois enshrined his body in his church at Aubigny.

Daniel-Rops, 74; Fitzpatrick, II: 75; Dubois, 98, 91; Benedictine Monks, 138.

Dympna and Gerebern
May 15   ? Seventh century

Dympna is Belgium's famous patroness of the insane. Everything else about the saint may be obscure except the efficacy of her prayer which is well known in the case of epileptics, the mentally disturbed, and those under malign possession.

The earliest known record of Dympna dates from the thirteenth century. Already her church had a hospice for the sick and popular veneration was so widespread the Bishop of Cambrai authorized one Pierre to write a life of

Dympna from oral traditions. Legend makes her the daughter of a Christian mother and a pagan Irish king. At the death of her mother, the bereaved king could find no one as beautiful except Dympna so he decided to make her his queen. Dympna fled, accompanied by her mother's chaplain, Gerebern, and a court attendant and his wife. At Gheel, some 25 miles from Antwerp, they were tracked down by the king and martyred.

Two ancient marble coffins preserved at Gheel are said to have contained the bodies of Dympna and Gerebern. In one of them, allegedly, there was a red stone with lettering deciphered as Dympna. Gerebern's relics are now enshrined at Sonsbeck in the Rhineland, having arrived there in a partially successful attempt made by the "holy robbers of Xanten" to acquire for themselves the remains of the two saints.

Ever increasingly, the town and the area around Gheel became an out-patient facility, with the inhabitants, generation after generation, devoting themselves to kindly provision and specialized care for the mentally ill. Today, Gheel's hospital for the insane is acclaimed the best in the world.

Ireland observes Dympna's feast day. She has a strong following in America. Three Belgian churches have altars dedicated to Dympna. She is more particularly venerated in Gheel where her relics are enshrined in a silver reliquary in the church that bears her name. On Dympna's festival hundreds of men and women "neither mad nor sick" make a great general pilgrimage in her honor.

The saint has a strong following in America. At Massillon State Hospital in Massillon, Ohio, the National Shrine of St. Dympna has a beautiful church and a beautiful outdoor votive shrine in honor of Ireland's saint of the mentally ill.

Kenney, 510; O'Hanlon, V; Benedictine Monks, 186.

Pellegrinus (Peregrinus)
August 1   Seventh century

Throughout the middle ages, the general designation "peregrinus" denoted an Irish religious wayfarer. The term, as used in Ireland, meant not the traveller who went on a definite pilgrimage to a definite shrine from which it was his intention, after paying his devotions, to return, but the man who, for his soul's good, departed Ireland to dwell for a space of years or for the rest of his life in a strange country.

Mt. Pellegrino in the Italian Alps is named for one of the Irish wayfarers who is known only by the name Pellegrinus, or Peregrinus, a solitary honored among the patrons of Modena and Lucca. Down the centuries his chapel has known both ruin and restoration. As time went on the site of his hermitage was expanded into a hospice and an inn in connection with the chapel. Some of the good offices performed in memory of the saint are the ringing of a bell in winter evenings to direct any traveller lost on his way, long poles to mark the road, a dog always kept ready for rescue work and free board and lodging for all poor for three days.

Tommasini, 346; Benedictine Monks, 468; O'Hanlon, VIII.

Etto (Eton, Ze)
July 10   c. 670

Belgian, Gallic and Benedictine Martyrologies and especially the Acts of the Saints of Belgium commemorate Etto who is brought into association with the Saints Amand, Vincent Madelgaire, Gertrude, Foillan and Ultan. He worked with Fursey in East Anglia, went on to Rome with him where he is said to have been consecrated bishop. His field was the Low Countires. As abbot-bishop, with the monastery of Fescan in the village of Dompierre for his headquarters, he labored to spread the faith in the canton of Avesnes; in Buinvilliers near Arras; in Liesse which as well as Fescan made his feast a great solemnity marked by a procession and a mounted escort for his relics. In 1630, confraternities in his honor under the name Ze were established in Dompierre and Buinvilliers. Cardinal Mercier, in his 1920 letter to the bishops of Ireland, named Eton among the Irish missionaries to whom Belgium was largely indebted for the greatest of all graces, the grace of belonging to Christ.

Kenney, 506; Fitzpatrick, I: 247, II: 76; Benedictine Monks, 209; O'Hanlon, VII: 181.

Roding (Rodingus, Rouin)
September 17   c. 680

Roding's biographer, Richard of St. Vannes who died in 1046, was the disciple-successor of another Irish saint, Fingen. Roding is said to have been an Irish companion of Columban and Gall who became the Abbot-founder of Beaulieu in the Argonne. His monastery is still in existence.

Kenney, 209; Tommasini, 80; Gougaud, 20; Benedictine Monks, 513; Butler, IX: 705.

Maugille (Madelgisilus)
May 30   c. 685

Maugille's chapel at Monstrelet in France was a parish church for a thousand years. Maugille worked beside Fursey in East Anglia, was his prior at Lagny and, finally, was his companion on the proposed visit to England. After Fursey's death, Maugille went to St. Riquiers at Centule, the monastery founded by the nobleman convert of the Irish monks, Caidoc and Fricor. But soon he was teaching and preaching with a little cell and an oratory on the banks of the Authie near Monstrelet, which afterwards was long a place of pilgrimage. It became the custom of the faithful, after Maguille's remains were entombed in the abbey church at Centule, to go in procession to Monstrelet on his feast day, occasions on which, according to old manuscript chronicles, remarkable cures occurred.

Kenney, 302; Gougaud, 19; Fitzpatrick, II: 75; Benedictine Monks, 385; O'Hanlon, V: 608.

Boethian
May 22   Seventh century

Laon in France lay well in the path of Irish pilgrims to Rome and the Holy Land and was later to have a celebrated colony of Irish men of letters. It was already a center of Irish missionary activity when the Irish ascetic, Boethian, came there to the church of St. Vincent in the seventh century. He built the monastery of Pierrepont near Laon and near there he was eventually martyred. His shrine is still a place of pilgrimage.

Fitzpatrick, II: 257; Benedictine Monks, 110.

Mombolus
November 18   Seventh century

Mombolus is an example of Gougaud's observation "From the very beginning of monasticism in Ireland, a strong tendency is noticeable towards the life of an anchorite. It was not unusual to see pious cenobites, in the very bloom of manhood or its decline, retire 'to the desert' or 'to a hard prison of stone' . . . in order to give themselves up entirely to absolute contemplation." Mombolus, one of Fursey's Irish monks at Lagny in the diocese of Meaux in France, succeeded to the abbacy only to resign very shortly because so many of the brethren considered his government too severe. He lived out the remainder of his days in retirement in a rigorous life of solitude and prayer. On his festival about the year 831 there occurred a re-enshrinement of his relics presided over by the bishops of Cambrai and Noyon.

Gougaud, 88; Fitzpatrick, II: 73; O'Hanlon, V: 145; Benedictine Monks, 432.

Turninus

July 17   Seventh century

The Irish monk Turninus, companion of Foillan in the Netherlands, labored there with unwearied zeal in the territory around Antwerp. At his death about the close of the 7th century, his relics were taken into the principality of Liege and were enshrined in a monastery on the Sambre.

Butler, VIII: 143; Benedictine Monks, 583.

Algise (Adalgisius)

June 2   c. 686

Gougaud mentions Algise as one of the many Irish pioneers who, although secondary to Fursey or Columban, are deserving of notice and still occupy a place in the folklore of the north and east of France. Algise and his brothers Gobain and Etto, all disciples of Fursey, settled in the forest of Thierache in Picardy and evangelized the country around Arras and Laon. Their hermitage became known as Cellula, or little cell or monastery and the town that grew up about them was named St. Algise. About the year 970, a later compatriot, Forannan, abbot of the monastery of St. Michael in Thierache, removed the relics of Algise to his church there.

The community of Algise is mentioned in connection with the financial support Ireland gave to her missionary projects on the Continent both early and late as in the case of Algise at Cellula in Picardy in the 7th century, and the foundations of Marianus Scotus at Ratisbon in the 12th.

Kenney, 506; Gougaud, 19, 134; *Benedictine Monks*, 7; O'Hanlon, VI: 15; Fitzpatrick, I: 247, II: 77.

Autbodus

November 20   Seventh century

The Irish missionary hermit monk Autbodus preached the Gospel in Artois, Hanault and Picardy. He died near Laon.

Benedictine Monks, 82.

Ultan

May 2   c. 686

"Ool-thawn" as it is pronounced, is a very old Celtic name still popular in Ireland. Although overshadowed by his more famous brothers, Fursey and

Foillan, Ultan was not less dedicated. He labored in Fursey's mission in East Anglia in England and then rejoined him on the Continent.

Ultan administered several Irish centers beginning with the monastery built for Fursey at St. Quentin. He governed Peronne in succession to Foillan. Mention of Ultan occurs in the Life of Amatus who had been unjustly banished by Theodoric: "Amatus found refuge in Fursey's monastery at Peronne of which Ultan was abbot at the time and rejoiced in the tranquillity of his retirement." Ultan taught liturgy, Scripture and sacred chant to St. Gertude's monks and nuns at Nivelles. Finally, and until his death, he ruled the hospice for pilgrims and the monastery erected at Fosses by Foillan through the generosity of Gertude's mother. Foillan's official feast day is the date of Ultan's vision of his martyrdom, although his remains were not recovered until two months later.

The monk of Nivelles who wrote the life of St. Gertrude tells that on the eve of her death which occurred March 17, 659, she sent messengers to Ultan at Fosses to ask his prayers. He sent back word to her to have no fear, that she would depart joyously the next day, that St. Patrick even then was making ready with the chosen angels of God to escort her into paradise on his own feast day.

Ultan rests at Fosses where he died about the year 686. Fosses, like Peronne, became celebrated as a monastery of the Irish, and like many another spot on the Continent, Brigid was remembered there. From a rise called the Hill of St. Brigid, a chapel dedicated to the saint of Kildare still looks down on the town of Fosses.

Daniel-Rops, 93; Tommasini, 79; Gougaud, 128; Fitzpatrick, II: 73; Butler-Attwater, II: 218.

Erhard and Others

c. 686

Writers all agree that besides the more famous of the Irish saints there were not only many men whose names have been handed down by more or less trustworthy records as followers of the same paths but also hundreds of others of whom all traces have long been lost in the debris of history. Gobain is a case in point. But for Bede, all knowledge of his Irish nationality would be lost.

Erard, commemorated on January 8, was a missionary bishop who died in Bavaria. His *Life* speaks of him as "Herhardus . . . genere Scoticus fuit." The future saint, Odilia, who was born blind is said to have recovered her sight at her baptism by Erhard. All through medieval times at Ratisbon a religious community of women known as Erhardinonnen kept up a perpetual round of prayer at the crypt of the saint.

Among the saints said to have been Irish is Hildulf, companion of Erhard in the Vosges mountain solitude, and abbot of the missionary center out of which he preached the faith. Arbogast, solitary in Alsace, abbot of Surburg and Shutteran monasteries and finally, bishop of Strasbourg, was at his own request, buried on a mountainside reserved for criminals, where, however, a church was soon built over his tomb. So many Irish pilgrims came to Strasbourg, Arbogast's successor, the Irish Florentius (November 7), built for them the church of St. Thomas outside the walls which became a monastery under the Irish rule and later a collegiate chapter of canons.

Beatus (May 9), an early Irish hermit venerated as an apostle of Switzerland, had his hermitage at the place now called Beatenburg. Germanus, a bishop from Ireland, suffered martyrdom near Amiens. There was Arnanus, an Irish recluse, the friend of Didier of Cahors. Romanus, "a holy pilgrim of God of the Irish race," was placed over Mazerolles by Ansoald of Poitiers. The bishopric of Angouleme was twice governed by Irish prelates, two centuries apart: Tomianus about 665 for whom Ansoald had reconstructed the church for Irish pilgrims, and Helias about 875. Donatus was bishop of Besancon. The Irish bishop Falveus who took the future abbot of Langrey, St. Cyran, on a pilgrimage to Rome is named in the latter's conversion. Bathilde, wife of Clovis II, went to Luxeuil to obtain the first abbot of Corbie and to the Columban abbey of Jouarre for the first abbot of Corbie and to the Columban abbey of Jouarre for the first abbess of her convent at Chelles. Celestine was abbot of the monastery of St. Peter of Mount Blandin in Ghent about 700. Dunchad, at once a bishop and a grammarian, taught literature in the Saint Remi monastery at Rheims.

Charlemagne needed not only teachers but well-written and faultless books for study and for the services of the church, work in which the Irish monks qualified on all counts. "So," says Gougaud "the Irish taught the Franks orthography and grammar . . . they commented the scriptures . . . they made numerous copies of such works on the Continent." More than one hundred manuscripts copied by Irish hands before the year 1100 are still preserved in Continental libraries. The poems of Sedulius name several of his Irish companions at Laon: Dermot, Fergus, Blandus, Marcus, Benchell.

Other scattered names are Praecordus or Precord, a hermit at Vesly-sur-Aisne; Brieuc (May 1), son of an Ulster prince, traveller to Rome, founder of a monastery at the present St. Brieuc in Brittany; Leutiern, a saint in Brittany identified as Irish; Mawes or Maudetus (November 18), an Irish saint with dedications in Brittany and in Cornwall; Menulphus or Menou (July 12), bishop of Quimper and founder of St. Menoux in Bourges; Ninnoca;

Cast; Osmanna, (September 9), patroness of Fericy-en-Brie; Tenananus, or Tinidorus, in Laon, either Irish or Irish taught; Vougay or Vio, (June 15), a bishop in Brittany; Vodoaldus (February 5), a missionary recluse near Soissans. Annals of the Abbey of Lorsch near Worms for the years 703–768, list in the obituary notices a number of Irish names: for the year 704, Conon, bishop; 705, Domnan, abbot; 706, Cellan, abbot; 707, Tigermal; 726, Dubdecris, abbot; 729, Macflatheus; perhaps Drocus in 708 and in 727, Daniel of Lagny. Ultan, (August 8), 8th century Irish monk-priest, a solitary of St. Peter's monastery at Craik, excelled in the art of illumination. One of St. Bruno's teachers was an Irish bishop Israel.

Gougaud; Kenney; Tommasini; Fitzpatrick; Benedictine Monks; Butler-Attwater, II: 208.

Kilian
July 8   c. 689

Cathedrals, chapels, wells, localities and mountains in different parts of Germany and Austria are named for Kilian. He is venerated in the dioceses of Würzburg and Vienna and elsewhere, including the country of his birth. In the city of Würzburg, July 8 is a great religious festival with an octave. For all the countryside between the Main and the Danube it is a great folk festival with more than a thousand years behind it. Formerly a three day right of asylum in the city was proclaimed by public herald.

Kilian was born about 640 in Mullagh in County Cavan. Forty years later with his brother monks, Colman and Totnan, he journeyed to the land of the Franks and in that still completely pagan land, planted a cross on a hill still called Kreusberg, the Mount of the Cross. A little later the three went to Rome where Pope Conon blessed their mission and commissioned Kilian a travelling bishop without a fixed see. They were back in Würzburg in the winter of 689.

All was going well, Christianity was taking root, converts were multiplying. One of them, Duke Gosbert, was married to his deceased brother's wife, Geilana, a union Kilian declared invalid. This ruling so infuriated Geilana she took the opportunity during an absence of Gosbert from Würzburg, to have assassins murder the three missionaries and carefully cover up all traces of them. But the Christianity they had planted survived. In 708, Gosbert's son Helon built within his castle walls a church which he dedicated to the Blessed Mother.

Some 50 years after the martyrdom the remains were recovered and transferred to what is now one of the oldest church sites in Germany. Boniface in 741 created Würzburg a bishopric in honor of Kilian. About 752, on July 8, with the permission of Pope Zachary for public veneration of the three martyrs, their relics were enshrined in the new cathedral erected on the spot of their martyrdom. The present day cathedral has a representation of the three companions on the facade. Their statues stand on the bridge that spans the river Main at Würzburg.

Before Luther's time almost every imperial city of Germany had churches and chapels dedicated to Kilian and his companions. Emperors from Charlemagne to Barbarossa visited his tomb which was from earliest times a special place of pilgrimage for his compatriots. They made Würzburg an emporium of Irish manuscripts. The greatest treasure, of course, is the ivory bound manuscript of the Gospels in Gaelic and Latin called *Kilian's Bible*, although scholars now assign it a slightly later period. In about 1880, there was discovered in a manuscript from the Irish monastery at Würzburg a copy of Muirchu's *Life of St. Patrick*, transcribed in 699. Until then the only known copy was in the *Book of Armagh*. Many Irish names occur in the Würzburg Annals. Clement, head of Charlemagne's Paris School retired to Wurzburg about 818. Marianus Scotus the Chronicler came from Fulda to be ordained near the tomb of Kilian. Macarius in 1134 founded the Irish monastery of St. James at Würzburg. One of his monks was the Irish David, chaplain to the Emperor Henry V and his historian on the imperial journey to Rome. The Jesuit, Stephen White, Irish antiquarian, was a professor at Würzburg about 1650.

Kilian remains the one named by an old tradition to intercede for the Franconians at the last judgment.

Kenney, 512; Stokes, 34; Gougaud; Tommasini; Porter, 64; Fitzpatrick; Butler-Attwater, III: 40.

Sidonius (Saens)
November 14   c. 690

It is interesting to know, as Tommasini remarks, that the surname of the French composer Camille Saint Saens originated from the 7th century Irish Sidonius, or Saens, who founded the monastery of St. Saens in the diocese of Rouen. "St. Sidonius of Irish origin" made his vows in the monastery at Jumieges, one of the important offshoots of Luxeuil whose founder, Philibert, had trained in the Columban Rule at Rebais, at Luxeuil and at Bobbio. At Irish-oriented Jumieges, although the rule combined the precepts of several of the monastic patriarchs, only to Columban did Philibert dedicate an altar in his church. Philibert's *Life* also has the item that a ship from Ireland came up the Loire carrying a load of merchandise out of which the brethren were supplied with shoes and clothing.

While he was at Jumieges, Sidonius was singled out for promotion by the archbishop of Rouen, St. Ouen, one of the three brothers Columban had blessed in their childhood, all of them afterwards distinguished in the church — ''Columban had only to bestow his blessing to win hearts forever.'' It was by the appointment of Ouen that Sidonius became the abbot-founder of the monastery near Rouen that was in after times called St. Saens.

Kenney, 495; Gougaud, 14; Tommasini, 78; Montalembert, I: 611; Benedictine Monks, 538.

Fredegand
July 17   Seventh century

The Office of Fredegand at Dorne in Belgium tells that he came from Ireland with other holy men to preach the Gospel around Antwerp; that he was with Foillan in the Low Countries. Another account connects him with Willibrord, the Anglo-Saxon who trained for 12 years in Ireland and who set out from Ireland for Europe. Monstier near Namur, St. Omer in the diocese of Arras, and especially Dorne honored Fredegand. In the 16th century during a great pestilence, the pastor of Dorne exhorted the people to ask the intercession of their holy patron and at the same time he ordered a new statue of the saint. From the moment of its erection on May 1, the plague ceased and in thanksgiving there was instituted a solemn procession with the Blessed Sacrament and the statue of Fredegand on each recurring anniversary.

Benedictine Monks, 247; Fitzpatrick, II: 73; O'Hanlon, VIII: 254.

Disibode
September 8   C. 700

Traditions of Disibode, handed down from generation to generation, describe him as austere of life, devoted to the sick and the poor, unfailing in answers to his prayer. He is said to have been a bishop in his native land and to have left Ireland accompanied by Giswold, Salust and Clement. The missionary center he founded in Germany near Bingen on a hill overlooking the Nahe was afterwards called Mount St. Disibode or Disenberg. Five centuries after his death, the German mystic Hildegarde, ''the Sibyl of the Rhine,'' who began her religious training at Disenberg wrote a life of Disibode which she attributed to her revelations. It recounted traditions already current. Another memorial from the 12th century, discovered about 1676, was an enamelled brass plaque made up of four plates. It depicted Disibode, incidents of his life and named his three original companions.

Tommasini, 80; Fitzpatrick, II: 92, 94; Gougaud, 20; O'Hanlon, IX: 196; Benedictine Monks, 176.

Corbican
June 26   Seventh century

The Irish monk Corbican flourished in the Low Countries in the 7th or 8th century, a solitary who devoted his days to instructing the peasantry in the faith. He is named by Gougaud among the Irish hermits, cenobites and missionaries who spread themselves throughout the North in Merovingian times.

Gougaud, 19; Benedictine Monks, 154; O'Hanlon, VI: 809; Fitzpatrick, I: 247.

Rupert
March 27   c. 718

Where Rupert was born cannot be said with certainty. Tradition assigns him an Irish origin. Colgan states he was Irish. The French de Barneval, writing of Irish missionary activity, says that Rupert before all others entered the valley of the Danube. Francis B. Bockwinkel, C.SS.R., whose Order once had charge of the Shrine of Our Lady of Alt-Oetting, speaks of the founder of that church as a young Irishman named Rupert and states he brought along with him from Ireland the statue of the Blessed Mother in that now world-famous shrine. Rupert built the strange little eight sided chapel about 698. Most of the original stone part and the original statue survive.

There are other not very convincing statements concerning the nationality of the saint: "it seems" he was French, not Irish. He was "presumably" a descendant of the Frankish-Merovingian royal line.

Rupert is first heard of as a bishop who had met with violent expulsion from Worms. Soon after, at the request of Theodo, Duke of Bavaria, he undertook missionary work in southern Germany, choosing as his episcopal see Juvavum, afterwards called Salzburg from the salt-mining he inaugurated there. His church and monastery, dedicated to Sanct Peter, functioned after the manner of Irish monasteries, not until later on becoming Benedictine. Irish monks were in his community and he is said to have gone to his native land (Ireland?) to recruit help for the Bavarian mission.

One of those he brought back with him was his sister or niece, Erintrude; whom he placed as first abbess over Nonnberg, the convent he founded for women on a hill high above Salzburg. She is commemorated June 30. Three hundred years after her death, her convent and church were rebuilt by the Emperor-Saint Henry in thanksgiving for a cure of epilepsy which he attributed to her intervention. Erintrude's convent is today probably the best publicized convent in the world as the setting for the opening chapter in the movie, *The Sound of Music*, the story of a novice-daughter of Nonnberg, Madame Trapp of the Trapp Family Singers.

Rupert preached the Gospel in Bavaria, Bohemia, Noricum, Styria, and when he died churches were rising everywhere. The Duchy of Salzburg cast Rupert's likeness with that of the Irish Virgilius on the coin of the realm. This coin, an old German rubentaler, is pictured under numismatics in the first *Catholic Encyclopedia*. Among the saints piously named to be called upon to present the nations they evangelized at the last judgment, Rupert of Salzburg is to speak for the Bavarians.

Kenney, 523; Gougaud, 141; Benedictine Monks, 141, 520; Butler-Attwater, I: 700, II: 677; de Barneval; *Catholic Encyclopedia; New Catholic Encyclopedia*.

Cummian (Bobbio)
August 19   C. 730

The inscription on the monument that commemorates Cummian at Bobbio asks that he be a powerful intercessor for the king, Liutprand, who erected the tomb. It further tells that Cummian, formerly a bishop in Ireland, was already well along in years when he came to Bobbio in Italy where he ended his days as abbot. Having labored there for a number of years, variously reckoned as 17 or 21, he died at the age 95, during the reign of Liutprand, King of the Lombards, 712–744.

In 1910, at the suggestion of Cardinal Logue of Armagh and with the offerings of the people of Ireland, the crypt of the basilica at Bobbio was completely renovated. Cummian's tomb was moved to a railed off part of the crypt and his relics, with those of some 20 other Bobbio saints, successors or disciples of Columban, were assembled under the new marble altar of the Bobbio church.

Kenney, 516; Tommasini, 315.

Wiro, Plechelm, Otger
May 8   C. 739

Patrick, Cuthbert and Columban were Wiro's models from earliest youth. Maelmuire (Votary of Mary) is given as the original Gaelic form of Wiro. He is said to have been born in County Clare. As for the statement that Wiro was a Scotsman, Irish writers are in complete accord: in his day the term applied exclusively to a native of Ireland. Plechelm, also, according to his Acts, was born within the confines of Scotia (Ireland). O'Hanlon says of Alcuin's supposed statement concerning Wiro's nationality, no such reference is to be found in any part of the poem cited for it. Butler's original *Lives* calls Wiro Irish and tells that a Northumbrian Pecthelm was sometimes confused with the Irish Plechelm.

Wiro and Plechelm, priests, and the (British?) deacon Otger started out as companions on a pilgrimage to Rome, continued together all the rest of their lives. Wiro and Plechelm were consecrated regionary bishops in Rome by the then Holy Father who is believed to have been St. Sergius. The two saints are on record as present at a synod called by that Pope in 697. Some time later after a period in their native land, the three returned to the Continent and settled in the Netherlands on land Pepin of Herstal gave them near Roermond. They named it St. Peter's Hill and on it they built a monastery and a church dedicated to the Blessed Mother. It was the base for long years of strenuous teaching and preaching, retirement and prayer that earned them the title, apostles of the Guelderland. It was Pepin's habit to go barefoot every Lent and occasionally at other times, to receive penance from Wiro or Plechelm. The three companions, especially Wiro, were named in old manuscript martyrologies and were otherwise honored in the Low Countires.

Kenney, 509; Butler-Attwater II: 253; Butler V: 100; O'Hanlon V: 120; Fitzpatrick II: 75.

Abel

August 5   c. 750

Tommasini and Gougaud both comment that Gaul chose more than one bishop from among the Irish strangers; that in 744, Pepin d'Heristal on the advice of Boniface summoned an Irishman named Abel from the Benedictine monastery at Lobbes, in Hainault, to the metropolitan see of Rheims, an appointment which Pope Zachary hastened to confirm. It was a post of high honor. The kings of France were crowned there.

But Boniface's troubles were not over. Charles Martel and his partisans, who had obtruded one Milo into the office, had no intention of relinquishing the rich revenues of that see. Abel was so obstructed in every way, even to dangers to his life, that he chose rather to retire from the contest than be the cause of scandal and bloodshed.

He returned to the abbey at Lobbes and to his missionary teaching and preaching. At his death his remains were accorded full honors of an Archbishop of Rheims and, to indicate the dignity of his see, emblazoned on his tomb with his archepiscopal cross was the fleur-de-lis of France. He is regarded as the patron of Liege and Hainault.

Kenney, 522; Gougaud, 22; Tommasini, 81; Benedictine Monks, 2; Fitzpatrick, II: 76; O'Hanlon, Aug. 5.

Eoban and Adalar
June 5   755

Two companions closely associated with Boniface in Germany were Eoban, the Irish priest monk he consecrated and named assistant bishop of Utrecht, and Adalar, said also to have been Irish. They were with Boniface on his way down the Rhine to Friesland and died beside him at Dokkum.

O'Hanlon, VI: 195, 197; Benedictine Monks, 6, 202.

Albuin (Wittan)
October 26   c. 760

Albuin, apostle of Thuringia and fellow laborer with Boniface in Germany, was an Irish monk from the monastery of Iona in Scotland. In 741, Boniface consecrated him bishop of Fritzlar in Hesse. Among several lesser commemorations, October 26 is the principal feast of the saint. He is also known by the German name of Wittan.

O'Hanlon, VIII: 380; Benedictine Monks, 25; Fitzpatrick, II: 92.

Martinus and Declan
December 1   Eighth century

The names of Martinus and Declan have come down as important contributors to the spread of the faith in German lands, workers in the continuing extended scale of Irish activity that played no small part in making possible the formal organization undertaken by Boniface.

O'Hanlon II, under Alto, Feb. 9; Fitzpatrick, II: 83.

Marianus and Anianus
November 24   Eighth century

As heralds of the faith in the region of Rot on the river Inn in southeastern Bavaria, Marianus and Anianus were yet another team of Irish missionary monks to be named apostles in German lands. They came there together on the return from a pilgrimage to Rome and at the end, departed this life almost together again. Marianus was martyred on the day of Anianus' death. Their remains afterwards were removed to the monastery of Rot to rest within its walls and to be accorded special honors there.

Kenney, 511; Fitzpatrick, II: 83, 91; O'Hanlon, IX: 103.

Alto
February 9 c. 760

The saint's Irish name is unknown. Alto, his Acts tell, signifies that he was born of an ancient family. He was a hermit missionary in a wood near Augsburg when King Pepin heard about him and made him the grant of land on which he founded the monastery afterwards called Altomunster in Bavaria. At the dedication in 750, Boniface would have prohibited women from both the church and the cloister, according to the Celtic rule. Alto however thought and wished otherwise and they were interdicted only from the monks' enclosure.

There is still in existence an ancient charter bearing the subscription "Alto reclausis" which is believed to go back to the saint's hermit days. After his time his foundation fell into ruins periodically but restoration always followed. Tradition holds Alto appeared himself in apparition to the Duke of Bavaria to ask the restoration in the year 1000. Since 1487, Altomunster has been a convent for Brigittine nuns.

Kenney, 514; Gougaud, 21; Tommasini, 80; Butler-Attwater, I: 290. Fitzpatrick, II: 83, 91.

Tuban
? c. 760

About the time Boniface arrived in Germany the Irish Bishop Tuban was founding near Strasbourg the island monastery of Honau, one of five principal Irish island monasteries in the Rhine river. Fourteen extant charters trace the former importance of the now completely submerged Honau which expanded into large possessions with eight dependent churches all governed by Irish clergy. The site and original endowments of the first 30 years of the monastery as set forth by six charters, came from Adalbert, Duke of Alsace and members of his family. Pepin, King of the Franks, in 755, confirmed Tuban in all of his possessions. Carloman, son of Pepin, in 770 exempted Honau from judicial interference.

Charlemagne, in 783, confirmed the exemptions of Carloman. His charter of 810 is signed by the abbot, seven bishops and one presybter, all Irish names. For over a period of 40 years, he concerned himself with the welfare of the Irish Honau. He confirmed all grants, past or present, documented or not. He exempted the monastery from tolls and imposts. He ordered all monastery possessions unlawfully seized to be restored at once "for the damage is done to the king when those under his protection are hurt." He declared the affairs of these Irish religious were of particular interest to him "for the kings of France had welcomed all of these Irish religious." He ordered that no one should come into possession of their churches but people of their own race. One of Charlemagne's last acts was, by the sixth canon of the Council of Tours in 813, to enjoin bishops to receive Irish strangers at their tables. Gougaud writes the twofold design of Charlemagne and his successors seems to have been to protect the Irish missionaries and to attract men of learning.

Kenney, 528; Fitzpatrick, II: 76, 93, 118, 281, 312; Gougaud, 21, 28; Tommasini, 80.

Rumold
June 24, July 3   c. 775

The Cathedral of Malines in Belgium is named for the apostle of all that region, Rumold, who for centuries has been accounted an Irish saint. Unfortunately, the life of the saint, written by Thierry of St. Trond in 1100, is so given to legends and the fabulous it is of little value. Added to that, the idea among scholars today seems to be if a missionary answered to the high repute of Irish missionaries, the people as a matter of course assumed him to have been Irish and paid him the compliment of an Irish birth. Rumold's Irish origin is assessed "a tribute to Ireland's reputation as an island of saints."

The *Martyrology of Mechlin* named Rumold a Scot from "that part of Scotia that is now called Ireland." Tommasini says of the Irish missionaries ". . . the 7th century found them scattered over modern Belgium. Rumold, or Rombaut, preached the Gospel in Malines." Gougaud tells that the Irish are to be found disseminated throughout Belgium; that from generation to generation the country people have mysteriously handed down the names of these strangers; that Rombault evangelized the people of Mechlin.

Rumold had gathered most of the country around Malines to the faith when he was slain on one of his missionary journeys. His body, said to have been miraculously recovered, is still preserved in a golden shrine behind golden doors above the high altar in the magnificent St. Rumold's Cathedral. Malines celebrates his feast June 24 with solemn pageantry, miracle plays based on his life, music from the world famous bells of St. Rumold. Ireland observes his festival July 3.

Kenney, 527; Gougaud, 20, 71, 147; Tommasini, 80; O'Hanlon, VII: 2; Butler-Attwater, III: 13.

Virgilius (Fearghal)
November 27   c. 784

The apostle of the Carinthians was Virgilius, "one of the glories of the Church of the 8th century." For 40 years, in association with many other Irish missionaries, he labored for the faith in Bavaria and Carinthia, converting Teutons and Slavs, founding monasteries, churches, and schools. During his time, in 774, the Council of Bavaria issued its first pronouncement on the establishment of schools.

The saint, known as Fearghal in Ireland, came to the Continent "pro amore Christi." With him came Dobdagrec and Sidonius, later abbot of a monastery at Chiemsee in Upper Austria, and bishop of Passau, respectively.

In Gaul the Irish monk's learning and ability attracted the favor of Pepin, the father of Charlemagne, and he was kept at the French Court for two years. About 743, Pepin sent him with letters of highest recommendation to Duke Otillo of Bavaria who from the first gave him his esteem and support. Within a year or two, Otillo placed him in charge of the diocese of Salzburg. With Dobdagrec to perform episcopal functions, Virgilius administered the diocese as priest-abbot of the monastery of St. Peter which Rupert the first bishop had founded at Salzburg. The epitaph on his tomb told he ruled for 40 years.

Of interest is the opposition from Boniface on more than one occasion. There was the question of the validity of baptism in a case in which a priest through carelessness or ignorance had used incorrect Latin wording. Virgilius and Sidonius held the error to be an accident of language, not of religious significance and that baptism so administered need not be repeated. Boniface, as Archbishop of Mainz, disagreed with the Irish theologians and carried the dispute to Pope Zachary who confirmed the view of Virgilius. He expressed surprise that Boniface should question it. Healy comments "this clear and emphatic expression of Catholic doctrine, as every theological student knows, we owe to Virgil and Sidonius."

Some time later on, Boniface again denounced Virgilius to the Holy See. Virgilius, "who was not one to call a comet the soul of a bishop going to heaven," had written a treatise on his cosmological theories which, far in advance of the learning of his time, moved Boniface to invoke ecclesiastical censure upon him. Although Pope Zachary in 748 directed Boniface to convene a council to investigate the strange, perhaps heretical, views of Virgilius, nothing more is ever heard of the matter. Virgilius was afterward consecrated bishop of Salzburg.

Virgilius enjoyed the high regard and support of three influential patrons, King Pepin, Duke Otillo of Bavaria, and Chetimar, Duke of Carinthia. He baptized two successive Slav Dukes of Carinthia at Salzburg and at the request of Duke Chetimar, sent missionaries for his territories, four religious under the Irish Modestus, following them up with other helpers. His mission penetrated far into the forest wilds of Carinthia, extending to the borders of Hungary where the Drava flows into the Danube, work he often shared with his monks throughout his vast diocese, doing much personally to confirm it to the faith. A Carinthian coin, an old Salzburg rubenthaler with the likenesses and the names of Virgilius and Rupert, was issued in the time of Chetimar.

Virgilius died on November 27, about 781, and was bured in the monastery of St. Peter at Salzburg. His formal canonization by Pope Gregory IX took place in 1233.

Kenney, 523; Gougaud, 21; Healy, 566; Fitzpatrick, II: 100; Butler-Attwater, IV: 436.

Patto and Irish Bishops of Verden

c. 788

The first ten bishops of the see of Verden in northern Germany are said to have been Irish. About the year 780, Charlemagne, in introducing the faith into Saxony, founded there two new bishoprics. Verden was one of them and in connection with it the Emperor established a monastery "for the Irish" at Anabaric. O'Hanlon has a partial list of the Irish bishops of Verden, men who came usually from the abbacy of Anabaric, but sometimes were outstanding missionaries from other parts of the empire, beginning with Suibert, Irish trained perhaps, but probably not of Irish nationality.

Second in line was the Irish Patto (March 30), abbot at Anabaric, who became bishop of Verden. He was succeeded by compatriots Tanco (February 16) who died in 808 and Erlulf (February 10) who died in 830, both of whom were martyred by pagan mobs. The list of Irish bishops continues: Cerelon, Kortyla (March 28), Isenger (March 21), Nortrila, Harruch (July 15). In all ten or twelve Irish bishops served at Verden.

In the year 1630, during repairs to the old cathedral at Verden, the remains of Suibert, Tanco, Patto, Cerelon, Nortrila, Erlulf and Harruch and a debris of mitres, sandals and other episcopal ornaments were found in the same tomb under the cathedral floor. The bishop had these relics collected into a new casket which, with his own seal of Francis William attached, was placed at the back of the high altar. Afterwards, in the time of the Swedish incursions into that part of the country, the same bishop took these relics with him when he fled in 1659 to the episcopal palace in Ratisbon.

Kenney, 785; Butler-Attwater, I: 342; Fitzpatrick, II: 94, 118; Benedictine Monks, 205, 282, 460, 557; O'Hanlon, II: 250, 569; III: 921, 991, 1015; IV: 573; VII: 245.

Beatus
May 9   Ninth Century

The modern name Scot, which anciently referred only to a native of Scotia (i.e., Ireland), has caused unfortunate complications in the history of the Irish saints. On the Continent, Scots (i.e., Irish) have been considered synonymous with Scots or English. Tommasini remarks that Irish annals and other historical documents are indexed under the rubric Angleterre in the Royal Library at Brussels and Mrs. Green tells us ''In Switzerland [the Irish traveller] will be told at St. Beatenberg by the guide-books that St. Beatus was British and by local tradition that he was Scotch. At the shrine of St. Pellegrinus in the Appenines he will hear praises of a 'Scotch' king's son. At Rome he will learn that England was 'the isle of the Saints.' ''

Beatus, venerated as one of the apostles of Switzerland, had a hermitage at the place now called Beatenberg near the lake of Thun.

The signature of perhaps that same Beatus as fourth abbot of the Irish monastery of Honau (with that of seven bishops and one presbyter, all Irish names) attests a confirmation grant from Charlemagne in the year 810 to Honau, the Monasterium Scottorum on an island in the Rhine, which at that time included widespread tributary churches.

Tommasini, 14; Benedictine Monks, 94; Fitzpatrick, II: 312–313; Green 47.

Clement
March 20   c. 826

A monk of St. Gall, Switzerland, believed to have been Notker Balbulus, tells that when Charlemagne began to reign alone in the West and when literature was everywhere almost forgotten, two Scots from Ireland, men incomparably skilled in human learning and Holy Scripture, announced in the market place they had learning for sale. In return they asked only food and shelter and pupils. They were Clement and Albinus.

On hearing of these venders of knowledge, Charlemagne sent for them and had them for some time at his Court. About 774, he established Clement in his Paris School and sent Albinus to Pavia to conduct the monastery of St. Augustine. Head of the Palace School at this time was England's scholar, Alcuin, pupil of an Irishman at York. In 796, on Alcuin's retirement to Tours, Clement succeeded him in the Palace School. One of Clement's pupils there was the future Emperor Lothair, noted afterwards for his great interest in the schools of Italy. Abbot Ratgar of Fulda sent Bruno, Modestus and Candidus to Clement.

Clement was one of many Irish teachers on the Continent at that time: Josephus, companion of Alcuin, the poet-astronomer Dungal, the grammarian Cruindmelus, to name some of those who enjoyed the favor of Charlemagne. Tommasini remarks that Continental contemporaries themselves considered the learning of the sons of Erin to be superior and realized that the progress made in spiritual and intellectual life was largely their achievement. To the known names, he tells us, there were a host of obscure monks who taught the elements and grammar; expounded the Holy Scripture; brought over from Ireland and copied on the Continent, biblical and liturgical manuscripts, cannons and penitentials. Alcuin's writings recalled the services rendered to Christendom by "the very learned Irish masters who enabled the Church of Christ in Britain, Gaul and Italy to make such progress." In 803, from his retirement in Tours, Alcuin commented, this time querulously, in a letter to Charlemagne, on the increasing influence of the Irish at the Palace School. According to Einhard, Charlemagne "had the Irish in special esteem" and he "loved the strangers."

Charlemagne's successors likewise invited the Irish teachers to their Court. Louis the Pious was the patron of the Irish geographer Dicuil; Lothair, of Dungal and of the Irish poet and scribe, Sedulius. Charles the Bald equalled his grandfather in his affectionate esteem for the Irish schoolmen. Under him, Elias taught at Laon, Dunchad at Rheims, Israel at Auxerre, and the greatest of all the Irish scholars, John Scotus Eriugena, was head of the Palace School. Irish schoolmen flocked to the places already known to them, to Reichenau, to St. Gall, to Bobbio, "a whole herd of philosophers" as one writer expresses it. The 9th century German scholar, Ermenrich, writing to Grimwald of St. Gall, extols the island "whence such brilliant luminaries have come to us . . .

for, teaching philosophy to little and great alike, they have filled the Church with their learning and doctrine.''

Kenney; Gougaud; Tommasini; Fitzpatrick; O'Hanlon, III: 905.

Donatus (Donagh)
October 22   876

The saint known as Donatus was the Irish Donagh who came to Fiesole in Italy on the return from a pilgrimage to Rome. He was bishop there for 47 years. With his compatriot Andrew as his archdeacon, Donatus served from 829 to 876, a long time in an episcopal office as difficult as it was insecure. Six years earlier the feudal barons had disposed of a predecessor by drowning.

As a man of letters, Donatus was particularly welcome to Lothair who had been the pupil of the Irish Clement. Lothair, now King of Italy, had in 825 set about establishing schools in his kingdom. Dungal of Ireland headed his school at Pavia. It is thought Donatus had charge of the Tuscany school at Florence. Several of Donatus's own literary works survive, including a manuscript in his own handwriting preserved by the Dominicans in Rome. Donatus wrote two lives of Brigid, one prose, one in verse, and also the preface for another life of the saint of Kildare, the one written by the Irish Coelan which Colgan found at Monte Casino.

History has five references to Donatus. In 840, as was expected of Italian churchmen, he led his own contingent of vassals in a military expedition for Lothair. In 844, he was present at the coronation of Louis, King of the Lombards, by Pope Sergius II. He sat in at this time on the dispute of the the bishops of Arezzo and Siena. In 862, he was a member of the Council of Rome convened by Nicholas I against John, Archbishop of Ravenna. In 866 he fought with Louis II against the Saracens. In 876 Charles the Bald confirmed all existing immunities, making Donatus independent of royal officials with the right to impose his own taxes and to hold his own court.

Fiesole was much frequented by Irish pilgrims on the way to Rome and Donatus fared well of their generosity. Between the years 829 and 850 he built at his own expense the historic St. Brigid's Church at Piacenza which has been a national monument since 1911. Donatus gave St. Brigid's to Bobbio in 850, in a document of transfer that stresses his devotion to Brigid and his affection for the community of Bobbio. It specifies in particular the hospitality he wished to insure at Bobbio for Irish pilgrims.

Donatus died in the year 876. The epitaph he had written for himself was cut on his now disappeared tomb on the heights of Fiesole. It told he was a

Gael, that for many years he served the kings of Italy, the great Lothair, the good Louis, taught grammar, meter, the lives of the Saints. Of the reader he asked not regrets, but prayers for his eternal happiness. In 1817, the relics of Donatus were transferred to the new cathedral of Fiesole to join the company of its other great bishops. The altar dedicated to Donatus is in the last chapel on the right behind the high altar.

Kenney, 602; Gougaud, 82; Tommasini, 383; Benedictine Monks, 183; Fitzpatrick, II: 317.

Fintan (Rheinau)
November 15   878

Irish calendars commemorate 55 Fintans. Leinster-born Fintan of Rheinau had been carried off by the Viking sea pirates. Confiding himself to the will of God and vowing a pilgrimage to Rome if he got away, he plunged into the sea in the Orkneys. He succeeded in making a landing in the north of Scotland where a kindly bishop took him in. Two years later, on foot, he accomplished his pilgrimage to Rome. Not long after he settled on the island of Rheinau in the Rhine river near Schaffhausen in the Black Forest.

There were Irish hermits there before Fintan but he is called the founder of Rheinau. He drew up the rule, peculiar to that community, whereby the brethren lived after the manner of religious in their native land. Fintan spent 27 years there, 22 of them in the utmost austerity as a solitary. He was given to visions and to hearing the voices of angels and of demons speak to him in his native tongue. Their words, as recorded by a 10th century biographer, are among the oldest specimens of Gaelic that have survived. Fintan's *Calendar* and his *Missal* are preserved respectively in the University Library at Zurich and in the St. Gall Library. The *Calendar*, which came from Nivelles, has numerous devotions to Irish Saints, especially to Brigid and to Brendan the Navigator. Fintan's relics were enshrined at Rheinau in 1446, and his feast is still observed there.

Kenney, 603; Daniel-Rops, 54; Gougaud, 88, 105, 110; Tommasini, 87; Butler-Attwater, IV: 350.

Maimbod
January 23   880

The Irish missionary monk, Maimbod, a pilgrim to the tombs of many saints, had labored to spread the faith in northern Italy and Gaul. He had met with cordial welcome in the home of a Burgundian noble, had been urged in vain to settle there. At his departure, the noble, convinced of the holiness of his visitor, pressed on him a pair of gloves as a reminder to pray for him. Eight miles from Besancon, Maimbod stopped to pray at the church of Domnipetra and only a little further on he met his death at the hands of robbers who thought anyone wearing gloves would have money.

He was buried at the church in which he had so lately prayed. When miracles began to occur at his tomb, Count Aszo of Montbeliard requested Bishop Berengarius of Besancon for the removal of the remains to Montbeliard. Berengarius granted the request, but because he had lost his eyesight, he delegated to his coadjutor, Bishop Stephen, the ceremony of the Translation. During the solemnities, the blind Berengarius was miraculously cured. His own cure and many other wonders prompted Berengarius to institute a festival in honor of Maimbod on January 23, the day of his death.

Maimbod's relics were destroyed in the 16th century, but observance of his feast day continued. His name is inscribed in the diptych of the Besancon church.

Fitzpatrick, II: 279; Benedictine Monks, 387; Butler-Attwater, I: 157; O'Hanlon, I: 403; O'Kelly, 74.

Eusebius
January 30   884

Whatever his Irish name, Eusebius is called "Scotigena" by Ratpert of St. Gall in Switzerland. Another St. Gall chronicler, Ekkehard, says he was a compatriot of the Irish Gall. Soon after his arrival at St. Gall about the middle of the 9th century, Eusebius retired to a life of solitude and prayer on nearby Mount St. Victor. He spent 30 years there, an edification to all who knew him, especially King Charles, son and successor of King Louis. In 883 Charles erected in Raetia for the Irish anchorite a "Monastorum Scottorum" on Mount St. Victor and two years later with the many Irish pilgrims in mind, the same prince made over to the same monastery, by royal charter, the revenues of one of his villas near Rottris in the Vorarlberg for a hospice which could accomodate 12 pilgrims on their way to Rome. Eusebius was slain by some of the peasantry he had admonished. In Ratpert's time the saint's feast day was celebrated at St. Gall.

Gougaud, 11, 82, 90; Tommasini, 76, 120, 126; O'Hanlon, Jan. 30; Butler-Attwater, I: 215.

Moengal (Marcellus)
September 27   c. 887

Moengal was one of a party of affluent Irish travellers returning from Rome who arrived at the Abbey of St. Gall in Switzerland during the abbacy of Grimwoald. Besides Moengal to stay on in St. Gall there was his uncle, Bishop Marcus, a man exceedingly learned in polite as well as sacred knowledge and versed in the seven liberal arts, especially music. He gave his horses and pack mules to the companions returning to Ireland. His books, his gold and his vestments he kept for himself and for St. Gall. Francoise Henry, eminent authority on early Irish art, suggests that the 8th century Irish *Book of Gospels* now in the St. Gall Cathedral Library (St. Gall Ms. 51) may have been one of the books the bishop gave to St. Gall.

Moengal, young and of brilliant talents, was given charge of the cloister schools. Among the boys he trained in the monastic life were the celebrated trio, Notker, Ratpert and Tutilo (the last, it is speculated, might have been Tuathal from Ireland). Under Moengal the music school of St. Gall became "the wonder and delight of Europe." Its scribes supplied all Germany with manuscript books of Gregorian chant, the copies very often priceless works of illumination art.

In the 11th century, the historian Ekkehard wrote "It is delightful to recall how St. Gall began to increase and flourish under the auspices of Moengal and his colleagues." Another German, H. Zimmer, writing in 1887 on the Irish element in medieval culture, said "In my opinion, there were very few men who in the middle of the 9th century exerted such a beneficent influence upon the German mind in the cultivation of the higher arts and sciences as Moengal and his followers." The Necrology of St. Gall has the entry for about the year 887: "Departure of Moengal, called also Marcellus, the most learned and excellent man."

Benedictine Monks, 392; Fitzpatrick, II: 290–95; Gougaud, 11; Tommasini, 76; Henry, II: 32.

Tutilo
March 28   C. 915

Tutilo is believed to have been Tuathal, a younger member of the party of the Irish Bishop Marcus and his nephew Moengal who came to St. Gall Abbey in Switzerland in the 9th century on the return from Rome. With Notker and Ratpert he was one of the famous trio trained up by Moengal when the music school of St. Gall was "the wonder and delight" of all Europe. Handsome, eloquent, quick witted, Tutilo was a universal genius, musician, poet, painter, sculptor, builder, goldsmith, head of the cloister school, teacher and composer of music for the harp and all of the stringed instruments. Charles the Fat thought it a great pity such a genius should be shut up in a monastery.

Paintings attributed to Tutilo, usually signed with an epigram or a motto, are still to be found in Constance, Metz, St. Gall and Mainz. He died at St. Gall, about the year 915. Afterwards the chapel of St. Catherine in which he was buried was renamed St. Tutilo for him.

Fitzpatrick, II: 296; Butler-Attwater, I: 696; Benedictine Monks, 583.

Columban (Ghent)
February 2   959

From his title of Abbot, it is thought this 10th century Columban had been either the leader of a missionary band coming out of Ireland or head of a community attacked by the Danes. On February 2, 957, he became a recluse in a cell in the cemetery near St. Bavo's church in Ghent in Belgium where he lived out his remaining days in prayer and in the most austere penances. February 2 is celebrated as his feast day rather than February 15, the day of his death in 959. He was buried in St. Bavo's cathedral. His name was included among the other patrons of Belgium in a Litany to be recited in time of public necessity or calamity.

Benedictine Monks, 149; Tommasini, 292; O'Hanlon, II: 247.

Maolcalain (Malcallan)
January 21   c. 978

In the 10th century, when Irish monasteries and hospices were multiplying throughout the Teutonic dominions under the fosterage of the emperors, when German monarchs studded their dominions with Irish foundations, Malcallan's company of missionary monks came out of Ireland to the shrine of Fursey at "Peronne of the Irish." They were made a grant of land in Thierache which received the name St. Michael's from the chapel they built there, dedicated to the archangel. Soon after, a second monastery was founded at Waulsort for Malcallan and his monks over which he placed Cadroe. Malcallan died in very old age at St. Michael's, regarded by all as a saint. In after times he was held in great popular devotion.

Benedictine Monks, 383; Fitzpatrick, II: 277; O'Hanlon, I: 387.

Cadroe (Cadroel)
March 5   c. 975

Armagh-trained Cadroe was the son of a Scottish (Irish) prince in Scotland. He came to St. Michael's in Thierache in the missionary band led by

Malcallan. When a second monastery was founded for Malcallan at Waulsort, he placed Cadroe at the head of it. A charter of Otho I, King of Germany, September 19, 946, made Waulsort the property of the Scotti (Irish) and specified an Irish monk was to be abbot in perpetuity as long as one remained in the community. Cadroe's government of Waulsort won him so high a reputation as a monastic organizer Bishop Adalbero I, in 953, called him to Metz to restore the decadent St. Clement's abbey. He raised it to a level never before known even in the days of its greatest glory. Afterwards an altar was built in his memory in the abbey church in which he was buried. A charter of Emperor Otto III in the year 991, refers to "Cadroel of blessed memory."

Fitzpatrick, II: 277; Gougaud, 83; Butler-Attwater, I: 502; O'Hanlon, III: 181.

Forannan
April 30   c. 982

Forannan was an Irish bishop who left his native land in obedience to a dream that led him to the abbey of Waulsort on the Meuse. He was elected superior the year of his arrival. Otto I of Germany had chartered Waulsort Irish property, over which an Irish monk was to rule in perpetuity as long as one remained in the community. It flourished and increased under Forannan with such an influx of postulants that he negotiated the annexation of the neighboring abbey of Hastiers. For his church he obtained from the Christian princes the "Truce of God," sanctuary and immunity from law to all bona fide pilgrims to Waulsort on the festival and during the octave.

Gougaud, 83; O'Hanlon, IV: 557; Butler-Attwater, II: 200; Benedictine Monks, 239.

Minborinus
July 18   986

Cologne in Germany had an important Irish colony dating from about 974. Because of Danish onslaughts at home, a migration of Celtic monks under Minborinus, in search of a place to settle, came to St. Martin's Abbey at Cologne, which is thought to have been Irish in its origin. Archbishop Eberger not only installed them in St. Martin's, he named Minborinus abbot and he gave the abbey over to them "in sempiternum." Great Irish activity flowed out of St. Martin's, as may be known to some extent from the dedications to Brigid. The Cologne parish church of St. Brigid, now destroyed, went back to that period. Four other churches, and seven chapels in the diocese of Cologne, were dedicated to the saint of Kildare.

Minborinus served for 12 years. In 986, he was succeeded by the Irish Kilian. During the abbacy of Blessed Elias, sometime after 1020, St. Panteleon's Monastery was given into the charge of the Irish at St. Martin's. Marianus Scotus, the Chronicler, was a monk in the community there for two years. His Chronicle names the abbots of St. Martin's from 974 to 1061, all of them Irish. Cardinal Moran of Australia came to Cologne in 1884 to obtain a relic of Brigid for his Brigidine nuns in Sydney. In the middle ages, when disaster was everywhere in Ireland, St. Martin's and its possessions were appropriated by the Scottish Benedictines of Scotland on the claim it was founded by Scots from Scotia. It was. But the names formerly applied solely to the Irish and Ireland.

Benedictine Monks, 427; Gougaud, 85, 107; Fitzpatrick, II: 279.

Fingen
February 5   c. 1005

The "Histoire Literaire de la France" tells that Fingen was a very celebrated Irish abbot who left Ireland to go the kingdom of Lothaire. Mabillon calls him a very religious man whom he considered to be a very great saint. The records of Metz list Fingen, a Scottus by race, derived by birth from Hibernia, celebrated in connection with that city. Kenney speaks of him as Fingen the Irishman, who became a reformer and restorer of monasteries in Metz.

The bishop of Metz was Adalbero II "who showed himself no less anxious than his predecessors to confide the religious establishments of his diocese to the Irish monks." About 991, he put Fingen, then abbot of St. Clements, in charge of the restoration of the old abbey of St. Symphorian, which was soon an exclusively Irish-staffed religious center. The Empress Dowager Adelaide obtained two charters, one from Pope John XVII and one from Otto III, signed at Frankfort in 992, that specified that Fingen, as first abbot, was to be succeeded only by Irish abbots who should not have any other than Irish monks as long as these could be found. Only in case they could not were monks of other nations to be admitted.

Fingen's final assignment was the rehabilitation of St. Vannes at Verdun. He took with him seven of his Irish colleagues. By 1001 it was flourishing and attracting applicants of high worldly rank, among them Frederich, Count of Verdun; and Richard, dean of the diocese of Rheims, who later succeeded to the abbacy at St. Vannes. The Necrology of St. Clement's at Metz at October 8 has an entry of praise of Fingen, abbot, buried in its church.

Kenney, 612; Gougaud, 84; Fitzpatrick, II: 278; Tommasini, 86; O'Hanlon, Feb. 5.

Colman (Austria)
October 13   1012

Four popes have granted indulgences to prayer at the shrine of Colman at Melk on the Danube: Paschal II in the 12th century, Clement VI and Innocent VI in the 14th, Leo X in the 16th century. In 1713, Melk publicly burned a wax candle weighing 70 pounds in petition to the saint for protection against the plague then devastating the land.

About 1012 Colman, who had left Ireland on pilgrimage to the Holy Land, was seized as a spy at Stockerau in Austria which was then at war with Bohemia and Moravia. Unable to speak the language or to explain about himself, he was subjected to tortures and finally, together with some robbers, was hanged in the public execution place. Wolves, dogs, birds of prey tore at the other bodies. For a year and a half Colman's remains swayed there, incorrupt and unmolested by bird or beast, on scaffolding which was said to have taken root and to have sent forth branches. One of those branches was preserved as a relic under the high altar of the Franciscan church at Stockerau.

The saint sleeps in the Abbey of Melk in a tomb erected for him by the emperor, Saint Henry. Besides Melk, which is one of the most frequented places of pilgrimage in Austria, other chapels that honor Colman are very numerous in the Palatinate, in Suabia, in Bavaria, in Austria and in Hungary. On the feast day, October 13, there is a great blessing of horses and cattle, while up until the 18th century, a chapel near Würtemberg was a place of pilgrimage from a dozen neighboring parishes on Whit Sunday. It was nothing unusual to count from 400 to 500 horses there for the traditional blessing. Colman has been invoked for husbands by marriageable girls, for every good, in every difficulty.

Gougaud, 90, 143; Kenney, 613; Tommasini, 88; Fitzpatrick, II: 365; Butler-Attwater, IV: 105.

Ailill (Elias, Helias)
April 12   1042

Ailill from County Monaghan became Elias in Germany. He was a distinguished musician. It is recorded of him he was the first to introduce Roman chant in Cologne. He came there about 1020, and was elected abbot of the community of St. Martin which Archbishop Eberger had assigned to the Irish in perpetuity. During the abbacy of Elias a second Cologne monastery, St. Panteleon, was given into the charge of the Irish religious.

Cathal O'Byrne; Gougaud, 86; Benedictine Monks, 195; Tommasini, 87; Fitzpatrick, II: 279.

Anatolius

February 3   11th century

Anatolius, whose Irish name is unknown, came into Burgundy about 1029 on the return from a pilgrimage to Rome. Near Salins in the diocese of Besancon, he came upon the oratory dedicated to St. Symphorian and there he lived out the rest of his life in a mountainside retreat overlooking a valley called Pagus Scotengorum, so named because it was a favorite stopover for Irish pilgrims. At Salins afterwards a church was built in honor of the saint. On account of their great number, an ancient writer of his Acts states, it would be impossible to treat of all the miracles of Anatolius.

Kenney, 614; Benedictine Monks, 46; O'Hanlon, II: 263.

Anmchadh

January 30   1043

One time when visitors came to Iniscaltra on the Shannon, the abbot Corcoran delegated Anmchadh to act as host. After the meal some of the guests, lingering sociably around the fire, asked for further refreshment, to which Anmchadh acceded, contrary to the rule. For this fault Corcoran banished him from Ireland. Anmchadh wandered about Europe until he came to the monastery of Fulda in Germany where he became a recluse. He lived out his life so, a contemplative shut up in a cell walled off from the world. Sixteen years afterwards, Anmchadh's more celebrated countryman, Marianus Scotus the Chronicler, became a religious at Fulda. His writings tell that for ten years daily he celebrated Mass over the tomb of Anmchadh and that around it supernatural light and heavenly psalmody were frequently seen and heard.

Kenney, 615; Benedictine Monks, 41; Gougaud, 89; Tommasini, 87; O'Hanlon, I: Jan. 30.

Paternus

April 10   1058

Two contemporaries, Peter Damien and Marianus Scotus, supply such facts as are known about Paternus, the Irish recluse in St. Meinwerk's monastery of Abdinghof in Paderborn in Lower Saxony. With the abbot's permission, he was enclosed in a cell adjoining the abbey in which he vowed to remain as long as he lived. All to no avail he deplored the evil rampant in Paderborn. The people only jeered when he foretold that as a consequence, fire would destroy the city within 30 days. On Friday before Palm Sunday in 1058, fires that broke out at the same time in seven parts of the city destroyed it. All of the brethren escaped harm except Paternus who, refusing to break his vow of enclosure, perished in his cell. Miraculously, a mat he had used was intact and afterwards was an object of veneration by the very people who had scoffed at his warnings. Marianus Scotus visited the ruins two weeks after the fire and knelt to pray on the mat upon which Paternus had died.

Gougaud, 89; Carty, 72; Butler-Attwater, II: 64; Benedictine Monks, 459.

John (Bishop of Ratzeburg)
November 10   c. 1066

An Irish bishop called John came to the Continent with Marianus Scotus about the middle of the 11th century. Five years after reaching Germany he was appointed bishop of Mechlinberg at Ratzeburg. At the request of Prince Gothescale in the time of Archbishop Adalbert of Bremen he worked among the Slavonians, baptizing thousands in the last outposts of German barbarism in the coastal regions between the Elbe and the Vistula. He was beheaded at Rethre in 1066.

Kenney, 614; Gougaud, 147; Benedictine Monks, 339; O'Hanlon, II: 688; Fitzpatrick, II: 26; Conyngham, 467.

Marianus Scotus (Chronicler)
December 22   1028–1082

The saint's Irish name was Maelbrigte, Votary of Brigid. He is believed to have been educated at Moville whose abbot in his time was Tighernach Boirceach: he tells in his *Chronicle* that once in reprimanding him for a slight fault, Tighernach reminded him that the abbot of Iniscaltra had exiled from Ireland a holy man (Anmchadh) all because he gave a little food to the brethren without permission. In 1056, Marianus came to the Irish monastery of St. Martin of Cologne. Two years later he entered Fulda where Anmchadh had died in 1043. Accompanied by Abbot Sigfried Marianus went to Würzburg to be ordained near the tomb of the Irish Kilian.

In his *Chronicle* Marianus states that Fulda was originally established by Irishmen, among whom he includes Boniface as of Irish descent. In our own day, Arthur Kingsley Porter catalogues as pure Irish the manuscript claimed to be the Bible which actually belonged to Boniface and he comments that an Irish book should have been venerated in the Abbey founded by Boniface himself.

Marianus's habitation at Fulda was a little cell, twelve by twelve, his schedule a life of prayer, penance, study and writing, walled off from the world but with access to his books. Every day for ten years he offered the Holy Sacrifice of the Mass over the tomb of his countryman, Anmchadh from Iniscaltra.

In 1069, upon being named Archbishop, Abbot Sigfried obtained the transfer of Marianus to Mainz with him. It was there the saint wrote his *Chronicle of the World*, an immense chronology in three books, the story of man from creation up to the year of Marianus's death, 1082. Many editions of his *Chronicle* have been published, many historians have made use of it. Book III has been published in Waits's *Historical Monuments* of Germany and in Migne's *Patrology*. The Vatican has one of the two extant 11th century manuscripts of the *Chronicle* (Vatican 380).

Healy, 256; Tommasini, 87; Porter, 65; Fitzpatrick, II: 379; Kenney, 614.

Marianus Scotus (Abbot)
February 9   1088

Professor Toynbee, in his monumental work *The Study of History* writes "The period of Irish cultural superiority over the continent and over Britain may be conveniently dated from the foundation of the monastic university of Clonmacnoise in Ireland in A.D. 548 to the foundation of the Irish Monastery of St. James at Ratisbon, circa A.D. 1090. Throughout those five and a half centuries, it was the Irish who imparted culture and the English and continentals who received it."

The founder of the Irish monastery at Ratisbon was Marianus Scotus, Abbot, as distinguished from his contemporary compatriot in Germany, Marianus Scotus, incluse and historian (the story of man from creation to 1082).

The Irish name of Marianus Scotus, abbot and originator of a congregation of monasteries long famous in southern Germany was Muiredach MacRobartaigh (MacGroarty). He came of a prominent Donegal family, hereditary keepers of Columcille's Book, the *Cathach*, or Battle Book, of the O'Donnells, at Bally-Macgroarty. The MacRobartaigh name figured prominently in the *Annals of Kells* of which Marianus was an alumnus. In his time lived his kinsman, Domnal MacRobartaigh, whose name is engraved on the 11th century silver case that encloses the *Cathach*.

About 1067, accompanied by John and Candidus, Marianus, in a party that included Clemens, Donatus, Magnoaldus, Ishac and Mauris, set out "for the thresholds of the Apostles Peter and Paul, after the custom of his nation." Marianus, John and Candidus, making a stopover at Bamberg in Germany, spent a year there at the foot of the mountain in small cells, in faithful observance of the austere rule of Irish "pilgrims for the heavenly kingdom" whose pilgrim's staff, leathern water bottle and a case of relics were the standard and usually the whole of their worldly goods. Bishop Otho, taking very favorable notice of the Irish religious, induced the three to be received into his Benedictine monastery at Michelsberg. After the bishop's death, continuing again on their way to Rome, they were warmly welcomed in the pilgrim's hospice maintained by the Abbess Emma at Ratisbon, a kindness that Marianus soon repaid. He was an accomplished scribe, quick, industrious and dedicated to the spread of learning. His flying pen turned out so many manuscripts "all without any wish for earthly gain" the abbess, in order to facilitate his work, settled the three companions in cells for themselves. John and Candidus prepared vellum from membranes. Marianus wrote over and over again the Old and New Testaments with explanatory comments and many smaller books, manuals and psalters. And the many miracles which were believed to attend his astounding output convinced the people Marianus was surely a special favorite of heaven.

After some little time, Marianus, having consulted with Muircetach, an Irish recluse in a cell at St. Peter's Church on the outskirts of Ratisbon, settled down to his writing and to the study of sacred literature at that same St. Peter's Church. Aventius, in the *Annals of Bavaria*, describes him as a distinguished poet and theologian second to no man in his time. One of the most prized works of the Saint is his *Commentary on the Psalms*, which the monks valued so highly it was not given out of the monastery library without a deposit large enough to ensure its safe return. The most famous of his works is his *Epistles of St. Paul*, Codex 1247 in the Imperial Library at Vienna, the original production of Marianus himself. This manuscript in his own handwriting has interesting details such as his name, Muiredach MacRobartaigh, the date of completion in 1078, and notations in Irish of the festivals of Irish Saints that occurred as he wrote. He asks the reader to say amen to his prayer "Amen God rest him" — to which a pious German complied in writing: "Amen, Got der Erleich."

About the year 1076, the Abbess Emma, with the consent of the Emperor Henry IV, gave Marianus the Church of St. Peter, and a Ratisbon citizen Bezelin built him a monastery with a cloister on an adjoining plot of ground. So began Marianus' monastery of St. Peter at Ratisbon and so began a new chapter in the history of Irish monastic institutions on the Continent. Soon there were coming to Marianus, chiefly from his native Ulster, many Irish monks already educated and trained in Irish monasteries. The Italian Tommasini remarks it is a curious coincidence that in the Germanies, those countries which had remained predominantly Catholic — the Rhineland,

Bavaria, Austria — are precisely those in which Irish missionaries expended the most intense effort and in which Irish monastic foundations were most numerous.

Marianus died February 9, 1088. His remains are believed to have been deposited in St. Peter's Church, but all traces of the Saint and his monastery were destroyed in the 16th century.

He left behind him a flourishing community to which fresh recruits continually arrived from Ireland. Six abbots from the north of Ireland governed successively after him. The seventh, also Irish, was from the southern part. Marianus' immediate successor was Dionysius in 1088. Under Dionysius came the first expansion of St. Peter's with a second more commodious monastery he dedicated to St. James. The Jesuit Stephen White, 1650, quotes an old Ratisbon Chronicle on the founding of St. James: Dionysius having delegated Isaac and Gervase, two Irishmen of noble birth, and two other Irishmen, Conrad and Liam, to go the Ireland to Conchubair (Conor O'Brien) King of Munster, obtained generous funds and other contributions from the king and princes of Ireland. This money from Ireland and further German contributions enabled Dionysius to purchase a new, larger site on which he built the new companion monastery, the Abbey of St. James, of which Domnus was put in charge. Completion was finally accomplished by a sale of costly skins and furs which one of Marianus' original companions, Mauris, and others of the brethren brought back from a long missionary journey they made to Kieff in the Ukraine in the company of traders. The old Chronicle wanted it known "that neither before nor since was there a more noble monastery. . . . because of the wealth and the money sent by the king and the princes of Ireland." Henry V granted privileges to St. James and in 1120 the monastery received a letter of protection from Pope Calixtus.

After Domnus at St. James, came Christian, a scion of the MacCarthys, princes of Desmond. Christian, ordained in Rome by Pope Innocent II, received from him a Bull declaring his protection of the Irish foundations at Ratisbon. Later Christian obtained a second Bull from Pope Eugenius, November 29, 1148, and set about enlargement of St. James. Like his predecessors he looked primarily to Ireland for aid and Christian himself was the choice of the brethren to solicit King Donncadh, a mission successfully concluded. But he fell ill and died in Ireland. He was buried in the Cathedral of Cashel.

It fell to Gregory, successor to Christian, to go to Ireland for the funds deposited with the Archbishop of Cashel for Ratisbon. And it was during Gregory's abbacy that there came to St. James the Irish monk Marianus who had taught liberal arts at Paris and had had for a pupil Nicholas Breakspeare afterwards Pope Adrian IV. During an audience in Rome, Adrian told

Gregory "I know not in the Catholic church an abbot who has under him a man as perfect in wisdom, prudence, and other gifts of God as my master Marianus."

St. James as head of the two Ratisbon communities became known as St. James of the Scots at Ratisbon. The Bavarian annalist Aventius wrote of Marianus and his companions and successors "By their devotion to the strictest religious exercises, and self-denial, by their writing and teaching, they earned unbounded respect, and became well approved patterns of piety. They were favorites of everybody. And with one mouth the whole people spoke loudly in their praise; kings and nobles built monasteries for them and invited them east and west." Out of St. James there issued twelve foundations propagated by Irish religious.

The first was at Würzburg. In about 1134, at the request of Bishop Embrico, Christian of St. James of Ratisbon established a hospice for Irish pilgrims at Würzburg, sending Macarius and a colony of Irish monks from Ratisbon to man the new foundation.

The Ratisbon prior, Carus, chaplain to King Conrad and Queen Gertrude, was chosen by those rulers to head a congregation in Nüremburg. They gave him St. Aegidius Church there as the nucleus of his foundation.

In 1142, another Irish colony from St. James of Ratisbon went to Constance. The Irish name of the first superior, Macrobius, is believed to have been Maelsuithain.

When Henry, Duke of Bavaria (1143–1154) built his castle in Vienna, he solicited many foreign merchants to set up in business there. The merchants from Ratisbon requested they be accompanied by some Irish religious. Henry erected the monastery of St. Mary for them and turned it over to Gregory, then the abbot in Ratisbon. In the monastery charter Henry makes only Scots (Irish) eligible for admission "because of their long and acknowledged piety." The magnificent abbey given the Irish monks was designed by Henry to be the burial place of his family and subsequently, his own tomb, that of his wife Theodora, daughter of the Emperor Emmanuel, and of his two sons, Leopold and Henry, and his daughter Agnes were to be seen in the church. The abbot that Gregory sent from Ratisbon to rule the Irish community in Vienna was called Santinus. His Irish name was Giolla na Naemh. Until the year 1418, the Vienna personnel was entirely Irish. A projected foundation of the Irish monks of Vienna at Kieff was not realized because of a Mongol invasion.

Mauris, or Muredach, in 1187, headed a company of twelve Ratisbon monks invited to Memmingen by Guelf, enemy of Henry, but friend of the Irish monks. Guelf chose them for the establishment he founded in memory of his only son who had died of the plague.

Similar Irish colonies came out of Ratisbon to other important beginnings — in Erfurt, Kelheim, Oels in Salesia, and, it is thought, Schottenburg in Upper Salesia — twelve of them in all, with the 12th and 13th centuries their most flourishing period.

A papal Bull constituted the twelve monasteries of the Irish in Germany a congregation and named the abbot of St. James of Ratisbon Abbot-General and Metropolitan of all those monasteries. King Henry bestowed upon the abbot-general of St. James the privilege of the Half Eagle of the Empire on his coat of arms, denoting his congregation ranked among the states of the realm.

But a strange fate was to befall the congregation of St. James of the Scots of Ratisbon. Irish contacts with Irish centers on the Continent, curtailed at first, were finally completely cut off by the woes at home where strange things also went on. In the Co. Kilkenny Cistercian Abbey at Jerpoint, governed by an English abbot, it was decreed in 1380 that no mere Irishman be permitted to make his profession at Jerpoint. This was not an isolated instance. And the world at large, including Rome, forgot that originally the term Scot was applied exclusively to Irish from Ireland (Scots from Scotia) and continued to be so applied long after the Irish colonization of North Britain that resulted in its being called the Land of the Scots and finally, Scotland.

The new Scotland began to lay successful, if false, claims to the achievements of the ancient Scots (Irish) all over Europe. The Scots of Scotland asserted to Rome that the foundations of Marianus Scotus belonged to their nation. They made the charge the Irish had thrust themselves in; their plea was admitted at Rome. Pope Leo X issued a Bull which "restored" the foundations to their "proper owners," the inhabitants of Scotland. The Irish were expelled after being charged among other things with having made "fraudulent" entry in the records that Ireland was Scotia Major.

The John Thomson who had been in Rome and had obtained the Bull from Leo X, in 1515 took possession of the Irish St. James of Ratisbon as superior with a company of Scottish monks from Dunfermline. The Scots of Scotland succeeded too in usurping the Irish monasteries of Constance and Erfurt. From that time down to their suppression in 1847, they were looked upon as belonging exclusively to the natives of Scotland.

The error lives on. The *Peoria Register*, September 1, 1949, published under the dateline München, an appeal to the Catholics of Scotland and Ireland to help rebuild "the famed Scots' Abbey, the Monastery of St. James . . . established by English and Irish monks during the early middle ages."

MacGeoghegan, 253; O'Hanlon II, Feb. 9; *Catholic Encyclopedia*, XV: 417; Tommasini, 88, 90; Stokes, 34; Fitzpatrick, II: 361; Gougaud, 89, 93; Toynbee, II: 329.

Macarius
December 19   1153

Four and a half centuries before Macarius, Kilian, an earlier Irish missionary was martyred at Würzburg. Kilian's statue, with that of his two Irish companions, stands on the bridgehead over the river Main there today. So many Irish pilgrim religious came to Kilian's tomb, Bishop Embrico appealed to Christian, abbot of St. James of the Scots (Irish) at Ratisbon, to establish a hospice for them at Würzburg. St. James of the Scots at Würzburg was the first of the twelve famous Irish Benedictine congregations that rose out of the original foundation of Marianus Scotus at Ratisbon. Macarius was named abbot of the "Würzburg monastery serving there from 1134 to 1153.

A man of ability and learning, Macarius is credited with having initiated at Würzburg the remarkable literary activity that has left that city one of the largest collections of Irish-Latin manuscripts in existence. In his time came the Irish David, historiographer and scholastic in charge of the Cathedral school, chaplain to Emperor Henry V, and his companion on the imperial journey to Rome. The successor to Macarius, Carus, was chaplain to King Conrad and Queen Gertrude. The third abbot, Declan, was chaplain to Conrad III and to Barbarossa. St. James at Würzburg had all Irish personnel until 1497.

Esteemed a holy man in his lifetime, Macarius was revered as a saint after his death. In 1615, his body was exhumed and transferred to the abbey church. Many cures, miraculous it was believed, occurred at this time. In 1818 his relics were moved into the Marienkapelle in Würzburg. The old Irish Abbey of St. James (Sanct Jacob) now belongs to the Salesians.

Fitzpatrick, II: 373; *Catholic Encyclopedia*, XV: 721; *New Catholic Encyclopedia*, 9: 40; Benedictine Monks, 383; Stokes, 35; Kenney, 619.

V

The Post-Viking Period

Into the Golden age of Ireland about the year 800, there descended the Viking sea pirates. It was the beginning of 200 years of burnings and plunderings of Irish monasteries and churches, wanton destruction of Ireland's precious books, wholesale murder of the brethren of Ireland's great monastic centers of religion and learning. All this was to pass. In 1014 at Clontarf, Brian Boru vanquished the Norsemen forever, but fell in the battle himself. Gradually the invaders were absorbed into the Irish life stream.

In the all too brief respite before the Anglo-Norman invasion, a resolute renewal marked all phases of Irish religious life. New churches and monasteries were built and old ones restored. There were many Irish-founded abbies all over Europe that were well stocked with writings of all kinds by Irish scribes and to these Brian Boru had sent overseas for books to replace those destroyed by the Viking invaders. Now Irish monks were turning out innumerable church documents. Abbots and kings prided themselves on great new manuscript Gospels and great new books into which scribes gathered the epics, poetry, history and science of the past. New metal work in gold and bronze produced such gems as the Cross of Cong, the Ardagh Chalice, the Tara Brooch. Great High Crosses sculptured in stone marked a new artistic bent of the age. Cormac's Chapel at Cashel, the doorway at Clonfert, speak of its architecture. Marianus Scotus's great new Congregation of Irish monasteries took rise in Germany. The forward wave brought episcopal and parochial rule to replace monastic authority in the Irish Church.

Ceallach (Celsus)
April 1   1129

One writer has declared that the ferocity of the Norsemen in Ireland was equalled only by the determination of the Irish to rebuild. Ceallach, who came into the abbacy of Armagh in 1105, stands at the head of the final phase of post-Viking renewal in the Irish church, reorganization into an episcopal and parochial system of government on the ruins of the old monastic church.

Armagh itself, the primatial see of Ireland, was held in lay ownership, a situation that went back to the pagan Turgesius who had installed himself as "abbot" of Armagh. From 957, Armagh had been held by powerful men who had at first come forward as stewards of the church property and defenders of the faith but afterwards usurped the abbey lands to secure the rich revenues for themselves and for their heirs. Lay abbots "learned enough but without Orders" ruled in hereditary succession, in full possession of title and all revenues. Regularly ordained clergy, unimportant in status, performed all religious functions. The family that posed the irregularities now produced the man who would set all to rights.

Ceallach, a 26 year old layman, came into the title of abbot of Armagh through hereditary lay succession that went back a century and a half in one family, the Clann Sinach. After his election, Ceallach took Holy Orders. The next year when the bishop of Armagh died, Ceallach acquired episcopal rank. Uncanonical as it appeared, Ceallach's objective was the restoration of Armagh to its rightful place at the head of the Irish church.

Mindful all of this time of the Irish bishops in the south, among them Malchus of Waterford and Gillebert of Limerick, who were already working toward a uniform liturgy and episcopal and parochial reorganization, Ceallach joined them, bringing his great name and influence to the movement. In 1106 at Cashel he was accepted by all as Archbishop and Primate of Ireland.

It was a difficult ministry. There was relentless harassment from kinsmen claimants to the see of Armagh. There was the now Christian Danish populace of Dublin who chose to have their bishops consecrated at Canterbury, who rejected the Act of the National Synod that subjected Dublin to the ancient see of Glendalough.

In 1129 Ceallach was taken ill in Ardpatrick in County Limerick. Knowing that his end was near and believing that his young bishop Malachy was of all others best fitted to succeed him as primate, Ceallach sent Malachy his crozier as proof of his choice of a successor. He died at Ardpatrick and was buried, as he had requested, at Lismore.

Curtis, 23, 28; Healy, 395, 471; O'Hanlon, IV: 46; Daniel-Rops, 141; Benedictine Monks, 135.

Christian O'Morgair
June 12   1139

Malachy's only brother, Christian O'Morgair, was bishop of Clogher. In his *Life of Malachy* , Bernard of Clairvaux describes Christian: "a good man, full of grace and virtue, second to his brother in fame, but possibly not inferior to him in sanctity of life and zeal for righteousness." Christian was buried at Armagh, under the great altar in the Abbey of St. Peter and St. Paul, where his relics were formerly preserved with great veneration.

Murphy, 102.

Gillebert
February 4   1140

The names Ceallach, Malachy, Gelasius, Laurence O'Toole, mark important milestones in the 12th century reform and renewal in the Irish Church. But earlier than those prelates was the band of native reformers who appeared in the south of Ireland, Irish bishops to whom the as yet uncanonically elected Ceallach came to join forces. In the forefront were Malchus of Waterford who had become a monk at Winchester, and Rouen-educated Gillebert of Limerick who was named apostolic delegate to Ireland in 1107.

The year of Gillebert's appointment to Limerick is inferred from an extant letter he wrote to Canterbury to congratulate the Italian Archbishop Anselm on having at last induced the untameable minds of the Anglo-Normans to observe the regular decrees of the Holy Father with regard to the election and consecration of abbots and bishops. Gillebert is reckoned to have been bishop of Limerick in 1106, or before, since that is the year Henry I of England settled his differences with Anselm.

About that same time, native reformers in the south, notably Gillebert of Limerick and Malchus of Waterford, joined by Ceallach of Armagh, launched reorganization of the Irish Church from monastic to episcopal rule. At the Council of Cashel the High King Murcertach signified his blessing with the gift of the famous Rock of Cashel to the church. One reforming synod succeeded another, a movement that came mainly from within with the leading part in it taken by Irishmen. At the National Synod of Rath Breasel in 1110 Ireland was divided into 24 dioceses. In 1139, "all things being in order," Malachy resigned Armagh to Gelasius. And in 1162, Gelasius decreed uniform liturgy as taught at Armagh for all of Ireland.

Gillebert is remembered for his "De Statu Ecclesiae," the tract written in the cause of ecclesiastical reform which outlined the episcopal and parochial reorganization and advocated the uniform liturgy adopted for all of Ireland.

O'Hanlon, II: 323; Curtis, 39; MacNeill, 283–286.

Malachy
November 4   1095–1148

More than half of Cistercian Eugenius III's troubled pontificate was spent away from Rome because of the hostility of the citizens. During this time the saintly Pope came to his former abbot, Bernard of Clairvaux for guidance. Bernard told him "study the life and follow the example of Malachy and all will be well."

Malachy O'More enrolled at Armagh about 1115. He was observed from the first with interest and approval by the Primate Ceallach. Malachy's father was the chief lector at Armagh. His mother's family held the Bangor lands in lay abbot succession. A brother, Christian, was "not inferior to him in sanctity and zeal." A sister occasioned much prayer on his part.

Ceallach advanced Malachy to the priesthood at the age of 25 and sent him to Lismore in the south of Ireland for instruction under Malchus of Waterford, one of the promoters of episcopal reorganization in Ireland. On his return, Ceallach at once assigned Malachy to Bangor which was in ruins from the Norsemen. Church, school, monks, 900 of whom had been slain on one occasion, all were gone. Only the lands and their revenues remained, held by a lay abbot, Malachy's mother's brother, who abdicated to become a monk under Malachy, who in turn resigned the revenues to others, a case of carrying the spirit of holy poverty too far, St. Bernard thought.

Malachy's way, ever, was to have nothing belonging to himself, no servants, no lay clerks, no revenues of any sort, to be constantly on the roads, always travelling on foot, going through the parishes to preach the Gospel, bringing to the work at hand a serenity, a gentleness and a power of attraction no one was ever able to resist. He raised Bangor out of its ruins, he founded the abbey of Iveragh in the south and then reluctantly, he accepted the episcopate when in 1125, Ceallach named him Bishop of Down and Connor, the latter especially having suffered from the Viking invasions.

Four years later, from his deathbed in 1129, Ceallach sent his staff and a letter to Malachy as his choice of a successor best fitted to administer the primacy.

At this point, the see of Armagh having been hereditary in the family of Ceallach for generations, a kinsman, Murtagh claimed the abbacy. Because Malachy refused to resort to force, it was not until 1132 that, urged on by the Irish church leaders, he assumed the primacy, but on a strictly spiritual basis, leaving the hereditary claimant in possession of the revenues. At the death of Murtagh, when a second lay abbot, Niall, succeeded to office, the reforming party and the princes who supported it came forward to fight the issue. About 1137, Niall relinquished the relics considered to be the very title deeds to

Armagh, the *Book of Armagh*, the Bell and the Staff of Jesus as Patrick's crozier was called. The break Ceallach had initiated thus became final. And now, all things being in order, Malachy, as he had been promised, returned to Down appointing Gelasius archbishop of Armagh who took office without opposition.

In the year 1137, on foot with three pack horses, Malachy and some companions set out for Rome. They went through Scotland where he had founded a monastery and where he was remembered for his prayer that cured a despaired-of-illness of the son of the Irish King David. In England he was given a very poor horse, "all that he had need of," he said. It was eminently in keeping with the turn-out of the Archbishop, so minus all the usual trappings of rank and importance. That was his introduction to Bernard of Clairvaux, whose writings lashed out at the luxury of prelates. The Irish bishop and the French abbot were immediate and lasting friends. Malachy later asked the Pope's permission to become a Cistercian under Bernard. The latter's admiration for Malachy is well known from his biography of the saint. (Modern historians point out, however, that Bernard "eulogized the hero at the expense of the good reputation of his compatriots, as if to the detriment of truth.")

Malachy was received in all honor by the Holy Father, Innocent II, who also had known intrigue and difficulty in the possession of his see. He promised Malachy palliums for Armagh and Cashel. He gave Malachy his own mitre and the stole and maniple he wore to say Mass. But Innocent refused Malachy's request to become a monk at Clairvaux. Instead he appointed him papal legate in Ireland. It was at this time, supposedly, that Malachy gave the Holy Father the famous prophecies about the Popes.

Malachy set out for Rome again in 1148, deputed to make formal application for palliums for the Irish churches from Pope Eugenius III. But Malachy was detained in England by King Stephen who was then in conflict with Rome. He was disappointed to find the Cistercian Pope had been in Clairvaux where he came to seek guidance of his former abbot, but had departed a short time before.

The saint fell ill at Clairvaux and died with Bernard at his side. When the monks were preparing him for burial, Bernard exchanged his own tunic for Malachy's which he afterwards wore on great feast days. Bernard sang the requiem. In the post-Communion prayer for the dead, he anticipated the formal canonization of Malachy by Pope Clement III in 1190. Bernard changed it into the prayer for a confessor-bishop "O God Who made the blessed Malachy equal in merits to Thy saints, grant we beseech Thee that we who celebrate the feast of his holy death may copy the example of his life. Amen." Later, he beckoned a boy with a crippled hanging arm and lifted the paralyzed hand to touch Malachy's hand with instant cure. "Malachy performed many miracles, but the first and the greatest was himself."

Bernard buried Malachy in the chancel at Clairvaux and was himself buried beside him. Since the French revolution, such relics as have been saved repose in a single reliquary in the Cathedral of Troyes.

Daniel-Rops, 138; Mould, 219; Butler-Attwater IV: 249; Healy, 393; MNab; Moran, 198; Tommasini, 237, 385.

VI

Henry II to Henry VIII in Ireland

In 1154, the Englishman Pope Adrian IV made his Donation of Ireland to Henry II of England with the provision that Henry lead Ireland back to religion and morality.

Archbishop Healy of Tuam said no Pope would do such a thing. The English Jesuit Herbert Thurston declares that the conquest of Ireland, projected by Henry in 1156, was carried out later with the full sanction of Alexander III, a sanction preserved in letters of unquestionable authenticity which concede in substance all that was granted by the disputed Bull of Adrian IV. Henry's ambassadors found the Pope at Benevento and with him John of Salisbury, also an Englishman. Salisbury is quoted that at his request, Adrian ceded and bestowed Ireland on Henry II to be possessed with hereditary right and that Pope Adrian sent by him a most beautiful emerald ring by which investiture the right of governing Ireland was to be made, a ring that was, in Salisbury's time, preserved by order in the public treasury. Henry, delayed by the disapproval of his mother, the Empress Matilda, and by political entanglements, did not act on the Donation until 1169 when his opportunity came in a request of the King of Leinster, Dermot McMurrough, for aid in his feud with the Irish princes. Thus the Anglo-Normans came to Ireland and with them, plunderings and burnings.

Henry II, by now the murderer of Thomas a Becket, arrived in Ireland in 1171. His "reforms" began with the confiscation of lands and holdings of the native Irish for such of the English as would benefit himself. Normans and English seized for their own candidates all Irish bishoprics and other worthwhile benefices. Laurence O'Toole wrested Dublin from the Danes only to have it taken over at his death by John Comyn, the politically oriented bishop of Henry II. Before long native Irish candidates were refused admission to many of the Irish monasteries. The creeping paralysis that began in 1169 would last until 1829.

Gelasius
March 27   1088–1174

When Malachy resigned Armagh to Gelasius all things pointed to a new and flourishing era in the Irish Church. But as it turned out, the primacy of Gelasius, 1137–1174, was to encompass the alleged Donation of Ireland by Pope Adrian IV to Henry II of England; the arrival of the first Anglo-Normans; Henry II's murder of Thomas Becket in 1170; Henry's own arrival in Ireland in 1171; Pope Alexander III's confirmation of everything granted by Adrian IV.

Gelasius (in Irish Giolla Iosa, Servant of Jesus) was abbot of Derry for 16 years, 1121–1137. His father was the foremost bard of his time, a man of learning and probably a professor at Derry where Gelasius is believed to have been educated.

In the calm before the Anglo-Norman invasion, literary, artistic and architectural activity flourished everywhere in the land. Celebrated Irish books survive from the time of Gelasius: the *Psaltair-na-Rann*, now in the Bodleian Library, Oxford; *Book of Gospels*, British Museum; *Book of Hymns*, Trinity College, Dublin; *Missal*, Corpus Christi College, Oxford; *Book of Leinster*, Trinity College. The O'Carrolls enshrined the *Book of Dimma* in the case which with its contents still survives in Trinity College.

Clonmacnoise, flourishing with such new additions as the O'Kelly sepulchral Church, the Tempul Kieran, the beautiful Nuns' Church, reached its peak as a school of art in the 12th century. Armagh was rebuilt on a grand scale. Derry Cathedral was completed. Twelve churches were built in Galway and Clare. Clonfert was rebuilt. In 1142 with Christian O'Conarchy as abbot, O'Carroll, Prince of Oriel, founded and endowed Mellifont, the first of 25 new Cistercian abbeys that took rise in Ireland before 1169.

Ireland was staffing, with Irish monks and Irish money, the foundations of Marianus Scotus of St. James at Ratisbon, the 12-fold Irish Congregation famous in Benedictine Annals of Southern Germany. A Bull of Adrian IV to Abbot Gregory of St. James of Ratisbon is dated March 19, 1157. Living a monk at Ratisbon at that time was a distinguished Irish ecclesiastic named Marianus who, while a professor of Liberal Arts at the University of Paris, had been the preceptor of the future Adrian IV. When Gregory was admitted to an audience at Rome, Adrian inquired, among other things, after "his Master Marianus" upon whom he heaped most extravagant eulogy.

Three Irish saints serving in Ireland in the time of Gelasius were Malachy, Concord and Laurence O'Toole, all of whom happened to die on French soil. Malachy and Laurence O'Toole were formally canonized, Concord beatified, through the initiative of the French people.

Gelasius, indefatigable in his ministry, was making visitations throughout Ireland, reorganizing old monasteries, witnessing charters to new foundations, convening synods, presiding over all "holding the Staff of Jesus (St. Patrick's Crozier) in his hands." Under Gelasius even Derry became an episcopal see with its abbot a bishop, a move long resisted by the Columban monks who deemed it an indignity to the memory of Colmcille that the abbot of one of his monasteries should be of higher rank than he had been.

Cardinal Paparo, papal legate to Eugenius III, in Ireland for the Synod of Kells in 1152, brought with him four palls for the archbishops of Armagh, Cashel, Dublin, and Tuam. In connection with this synod is found the first reference to tithes in Irish annals. All other decrees passed unanimously but not one ecclesiastic is on record as having approved of the cardinal's unheard of new system of obtaining a maintenance. This matter of tithes and especially of Peter's Pence is said to have been an important consideration in subsequent negotiations between Adrian IV and Henry II.

Norse invasions and settlement had made Dublin a Norse city with the now Christian Norsemen turning to Canterbury rather than to Armagh. In 1162, however, Lawrence O'Toole went to Armagh to be consecrated Archbishop of Dublin by Gelasius. In that same year, at the Synod of Clane in County Kildare, a uniform liturgy was assured by the enactment that only Armagh-trained or Armagh-accredited teachers of divinity were to be permitted to teach in any school attached to a church in Ireland. And in 1169, Roderick O'Connor, King of Ireland, established and endowed at Armagh a new professorship for the benefit of students from Ireland and Scotland, allocating funds from himself "and from every king that should succeed him forever." It is now history that the enactments for a uniform Irish liturgy, along with Roderick O'Connor's endowment in 1169 were soon a part of the debris of the native Irish Church. 1169 was the year the first of the Anglo-Normans arrived in Ireland.

On the political side of the picture, Gelasius convened a synod in Armagh in 1170 in the vain hope of concerting means to expel the Anglo-Normans while it was still possible. Henry II himself, out with the Papacy at the time, over the martyrdom of Thomas Becket, came to Ireland late in 1171, not to proclaim the Bull of Adrian but to enter upon a winter of lavish entertainment. The Synod of Cashel which was convened by the papal legate, Christian of Lismore, at Henry's insistence, was attended by most of the Irish prelates as well as the several high ecclesiastics who accompanied Henry to Ireland. At Cashel Henry presented his decrees for the "uplift" of the Irish Church (merely an echo, says MacNeill, of the words in which Bernard of Clairvaux describes the reforms already effected by Malachy.) Nothing was said concerning any claim of Canterbury and the supremacy of Armagh over

Ireland with final obedience to none but Rome was unchallenged. But the day of native Irish liturgy was over. Decree Eight imposed upon the Irish Church the celebration of divine offices according to the usage of the Church of England.

Neither the princes of the north nor Gelasius were in attendance at Cashel. Gelasius was occupied in a visitation of Connacht and Ulster in a last attempt to organize with the High King a defence of Ireland. But he saw Henry accepted by the many princes of the country who were badly mistaken as to Henry's true designs. He saw Henry's religious decrees accepted by prelates such as Lawrence O'Toole, whose acceptance is explained as obedience to the mandate of Adrian IV. Only then did Gelasius go to Dublin to meet with Henry.

In April of 1172, Henry left Ireland, recalled by the threat of Papal interdict for Becket's murder. But a penitent Henry walked bare-foot to the shrine of the martyred Archbishop and royal envoys reached Rome with word of the fine reception tendered the English king and his decrees for the uplift of the Irish people. In May Henry was reconciled with the Papacy and in September came Alexander III's confirmation of the Donation of Ireland made by Adrian IV.

Gelasius died March 27, 1174, honored as a saint by the entire people and by the Church in Ireland. Armagh held out for a while but in vain. The last mention of the School of Armagh in Irish annals is in 1188. The last native prelate of Armagh until the Reformation was Nicholas Maoliosa, 1272–1313.

From Geraldus Cambrensis, chaplain to King John, comes an assessment of this phase of Irish history as related by Eoin MacNeill: "Years afterwards, when Henry was dead, he addresses his successor John, reminding him of his father's pledge to Pope Adrian, then also dead — the first pledge made by an English ruler in regard of Ireland, whereby, he says, Henry 'secured the sanction of the highest earthly authority to an enterprise of such magnitude, involving the shedding of Christian blood.' This pledge, he says, has not been kept. On the contrary, 'the poor clergy in the island are reduced to beggary; the cathedral churches, which were richly endowed with broad lands by the piety of the faithful in the olden times,' and which, we may add, supported on these endowments the schools already mentioned, 'now echo with lamentations for the loss of their possessions, of which they have been robbed by these men and others who came over with them or after them; so that to uphold the Church is turned into spoiling and robbing it.' Even the revenue, the Peter's Pence, promised by Henry to the Pope was not paid, and Geraldus pleads that it should be paid in future, 'in order that some acknowledgement and propitiation may be made ot God for this bloody conquest *and the profits of it.*' " [Italics added]

Kenney, 18; MacNeill, 286–8; Stokes, 70; Healy, 121; 358; O'Hanlon, III: 965; *Catholic Encyclopedia*, I: 158; VIII: 639.

Concord
June 4   1120–1176

In 1854 Archbishop Dixon of Armagh was in Rome for the ceremonies of the decree of the doctrine of the Immaculate Conception. In scanning a French newspaper published in Chambery, he came across a report of the examination in that year by Vatican authorities of the remains of St. Concord, Archbishop of Armagh, who had died in Lemnec in Savoy seven centuries before but whose brain was still incorrupt.

The Irish Archbishop knew no such name in the list of prelates of Armagh. He returned home by way of Lemnec in order to learn the full particulars of this predecessor so strangely forgotten in his native land. Not so strangely, perhaps, in view of the burning and demolition going on in Ireland in Concord's time.

Concord of Lemnec was born Conchobhar MacConchaille in Armagh, December 17, 1120. He became an Augustinian canon at Armagh in 1140, abbot in 1151. He is listed as Cornelius in succession to Gelasius as primate in 1174. In 1175 he made a pilgrimage to Rome where he pleaded the cause of Ireland before Alexander III.

On the way home he fell ill at Lemnec. He told them he had served the Church of St. Peter in Armagh, he had visited the Church of St. Peter in Rome, and that he would be buried in the Church of St. Peter at Lemnec. A few days later on June 4, 1176, he died.

Miracles at Concord's tomb brought such fame the people named him their patron. They established a St. Concord's Confraternity that flourished throughout five succeeding centuries. In 1671, Pope Clement X confirmed the confraternity and formally approved religious veneration of Concord. With the approval of Rome, a white habit with purple cincture was adopted by confraternity members to be worn at church functions. Recorded in 1689 were foundations for masses to be celebrated for 300 years in the Chapel of St. Concord. Six centuries after his death sick people daily invoked his prayer.

When Concord's remains, together with documents relating to his life, were taken to Rome for examination, the relics were encased in a waxen lifelike bust which on the return to Chambery, was vested in archiepiscopal mitre and chasuble. The religious of St. Peter having obtained from the Holy Father an Office and Mass for Concord, grand solemnities marked the celebration of the feast of the saint in the year 1854, a feast observed there each recurring June 4.

Relics of Concord are now enshrined in the Sacred Heart Convent, Armagh, and in the Presentation Convent, Drogheda.

Carty, 58; O'Hanlon, VI: 96; Healy, 122; Neeson, 108.

Laurence O'Toole
November 14   1128–1180

Lorcan Ua Tuathail anglicized is Laurence O'Toole. Tuathail is a very old Celtic name. Second century Tuathail was one of the great ancient Irish kings. Another Tuathail reigned in 533. One of the seven churches at Glendalough entombed long generations of the royal line of O'Toole. Laurence's father, Murtagh O'Toole, was a prince of southeast Kildare, his mother a daughter of O'Byrne of northeast Kildare. The tall, too slim young archbishop is remembered for his seemly dignity, for his abstemious life, for his love of his native land whose wounds he tried so hard to heal, wounds brought on by internal dissensions and by foreign foes.

Laurence O'Toole knew political intrigue from the time he was ten years old when Dermot McMurrough, King of Leinster, forced Murtagh O'Toole to deliver up his son as a political hostage. After two years O'Toole negotiated Laurence's transfer into the custody of the bishop of Glendalough. And when Murtagh O'Toole would have cast lots as to which of his four sons he should give to the Church, Laurence asked to be chosen. He spent 22 years at Glendalough, as student, novice, monk, and from the age of 25, as abbot. When the clergy and people would have made him bishop of Glendalough, he refused on the grounds he had not reached the canonical age. Eight years later in 1161 when Gregory of Dublin died, Dane and native Irish, clergy and laity, the High King O'Loughlin, Dermot McMurrough, his former captor and husband of his sister Mor, all united in the choice of Laurence O'Toole.

Dublin had become a wealthy foreign port of Norse enterprise. Norse Christians dedicated their Dublin churches to St. Mary of the Ostman, St. Olaf, St. Michan. They looked to Canterbury rather than to Armagh. Dublin's Christ Church, founded by Sitric the Dane, had never known an Irish ordained prelate until Laurence O'Toole brought Gelasius from Armagh to consecrate him bishop. All succeeding bishops of Dublin, Anglo-Normans notwithstanding, went to Rome through Armagh, not through Canterbury.

In the still half-pagan Danish Dublin, the young Archbishop converted his secular priests at Christ Church into Augustinian canons, he donned the white habit with them, shared the strict community rule and set an example few could follow. Long after midnight matins he would still be kneeling before the Crucifix which was said to have spoken twice. He spent Lent as he had spent it in Glendalough, in Kevin's mountainside shelter.

Although Dermot McMurrough was later to open the flood gates to Anglo-Norman adventurers, his name occurred often with that of Laurence O'Toole as the generous donor in much of the great expansion program that was to be sabotaged even in the Archbishop's own lifetime.

It all began when Dermot McMurrough, King of Leinster, abducted by her own invitation, Dervorgilla, wife of the Prince of Brefni, Tiernan O'Rourke, who never forgave the injury. In 1166, O'Rourke and other Irish princes having to all appearances reduced McMurrough to ruin, the Leinster king sailed to England for help, taking with him his daughter Eva, Laurence O'Toole's niece, whose beauty and rank made her a matrimonial prize. Henry II, although involved in Aquitaine at this time (and in waging his continuing bitter conflict against Thomas Becket who had fled to France in 1164), was prompt to authorize a project made to order for his own designs upon Ireland. Richard de Clare, Earl of Pembroke ("Strongbow"), was won over by the promise of marriage to the beautiful Eva, and with her, succession to the throne of Leinster.

Irish annals say of the first contingent of Anglo-Normans in 1169; "The fleet of the Flemings came to Erin, they were ninety heroes dressed in mail and the Gaels set no store by them." Others followed, and de Clare and his men-at-arms in 1170, and with McMurrough they attacked and took Waterford. Earl Richard claimed Eva as his bride in the Waterford Cathedral and with her succession to the kingship of Leinster.

At this point, Roderick O'Connor, King of Ireland, assayed negotiations with McMurrough with Laurence O'Toole as mediator, a role that would make increasingly heavy demands upon the Archbishop as long as he lived. Even as negotiations concerning Dublin were in progress, Normans burst into the city filling the streets with the dead and the dying. Laurence O'Toole, rushing from the parley to try to stop the carnage, could only give absolution to the dying and help to care for the dead. Thoroughly aroused for his country, the saint urged a united front under Roderick O'Connor, something that never quite materialized.

Suddenly in July of 1170, Henry II made his short-lived peace with Thomas Becket who returned to England December 1, only to be murdered in his own cathedral by "the king's men" on December 29, 1170. Henry arrived in Ireland in October of 1171 to look to his own interests, the move long brewing and now facilitated by Dermot McMurrough.

Ostensibly, Henry was the benevolent king, come purely on a mission of welfare. He publicly denounced English misconduct in Ireland. He extended the hand of most cordial friendship — markedly ignored by the Primate Gelasius, the High King Roderick O'Connor and the princes of the north but accepted as genuine by the princes of the south. Henry did not proclaim his

Laudabiliter at this time. But he projected the religious character of his campaign. He arranged with the papal legate, Christian of Lismore for a Synod at Cashel. It is supposed the king's rights under a papal concession had been made known to Christian, the Archbishops of Tuam and Cashel and especially to the patriot Archbishop Laurence of Dublin. Henry's decrees presented little not already in observance in Ireland with the one exception, that the divine offices be celebrated according to the usage of the Church in England, with, however, the supremacy of Armagh over the whole island and final obedience to none but Rome. On the strength of such fair assurances the leaders of the Church and the State accepted Henry.

The preliminaries out of the way, Henry effected the first of his "reforms," the granting out of lands as Crown properties, before his recall from Ireland in April, 1172, by the threat of excommunication for the murder of Becket. But royal envoys reached Rome to report Henry's fine success in Ireland. And Henry himself, powerful king though he was, walked barefoot in public penance for the martyred Becket. In May of 1172, Alexander III reconciled Henry with Rome.

In 1175, the aroused Irish having almost extinguished the English forces in Ireland, Henry resorted to his papal letters, dispatching emissaries to read them to the assembled prelates. King Roderick O'Connor sent ambassadors headed by Laurence O'Toole to negotiate with Henry a formal treaty regulating the relations that were to exist between them, a treaty the English king violated almost before the ink was dry. It was on this visit to England that Laurence O'Toole was felled by a blow from a club as he was saying Mass. Unlike the martyred Becket, he was able to return to the altar to finish Mass. Traces of the blow on his skull were verified in 1876 by the Cardinal Archbishop of Rouen.

In 1178, Henry II created his son John "Dominus Hiberniae." A royal title had been designed by the Papacy, but Henry considered a lesser title better suited to keeping Ireland subordinate. That year, Cardinal Vivian, papal legate to Scotland and Ireland, arrived in Ireland. He saw with indignation and horror the incursions and slaughter of the invader de Courcy. He admonished de Courcy in vain to withdraw his army and then the Cardinal exhorted MacDunlevy, King of Ulster, to defend his country against the invaders.

That same year, Alexander III called the third general Lateran Council for the first Sunday of the following Lent, 1179. Laurence O'Toole and five other Irish bishops, more than attended from Scotland and England together, are signatories of that council. Henry allowed their passage through England only after exacting of them on oath they would seek nothing at the council prejudicial to him or his kingdom. Laurence did however secure from the Pope the independence of the Church in Ireland, forestalling the condition

Henry in 1177 had forced upon the prelates and abbots of Scotland, obedience to the Archbishop of York.

Alexander III appointed Laurence papal legate in Ireland. He at once set about vigorous use of his new authority, especially in the problems and abuses presented by Danish paganism and the Norman adventurers. He sent 140 offenders to Rome. Henry, observing this, remembered Thomas Becket.

Soon after this Henry's wrath again flared against Roderick O'Connor. Once more the Irish king turned to Laurence O'Toole to negotiate in person with Henry. But by now, Laurence, too, had fallen under the king's displeasure. Henry refused to see him, he forbade his return to Ireland, and then he sailed away to Normandy. After three weeks of virtual imprisonment in the monastery at Abingdon, Laurence followed Henry to France.

The place of his landing in Normandy is still called Saint Laurent. He had been very ill setting out from Dover and he was barely able to travel the short distance to the monastery of the Canons of St. Victor at Eu, a branch closely related to his own Canons at Dublin. A priest companion sent to find Henry brought back word that the English king would again meet with the king of Connaught. Laurence O'Toole had done all he could. One of those around him, knowing his high connections in Ireland, suggested he make his will. He told them "I declare before God I have not one penny under the sun to dispose of, not one penny." He died at Eu in Normandy November 14, 1180.

So many wonders were reported at the tomb of Laurence O'Toole, his remains, four and a half years after his death, were enclosed in a crystal case and transferred to a place of special honor before the high altar of the church. Formal canonization was forwarded by the Canons Regular and the faithful at Eu. And at the request of the Archbishop of Rouen, Pope Honorius III ordered the usual investigations. In 1225, forty-five years after his death, Laurence O'Toole was formally declared a saint.

Catholic Encyclopedia; Kenney, 18; Curtis, 54, 57; Sullivan, 122; Healy, 432; Butler-Attwater, IV: 633–4.

John Duns Scotus

1266–1308

About the year 1300 the most famous teacher and lecturer in the universities of Cambridge, Oxford and Paris was the Franciscan friar, Father John Duns Scotus. And 500 years before the official promulgation of the doctrine of the Immaculate Conception he triumphantly championed the prerogative of Our Lady which the Church in 1854 declared a dogma of the faith. At the time of the great Disputatio held about 1306 at the University of Paris for the examination of the doctrine of the Immaculate Conception, he was called upon by the Holy See to be the Defender of the Thesis.

On the way to his great single-handed triumph, Duns Scotus knelt before a marble image of Our Lady in the hall where the Disputatio was to be held. "Dignare me laudare. . . Make me worthy to praise thee Holy Virgin. Give me strength against thine enemies" he prayed, and in the presence of the great assembly, the head of the statue slowly inclined, as if in gracious approval. The miraculous statue was long preserved as an object of great veneration.

According to the Franciscan Book of Saints, John Duns was born in 1266 of an Irish family that settled in Littledean in Scotland. His birthplace is now called Duns. He received his early education from his Franciscan uncle, Father Elias Duns in the friary at Dumfries and was ordained on St. Patrick's Day, March 17, 1291. After some eight years of studies at Paris and Oxford came years of teaching and lecturing at Cambridge and at the Sorbonne, Paris. In 1307 he was sent to Cologne and there he died and was buried. The day of his death was November 8, the year, 1308, or perhaps later.

In recent times there was discovered in the summer retreat of the Holy Father, Castel Gandolfo, two paintings that commemorate the Franciscan Duns Scotus. One is of the Blessed Mother and the Infant Jesus; St. Francis stands on the right with John Duns Scotus behind him; on the left is St. Patrick backed by a representation of Ireland to which the Infant is shown handing some now indistinguishable object. The other painting, by the Flemish artist von Heche, portrays the translation of the remains of Duns Scotus to his resting place behind the high altar of the Franciscan church in Cologne in 1619, the date also of the painting.

Throughout the centuries, large numbers of the faithful have visited the tomb of John Duns Scotus and confirmation by the Holy See of his cult as Blessed is now being sought in Rome. He is venerated in the Franciscan Martyrology and in the diocese of Cologne and of Nola in Italy which since 1710 at least has observed the feast of John Duns Scotus with an Office and a Mass on November 8th. Now underway is a new and critical edition of his writings, the first volumes of which have been published, material it is hoped, that will speed the cause of his sanctification.

Habig; Concannon, II: 234; New *Catholic Encyclopedia*, 9: 224.

Thaddeus MacCarthy
October 24   1455–1492

The MacCarthys built Drishane Castle, the Franciscan Abbey and Castle at Kilcrea, Blarney Castle, Kanturk Castle, now a national monument, and the

Cistercian monastery of Maur de Fonte Vivo. Muckross Abbey, refounded by Donal MacCarthy in 1440, was the burial place of the MacCarthys for centuries. MacCarthy lineage goes back to a 3rd century Irish King of Munster, Oilioll Olum, who had two sons, one of whom inherited north Munster (Thomond) and the other, south Munster or Desmond. In the 11th century when surnames came into use, the king of Desmond was Carthaigh and from him comes the name MacCarthy. In the National Museum, Dublin, may be seen the Limoges enamelled Crozier of the King-Bishop Cormac MacCarthy, builder of the Chapel on the Rock of Cashel of the Kings, who died in 1138. The carved stone sarcophagus in the Chapel is believed to have been his tomb. Cormac's Chapel, described as the culminating point of Irish Romanesque, is one of the surviving glories of pure Hibernian art. In spite of Anglo-Norman encroachments, the MacCarthys retained the title of Kings of Desmond until 1395.

Blessed Thaddeus MacCarthy's time was one of turbulent political dissension between the native Irish MacCarthys and the Norman Fitzgeralds. From the time he was 13 until long after his death, the most powerful figure in Ireland was Gerald, Earl of Kildare, the man all Ireland could not rule, of whom Henry VII said "Then let him rule all Ireland"— the same who excused his burning of the Cathedral of Cashel by explaining he thought the Archbishop David Creagh was inside it.

Thaddeus was educated with the Friars Minor of the Abbey of Kilcrea and was ordained in his native Cork by Bishop William Roche. He was in Rome in 1482 when word reached Pope Sixtus IV of the death of Domnal, Bishop of Ross. Sixtus, impressed with the great merits of Thaddeus, named him bishop of Ross, dispensing him at the same time from the impediment of insufficient age in canon law. He was consecrated bishop in Rome.

Back in Ireland in the meantime, Domnal of Ross, before his death, had resigned his See to Odo whom he delegated to go to Rome in person to acquaint Sixtus IV of the resignation. Thaddeus returned to Ireland to find his post already filled. Both Thaddeus and Odo considered themselves rightly appointed. Matters were further complicated by the death of Sixtus IV.

Thaddeus, supported unavailingly by Edmund de Courcy, Bishop of Clogher, took refuge in the Cistercian Abbey of Fonte Vivo.

The Anglo-Normans denounced Thaddeus to Pope Innocent VIII as a friend of the Bishop of Clogher and an intruder into the see of Ross. Innocent in a Bull of August 21, 1488, declared Thaddeus a son of iniquity, interdicted and excommunicated. Rather than in any way scandalize the faithful, Thaddeus requested of Innocent an inquiry be instituted, and on the report of that inquiry, Innocent issued three Bulls, dated April 21, 1490.

The first declared Odo by priority Bishop of Ross. Domnal, having resigned in favor of Odo, had died before Odo reached Rome. The second appointed Thaddeus Bishop of Cork and Cloyne of which he was worthy by reason of the honesty of his life and manners, his prudence and the many talents and virtues that adorned his character. The third, in order to forestall any and all further disagreement, decreed the said appointment should be fully valid through the death of Bishop William Roche or for any other reason whatsoever.

Although Bishop Roche resigned freely and without hesitation, Thaddeus MacCarthy, Bishop of Cork and Cloyne, returned to fresh and equally insurmountable difficulties. The property of his episcopal see had been seized by the same Anglo-Normans who had opposed him in the bishopric of Ross. Exonerated by Rome, armed with incontestable papal documents, he went wearily from village to village for two years. In desperation he finally returned to Rome.

Innocent gave him another document dated July 18, 1492, which sternly enjoined upon Gerald, Earl of Kildare, and other persons the duty of protecting Thaddeus from interference with the property of his diocese and from trampling under foot the rights of the new bishop.

Thaddeus was to be spared further frustration.

He set out from Rome in that age of pomp and splendor as devoid of all insignia of rank, lay or ecclesiastical, as the most obscure pilgrim. He travelled alone, on foot, in a course habit and hood, wearing the oyster shell emblem that insured safe passage to pilgrims to shrines. A wallet, a leathern water bottle, a pilgrim's staff were his sole possessions. He travelled the Via Romano that led from Italy into the Gauls, passing through Ivrea and on to Hospice XXI — it accommodated twenty-one guests — on the northern outskirts, a hostel maintained by the Canons of St. Ursus of Aosta, his 6th century compatriot. The rector, Father Chabaud, received him charitably, without scrutiny, almost without notice. And Thaddeus retired immediately for the night.

At dawn servants investigating a light in the cell occupied by Thaddeus found him there, peacefully asleep in death. The rector, searching back over the meager details, was deeply disturbed that the poor traveller had not been ministered to in death. The bishop upon being notified came at once. His own night had been made sleepless by a dream, profoundly real and vivid, of a stranger bishop ascending into heaven. The pilgrim's wallet yielded a bishop's ring, a pectoral cross and the papal document testifying to the rights of Thaddeus MacCarthy, Bishop of Cork and Cloyne.

Reverent hands clothed him in episcopal robes with his ring and his pectoral cross in place for all to see. He was carried in procession to the Cathedral of Ivrea to lie in state for the visitation of the people among whom cures were reported. Entombed at first under the altar dedicated to St. Eusebius, his relics were removed in 1742 to the chapel of the Blessed Sacrament. They were moved once more, to their present place of great honor, under the high altar in the Ivrea Cathedral.

The title of Blessed is now official but Ivrea bestowed it from the first. Four centuries after the death of Blessed Thaddeus, another Bishop of Cork who had been many years in Rome, the Dominican Monsignor O'Callahan, petitioned in association with Bishop Richelmy of Ivrea, later Cardinal, for official recognition of the veneration paid for long centuries to Blessed Thaddeus. It was approved by the Congregation of Rites, and confirmed by Pope Leo XIII in 1895.

Tommasini, 433; Curtayne; *Capuchin Annual*, 1948; Porter, 24; Neeson, 149; Stokes, II: 64–66.

VII

The Martyrdom of Ireland

Persecution for the Faith began in Ireland in 1535 when Henry VIII set in motion three centuries of atrocities in the name of religion. Henry, Elizabeth, Cromwell, the Penal Laws all concentrated on woes to the Irish Catholic. Catholic Emancipation did not come until 1829.

Queen Elizabeth decreed "Every Romish priest found in the island is deemed guilty of rebellion. He shall be hanged until half dead, then his head taken off, his bowels drawn out and burned and his head fixed in some public place."

Cromwell landed in Dublin in 1649 with eight regiments of foot soldiers, six regiments of cavalry, several troops of dragoons. Arthur Wood, Oxford historian, describes the seige of Drogheda where English soldiers murdered 3000 men, women and children: "Each of the assailants would take up a child and use it as a buckler of defence to keep himself from being shot or brained." In Cromwell's report to London on "the righteous judgment of God upon the barbarous wretches and the mercy vouchsafed the English, a great thing done, not by power or might but by the spirit of God," he asked that all honest hearts give the glory of it to God alone.

Sons and daughters of the noblest Catholic families were sold as slaves to the tobacco planters of the West Indies. English merchants contracted in 1653 with the government for a consignment of 250 women and 300 men, ages 14 to 45, to be captured in the neighborhood of Cork, Youghal, Kinsale, Waterford and Wexford. Lord Broghill, considering it unnecessary to make such a hunt for a cargo of "mere Irish" supplied the whole number from Cork alone. In a consignment of 1655, all the Irish of Lachagh, County Kildare, were seized. Of them, four were hanged and the rest, including two priests were sent as slaves to Barbadoes.

Irish youth were not intimidated. By the hundreds they slipped away to Irish colleges in the Low Countries, Spain, Portugal and Rome. Non-Catholic Mitchell writes of them "Imagine a priest ordained at Seville or Salamanca, a gentleman of high old name, a man of eloquence and genius who had sustained disputations in the college hall on questions of literature or theology and carried off prizes and crowns — see him on the quays of Brest bargaining with some skipper to work his passage. He throws himself on board, does his full part of the hardest work, neither feeling the cold spray nor the fiercest tempest. And he knows, too, that the end of it all for him may be a row of sugar canes to hoe under the blazing sun of Barbadoes. Yet he pushes eagerly to meet his fate, for he carries in his hands a sacred deposit, hears in his heart a holy message and must tell it or die. See him at last springing ashore and hurrying on to seek his bishop in some cave or under some hedge — but going with caution by reason of the priest-catcher and the bloodhounds.''

Abbot and Brethren of Manisternenay

1579

Conyngham in his *Irish Martyrs* pictures the last days of Manisternenay, County Limerick, whose Cistercian abbot and brethren are named under the year 1579 in Ireland's list of martyrs.

In that year when Elizabeth's soldiery were spreading devastation and ruin all about them, the monks of St. Mary, Nenagh, resolved to remain to the end in the hallowed cloister which had so long been their home. The soldiers found them in the church praying about the altar. It was the vigil of the Assumption.

A lay brother who had been absent returned that evening only to find the monastery in ruins and the church streaming with blood. Throwing himself prostrate before the mutilated statue of Our Lady, he poured forth his lamentations that her monastery was no more and her glorious festival which should then be commencing would pass in sadness and silence. He had scarcely breathed his prayer when he heard the bells of the monastery toll and lifting his head he saw his martyred brethren each taking his accustomed seat. The abbot intoned the solemn vespers, and psalms were sung as usual on their festival days. The enraptured lay brother knew not whether he had ascended to heaven or was still on earth, till the Office being completed, the vision ceased and he once more contemplated around him the mangled and bleeding remains of the religious.

Robert Sherlock and Christopher Eustace

1581

In his *Irish Martyrs of the Penal Laws*, Father Miles Ronan has an interesting account of the journey to the scaffold of Robert Sherlock and Christopher Eustace, two names to be found under the year 1581 in Ireland's list of Martyrs, material he discovered in the State Papers, Public Record Office, London. It was the report of one Thomas Jones, a Protestant minister sent by the English government to induce victims to deny their faith and so win a reprieve. Jones had accompanied three young gentlemen of the Pale, Robert "Scurlock," George Nenterfild, Christopher Eustace and the serving man, John Scurlock, to their place of execution. His version follows.

"Nenterfild and Scurloche wyninge together at ye castle gate began with the Lady Spalter (Psalter, or Rosary) and sayd it verse by verse, one answering the other throughout the streets of Dublin." To the minister's exhortations, Nenterfild would only say "Vade Satana, vade Satana, vade post me Satana." When Jones attempted to persuade the servant Scurlock to conform "Nenterfild and Scurlock espying that sayd both on this wise. Remember God, John Scurlocke, John Scurlocke remember God and praie that you be not deceyved by this tempter." . . . Eustace, at the place of execution, "being likewise moved to aske God forgynesse, he did so, but being moved to aske the Queene forgynesse, he thereby refused to do it. Going up the ladder being moved to praie for the Queenes Majestie, I will sayd he and therwyth he sayd: God amend Hir; God amend Hir, this was all we colde gett of him."

Our Lady of Youghal

1587

Following the Smerwick massacre Sir Walter Raleigh was granted 40,000 acres of land in County Cork. He chose Youghal for his manor house and in 1587 he destroyed the Dominican church and priory there. The Dominicans however, managed to save their precious miraculous ivory Mother and Child and neither paid spies nor organized espionage ever succeeded in gaining possession of it. From the Dominican Father Urban Flannigan comes what is believed to be its authentic history.

The little image, one of the finest known specimens of the ivories made in northern France about 1300, belonged to Archbishop O'Carroll of Cashel who wore it on a chain around his neck in life and asked that it be buried with him. He died at Youghal in 1316.

Towards the end of the next century, evil times and threatened extinction had come upon the Anglo-dominated Youghal Dominican community, described as "Deprived of friars . . . contaminated by bad customs." About 1484, Maurice O'Mochain obtained independence from English jurisdiction and was made the first Irish provincial. About the same time, one of the Youghal brethren while travelling in Ulster had a vision of the Blessed Virgin in his dreams. She told him the little image, if recovered from the tomb of the Archbishop, would cause the poverty of the community to be speedily relieved and added that the corpse, incorrupt when the image was attached to it, would crumble away on removal of the holy keepsake. He hurried back to Youghal and all of these things happened as foretold to him by the Blessed Mother in the vision. Youghal was soon a place of great pilgrimage and "Our Lady of Grace and Miracles" became famous all over Ireland.

Since about 1823 Our Lady of Youghal has been in the Dominican convent in Cork. In 1895 the precious ivory was enshrined on the Rosary altar of the Dominican church there. Time and the touch of many hands have worn and damaged the image, but still, after 600 years, it shows "a quality and sculptural assurance . . . a nobility and simplicity almost unsurpassed."

John Cornelius, Patrick Salmon, John Carey
July 4   1594

Because of his priestly ministry and eventual martyrdom in England, the cause of John Cornelius and the two Irish serving men who had aided him was included with those of the English martyrs and with them, the three Irish martyrs were beatified by Pius XI. Blessed Patrick Salmon and Blessed John Carey were hanged, the young Jesuit, Blessed John Cornelius was hanged, drawn and quartered at Dorchester, July 4, 1594.

John Cornelius was born of Irish parents at Bodmin in 1557. He began his studies at Oxford, but because of the "new learning" there, he departed overseas, first to the English college at Reims in France and later to Rome where he was ordained for the English mission. He labored out of Lanherne for about ten years and "both then and earlier he had been known as a man of unusual zeal and recollection."

Taken to London April 25, 1594, John Cornelius was tried before the Privy Council and ordered, unavailingly, to be racked to extort betrayal of those who had shielded or assisted him. Back in Dorset, on July 2, he was found guilty of treason, Patrick Salmon and John Carey of felony and all were offered reprieve if they would apostatize. They were executed two days later. At the gallows John Cornelius kissed the feet of his compatriot martyrs who preceded him to the scaffold. He declared he had been admitted into the Society of Jesus and would have made his novitiate in Flanders but for his arrest.

Butler-Attwater, III: 18; *New Catholic Encyclopedia.*

John Burke
                                                                                    1606

Memory of John Burke of Brittas lives on today at Belem, outside Lisbon,

Portugal, in Bom Successo, the oldest Irish convent in the world, a foundation that owes its origin to a unique chain of events that began with the martyrdom of Sir John in 1606.

John Burke's "misdemeanors," activities for the Catholic faith in Limerick, had earlier won him a prison term in Dublin Castle, an interim he devoted to prayer, especially the rosary. All through the Penal years, the rosary was "treasonable furniture" but regardless, upon Burke's release, at his solicitation the Dominican Father Hallaghan established a branch of the Rosary Confraternity in Brittas. On the fateful great first "Rosary Sunday" Brittas Castle was raided. The congregation dispersed and the chaplain escaped to safety but John Burke was captured and hanged.

As a last request, he asked his wife to dedicate their unborn child to St. Dominic. The child was a girl, Eleanor, and there were no convents of Dominican nuns in Ireland to receive her. The beginning of Elizabeth's reign saw 1000 Dominicans in Ireland, the end just four. Eleanor became a Dominican Tertiary, however, and with a cousin, lived a holy, conventual life in Brittas Castle. There a young Tralee Friar, Domhnall O'Daly, in religion Father Dominic of the Rosary, found them with happy outcome.

In 1629, while travelling on the business of his Order in Belgium, Spain and Portugal, then all a part of the Spanish Empire, Father O'Daly prevailed upon Phillip IV to establish a house for Irish Dominicans at Lisbon, Corpo Santo, of which Father O'Daly was made the first prior. His little church became the center for a branch of the Confraternity of the Rosary, the first Sunday of the month became "Confraternity Sunday" and all classes, beginning with Margaret of Mantua, wife of the Viceroy, her Court and Portuguese aristocracy, marched in the Rosary processions.

Among the sodalists was the widowed Countess Atalaya who came to Father O'Daly for counselling as to a worthy disposition of her large fortune. He told her of the crying need for a convent in which Irish girls might receive the habit of St. Dominic, a suggestion she readily accepted. One last requisite must be met, the royal charter from Phillip IV. The Annals of Bom Successo record the unusual condition the King attached to his grant, "200 Irish soldiers for his Spanish army." Back went Father O'Daly to his native Tralee. Phillip IV was so taken with the gallant Kerry brigade, he asked for, and got, a second 200 Irish boys.

And so, step by step to 1645, John Burke's dying request, a holy daughter, a Dominican friar, a Portuguese Countess, 400 of Ireland's "Wild Geese," make up the story of the origin of Our Lady of Good Success, the formal title of Bom Successo. Among the first postulants were John Burke's daughter Eleanor and her cousin Ursula from Brittas Castle and Lisbon's more than 300 years old Irish Dominican convent is still in operation. As of 1971, Bom

Successo had 500 pupils, juniors, seniors, kindergarden and an international school, students of the latter being mostly Americans.

O'Kelly, 220; Concannon, II: 118, 136; Sr. M. Cecelea, Archivist; Bom Successo.

Patrick Fleming, O.S.F.
November 7   1599–1631

Franciscan Christopher Fleming, Patrick in religion, was one of the many Irish boys who slipped out of persecuted Ireland to study in the more than 20 colleges under Franciscan, Dominican, Jesuit auspices for the Irish on the Continent. He came at the age of 14 to his uncle, Father Christopher Cusach, founder and rector of St. Patrick's College at Douai, France. Five years later in 1617, at another Irish College, St. Anthony's in Louvain, he became a Franciscan on March 17, taking the name Patrick. He spent six "most exemplary" years at St. Anthony's. From 1623 to 1626 he was with Father Luke Wadding, founder of St. Isadore's Irish Franciscan College in Rome. Father Wadding's rule was so strict St. Isadore's got the reputation its brethren could not sin: the devil could never, never find them idle. After his ordination in Rome, Patrick Fleming was named professor of Philosophy and Theology at Louvain.

Disaster was everywhere in his native land. The Gaelic language was forbidden and penalized. Laws decreed death to any person in possession of an unsurrendered Irish manuscript. So sweeping was the destruction of Ireland's precious books, the Irish Franciscans undertook to collect and write a history of Ireland "lest should it be neglected at that time it would not again be done even to the end of time." The Franciscan monastery of Donegal had been occupied in 1601 by 500 English soldiers and subsequently reduced to ruins. In the return of the friars during the comparative peace in the time of Charles I, they occupied such shelter as could be found near the ruins. In these makeshift habitations, the lay-brother Michael O'Clery and three principal collaborators compiled in the years 1632–1636 the gigantic work, the *Annals of the Four Masters.*

Father Patrick Fleming was deputed to gather originals, or make transcripts, wherever they could be found in Europe. His search took him to St. Gall, to Bobbio and other monasteries and on to Rome in the years 1623–1626. Back to Ireland went letters on lives and works of Irish saints and a Chronicle of the Irish monastery of St. James of Ratisbon. The richest finds were at Bobbio, important documents on Columban, including the *Life* by Jones. These were printed for the first time in his *Collectanea Sacra,* finished but not published before his death.

Ferdinand II of Austria having granted to Irish Franciscan emissaries their choice of a site for a college for the overflow of aspirants to the order at St. Anthony's and St. Isadore's, Prague was duly chosen. Father Patrick Fleming, as head of a community of six priests, was sent there from Louvain in 1630. In July of 1631 the Irish Franciscan College at Prague was inaugurated by the Cardinal Primate of Bohemia.

That same year, in the advance of the Protestant army of Saxony against Prague, Patrick Fleming and his young deacon, Matthew Hoare, were murdered at Benesabe, Bohemia, by a band of armed Lutheran peasants. The day was November 7. Patrick Fleming was 32 years old. His name, introduced in 1903, is among those whose cause for sanctification is now in progress.

O'Kelly, 146; Tommasini, 16; McCarthy, xi; *Catholic Encyclopedia*, VIII: 167.

John Meagh, S.J.
May 31   1639

John Meagh had fled English persecution of the faith in his native Cork and in far away Naples was debating what to do next. He was troubled about his vocation. One day he picked up a book on the lives of the saints and opened it at random with a prayer the page would help him to decide his future. It opened to Dympna, virgin martyr, which seemed far removed from the problem at hand. But the thought of her martyrdom persisted. Perhaps martyrdom was to be his own fate.

He decided to try for the priesthood in the Society of Jesus and very soon the Superior General had him training for a return to Ireland in the Bohemian Jesuit College in Guttenberg near Prague.

In 1639, when the college was destroyed by Swedish troops, Protestant peasants on May 31 attacked the fleeing Jesuits about a mile from Guttenberg. All of them escaped but one, John Meagh, dead of a bullet wound. His cause for canonization was begun in 1904.

Carty, II: 37; *Catholic Encyclopedia*, VIII: 167.

Honoria Magan and Honoria de Burgo
                                                                            1653

From the age of 14 until she was old and decrepit, Honoria de Burgo and a little band of Dominican tertiaries lived the religious life in a small house built for her near the Dominican Friary of Burrishoole in County Mayo. They continued undetected during the reigns of Elizabeth, James I and Charles I.

But in the Cromwellian regime, Honoria Magan, Honoria de Burgo and an attendant fled in vain from fanatical Puritan soldiers. They were beaten, stripped of their clothing and left to perish in freezing February weather. The strong young sister attendant carried Honoria de Burgo back to their convent, laid her down in front of the statue of the Blessed Virgin and then returned to Honoria Magan whom she found frozen to death in a hollow tree. On her return to the convent with Honoria Magan's body, she found Honoria de Burgo kneeling upright before the Blessed Mother, "placidly asleep in the Lord."

Concannon, II: 112.

Oliver Plunket
July 11   1625–1681

Plunket generations had intermarried with the wealthiest families of the Pale, had enjoyed continuing prosperity and high offices of state, little touched by the persecutions and confiscations of Henry VIII and Elizabeth that were the tragic lot of the native Irish nobility.

Blessed Oliver, son of Thomasina Dillon and Sean Plunket, was closely related to the Earl of Roscommon, who had converted to the Church of England, and to Christopher, Earl of Fingal, two of the greatest of Anglo-Irish noblemen; to Nicholas Plunket, prominent barrister and to the Cistercian Abbot Patrick Plunket, later bishop of Dublin, who educated him until his 16th year.

At this time, largely through the instrumentality of Father Luke Wadding, who was working tirelessly in Rome for the Irish cause, Pope Urban VIII sent as his special representative to Ireland Father Peter Scarampi. On his return to Rome Father Scarampi took with him five Irish boys destined for the priesthood, among them John Brennan, later a bishop in Ireland, and Oliver Plunket, the future primate.

Oliver Plunket and John Brennan, ordained to the priesthood in Rome, progressed from honor to honor there. They had no plans for return home in the face of the appalling news from Ireland month after month. It was high treason for a priest to be found in the land and treason for anyone to harbor a priest. Through Father Scarampi, Blessed Oliver was appointed, and continued, professor of theology in the College de Propaganda Fide for 12 years.

In March of 1669 the Irish Primate Edmund O'Reilly, who had been able to spend only two of the twelve years of his episcopate in Ireland, died in exile. In July of that year, Pope Clement IX nominated Oliver Plunket Archbishop of Armagh. He asked one last privilege, to receive consecration in Rome, but for reasons of prudence and secrecy, Belgium was decided upon as less subject to scrutiny. A memorable farewell was that of a holy Polish priest who said to Oliver "My Lord, you are now going to shed your blood for the Catholic Faith."

Blessed Oliver was consecrated in the private chapel of the Bishop of Ghent, in the greatest secrecy, November 3, 1669. Passing safely through England where he performed ordinations and consecrations, he entered Ireland all unobserved, he thought, in the guise of an army Captain Brown. All of the Plunkets were gathered at the house of Sir Nicholas to welcome him — among them young Michael Plunket who aspired to the priesthood; Bishop Patrick who had tutored Oliver; and a servant, James McKenna.

The reunion was cut short by a delivery boy who brought gossip from the royal castle. The archbishop's arrival was expected and plans were afoot to apprehend him. Bishop Patrick in all haste appealed to the Protestant Earl of Roscommon who interceded and went bail for the new primate. But he warned them a priest who had lately come from Rome must needs walk warily. When Blessed Oliver set out for Armagh he was accompanied by young Michael, whom he would train for the priesthood, and James McKenna, whose devotion would go with him to the scaffold.

He soon learned how very warily indeed a priest must walk. Now "on the run" himself, he welcomed with a new appreciation the protection of the rapparee Redmond O'Hanlon, whose bandit ways he had once denounced — "the hero of the North," gentle of birth and education and with a reward from the English Government of 200 pounds on his head. He was an outlaw just as the clergy were outlaws on lands that might still be theirs had their fathers renounced the Faith. Oliver Plunket and John Brennan, both of them now in health broken by hardships and the direst of poverty, were often companions afoul of the law. On one occasion they shared week-long concealment cramped into a cheerless unheated loft. The primate's letters make mention of the bishop's rheumatism and his own unceasing toothache. The maximum yearly income the primate ever received was 62 pounds.

Blessed Oliver's whole devotion centered in his church and clergy, in trying to carry on in the chaos everywhere. The Protestant gentry and officials, recognizing his complete non-participation in politics, would have been glad to close their eyes to his presence in Ireland. On the other hand their very cordiality gave rise to suspicion within the native fold and on one occasion Rome wrote to the primate's friend Bishop John Brennan for an unbiased appraisal of affairs.

The great Popish Plot of Titus Oates that originated in England was extended to include Ireland, and the primate became the logical choice on whom to fasten the guilt. It was reported back to England that the most ultra Protestant would deny such a charge but the order went out, regardless, to arrest the Archbishop. Pardon was offered to any criminal, murderer, tory or traitor, who would supply the necessary evidence against Blessed Oliver. And witnesses for the Crown appeared from all sides, ready to swear or not swear whatever was required. Redmon O'Hanlon's type preferred 200 pounds on his head or a place of his own, perhaps, on the scaffold. An all-Protestant jury declared the primate innocent and the Crown witnesses gross perjurers. London then directed the primate be brought to England where no such squeamishness of jurors would interfere with ''justice''.

On June 8, 1681, Oliver Plunket was arraigned and convicted. He was sentenced to be drawn on a hurdle to Tyburn, to be hanged, cut down while alive, his body quartered and the entrails burned.

Florence MacMoyre, the last hereditary keeper of the Book of Armagh, pawned it for five pounds to pay his way to London to testify against the primate. His anticipated reward failed to materialize, however, and he ended up in Dublin prison, loathed and avoided by all.

For 11 years, James McKenna had ministered to the primate: served his Mass, accompanied him in the arduous visitations, shared his imprisonment in Dublin Castle, waited patiently at the door of Newgate prison for a chance to see the martyr. He slept in the primate's cell his last night on earth and called him from a tranquil sleep to prepare for the execution. On the way to the scaffold Oliver Plunket handed his rosary, his sole earthly possession, to James McKenna, a precious gift still preserved by the McKenna heirs.

Elizabeth Seldon, ''impelled by some irresistable force,'' had obtained from the king permission to bury the martyred primate. She came provided with receptacles for the dismembered body, among them one for the martyr's head which is now enshrined in Drogheda. With the help of a surgeon, John Ridley, all were buried, as the primate had requested, in St. Giles Churchyard near the five Jesuit victims of the Titus Oates Plot.

Father Corker, a fellow prisoner later released; Bishop John Brennan; Monsignor Cybo and Cardinal Norfolk in Rome; Hugh McMahon, a young student in Rome later primate of Armagh; George Crolly of Maynooth, Cardinal Moran, interested themselves in the canonization of Oliver Plunket. On March 17, 1918, the Declaration of Martyrdom was solemnly read in Rome. Benedict XV spoke in the name of the Church, Monsignor Michael O'Reardon in the name of Ireland. Beatification, the last step before canonization, took place May 23, 1920.

Concannon, II; Butler-Attwater, III: 73; McManus, 402.

Irish Confessors and Martyrs

From the first catalogue of Irish Martyrs compiled in Portugal 1588–1599 by Father John Houling S.J., to *Our Martyrs* by Denis Murphy, which appeared posthumously in 1896, many historians have brought out extensive contributions. After many difficulties and many delays, on March 16, 1915, there was at long last published in Rome the decree ratified by the Holy Father which instituted officially a commission for the Introduction of the Beatification of 259 Servants of God. This list covers the centuries from Henry VIII to the death of Queen Anne, 1534–1714.

1572

Edmund O'Donnell, Jesuit, first definitely recorded martyr for the faith in Ireland under Elizabeth; hanged, drawn and quartered, Cork, October 25.

1575

Conor Macuarta and Roger MacConnell, Franciscans at Armagh; flogged to death. Franciscan guardian, Fergal Ward, Armagh; hanged with his own girdle.

1576

Franciscans John Lochan, Donagh O'Rorke, Edmund Fitzsimon; hanged, Downpatrick.

1577

William Walsh, Cistercian Bishop of Meath; after imprisonment, died in exile at Alcala. Thaddeus O'Daly, Franciscan; hanged, drawn and quartered at Limerick. Bystanders reported that his head when severed from his body distinctly spoke the words: "Lord show me Thy ways." John O'Dowd; for refusing to reveal a confession, put to death, his skull compressed with a twisted cord.

1579

Patrick O'Healy, Franciscan Bishop of Mayo who said he could not barter his faith for life or honors; his brother Franciscan Cornelius O'Rorke; tortured and hanged, Killmallock. Cistercian abbot and brethren, Manisternenay, County Limerick; slain.

1580

Lawrence O'Moore, secular priest; tortured and hanged, Smerwick. William Walsh and Oliver Plunkett, laymen; executed with O'Moore. Eugene Cronin, secular priest; executed, Dublin. John Kieran of Tuam, Premonstratensian; hanged. Galasius O'Cullenan, Cistercian abbot of Boyle; hanged, Dublin.

Daniel O'Neilan, Franciscan; fastened around the waist with a rope and with weights tied to his feet was first thrown from one of the town gates at Youghal and then, fastened to a mill wheel was torn to pieces.

1581

Richard French, secular priest; died in prison, Wexford. Nicholas Fitzgerald, Cistercian; hanged, drawn and quartered in Dublin. Mathew Lamport, Wexford layman; hanged for harboring a Jesuit. Robert Meyler, Edward Cheevers, John O'Lahy, Patrick Canavan, all Wexford laymen; hanged for conveying priests to France. Patrick Hayes, ship owner of Wexford; charged with aiding bishops, priests and others, died on release from prison. Maurice Eustace, nobleman and Jesuit novice in Flanders against his father's bitter opposition, returned as a lay apostle in Ireland. Informed on by his servant, he was arrested for "high treason." If he would but accept the reformed religion, the Protestant archbishop of Dublin offered him his daughter in marriage and a large dowry. Unshaken by bribery or persecution he was hanged, drawn and quartered. Daniel Sutton, John Sutton, Robert Sherlock, Robert Fitzgerald, William Wogan, laymen; executed, Dublin, May 26. Walter Aylmer, Thomas Eustace, son Christopher, and brother Walter, laymen; hanged, Dublin.

1582

Aneas Penny, parish priest, Killagh; slain by soldiers while saying Mass. Philip O'Shea, Maurice O'Scanlon and Daniel Hanrahan, Franciscans; slain at Lislactin. Charles MacGoran, Roger O'Donnellan, Peter O'Quillan, Patrick McKenna, James Pillan and Roger O'Hanlon, Franciscans; died in prison, Dublin Castle. Phelim O'Hara, Franciscan lay brother; strangled before the altar. Henry Delahyde, Franciscan lay brother; suffered with O'Hara. Thaddeus O'Meran, Franciscan guardian of Enniscorthy; tortured to death.

1584

Dermot O'Hurly, bishop; tortured and hanged, Dublin. He had studied at Rheims, Louvain and Rome where he was consecrated bishop of Cashel. Intercepted on the way and committed to Dublin Castle, he was tied to a tree in Stephens Green where his clothing, even his body was saturated with oil and alcohol, his legs encased in boots filled with oil and salt. Lighting a fire beneath him, alternately they quenched and lighted the flames, prolonging his torture for four days. All this time he prayed "Jesus, have mercy on me" and steadfastly refused to deny his faith. He was finally removed by his torturers who pulled off his boots stripping the flesh from his bones and so returned him to prison. He was hanged near Stephen's Green, Dublin. Prior and brethren,

Graiguenamanagh, Cistercians; slain. Franciscan John O'Daly; trampled to death by cavalry. John O'Grady, secular priest; executed. Thaddeus Clancy, Ballyrobert, layman; beheaded. Eleanor Birmingham, laywoman, the only recorded woman sufferer for the faith during the times of Henry and Elizabeth; died in Dublin prison.

1585

Maurice Kenraghty, secular priest, taken by Ormond, was chained to one Patrick Grant and imprisoned at Clonmel. A local Catholic, Victor White, bribed the jailor to release him overnight to say Mass and give Communion on Passion Sunday, which the jailor did and informed the authorities who arrested all at Mass. Father Kenraghty escaped but later gave himself up to save White's life. He was hanged as a traitor and his head was impaled in the Clonmel market place. Patrick O'Connor and Malachy O'Kelly, Cistercians; hanged, drawn and quartered at Boyle.

1586

Richard Creagh, bishop of Armagh; died, after 18 years imprisonment, Tower of London. Donagh O'Hurley, Franciscan sacristan, Muckross Convent; tortured to death.

1587

Murtagh O'Brien, bishop of Emly; died in Dublin prison. John Cornelius, Franciscan of Askeaton; died under torture.

1588

Dermot O'Mulrony, guardian, and two brother Franciscans; beheaded at Galbally, County Limerick. John O'Molloy, Cornelius O'Doherty, Geoffrey O'Farrel, Franciscans, hanged, drawn and quartered at Abbeyleix. Thaddeus O'Boyle, guardian, Franciscan Convent, Donegal; killed by English soldiers. Peter Meyler, layman; executed at Galway or Wexford on his way from Spain.

1589

Patrick O'Brady (or Ward), Franciscan prior and six friars; slain in Monastery of Monaghan. Uncertainty of date.

1590

Matthew O'Leyn, Franciscan of Kilcrea Convent, Muskerry; killed by English soldiers. Christopher Roche, Wexford layman; killed by torture, London.

1591

Franciscans Terence Magennis, Manus O'Fury, Loughlan MacKeagh; died in prison. Michael Fitzsimmon, layman of Fingall; put to death.

1593

Edmund MacGauran, bishop of Armagh; slain at Tulsk.

1594

Andrew Stritch, secular priest; died in prison, Dublin.

1596

Bernard Moriarty, secular priest, vicar-general; his thighs broken by soldiers, died in prison, Dublin.

1597

John Stephens, secular priest, County Wicklow; convicted of saying Mass, hanged and quartered. Walter Fernan, priest; torn on rack, Dublin.

1599

George Power, secular priest, vicar-general of Ossory; died in prison Dublin.

1600

John Walsh, vicar-general, Dublin; died in prison at Chester. Nicholas Young, secular priest of Trim; died in Dublin Castle. Thomas MacGrath, layman; beheaded.

1601

Raymond O'Gallagher, bishop of Derry; slain. Daniel Molony, secular priest vicar-general of Killaloe; died under torture, Dublin Castle. John O'Kelly, Connacht priest; died in prison. Donagh O'Cronin, secular priest, cleric; hanged, drawn and quartered, Cork. Brian Murchertagh, secular priest, archdeacon of Clonfert; died in prison, Dublin. Donagh O'Falvey, secular priest; hanged, Cork.

1602

Dominic Collins, Jesuit lay brother; hanged, Cork. As he was led out to execution, his hands tied behind his back, a halter about his neck, he exhorted the faithful "Look up to heaven and, worthy descendants of your ancestors who ever constantly professed it, hold fast to that faith for which I am this day to die." He was not allowed to hang long on the gallows by his executioners who cut open his breast and, taking out his heart, held it up to the view of the people uttering the usual "God save the Queen."

1603

Eugene MacEgan, bishop of Ross; slain. Patrick Brown, convert, alderman of Dublin; died in prison. Dominican communities, 21 members at Coleraine, 32 members at Derry; put to death at unknown date in reign of Elizabeth.

1606

Bernard O'Carolan, secular priest; hanged in Dublin. Cistercians of Assaroe, Donegal, Eugene O'Gallagher, abbot, and Bernard O'Trever, prior; slain by soldiers. John Burke, lord of Brittas, layman; hanged.

1607

John O'Luin (O'Lynn), Dominican; hanged at Derry.

1608

Donagh O'Luin, brother of John O'Luin (1607), Dominican prior at Derry; hanged and quartered there.

1609

Donagh MacCreid, secular priest; hanged, Coleraine.

1610

John Lune (Lyng) of Wexford, secular priest; hanged and quartered, Dublin.

1612

Franciscan Cornelius O'Devany, bishop of Down and Connor and one of those who gathered information on Ireland's martyrs up until his own time; hanged, Dublin. Catholics lined his route to the gallows to beg his blessing even as Protestant clergymen made last efforts to turn him from the faith. He kissed the gallows and turned to exhort the Catholics to constancy whereupon he was thrown off, cut down alive and quartered. Patrick O'Loughran, secular priest; hanged with Bishop O'Devany.

1614

William MacGallen, Dominican; executed at Coleraine.

1615

Louglin O'Laverty, secular priest; hanged, Derry. Brian O'Neil, Art O'Neil,

Rory O'Cane, Godfrey O'Kane and Alexander MacSorley, laymen; hanged with O'Laverty at Derry.

1617

Thomas Fitzgerald, Franciscan commisary and visitator of the Irish province died in Dublin prison. Franciscan John Honan (MacConnan), Connacht; tortured, hanged, drawn and quartered, Dublin.

1618

Patrick O'Deery, secular priest; hanged, Derry.

1620

James Eustace, Cistercian; hanged and quartered.

1622

John O'Cahan, Franciscan, Buttevant convent; died in prison, Limerick.

1628

Edmund Dungan, bishop of Down and Connor; died in Dublin Castle.

1642

Philip Cleray of Raphoe (?) secular priest; slain. Cistercian Malachy Sheil; hanged Newry. Peter O'Higgin, Dominican prior of Naas; hanged Dublin, March 24. Cormac MacEgan, Dominican lay brother; hanged. Raymond Keogh, Dominican of Roscommon priory; hanged (1643?). Stephen Petit, Dominican subprior, Mullingar; shot while hearing confessions on the battlefield. Hilary Conroy, Franciscan of Elphin; hanged Castlecoote. Fulgentius Jordan Augustinian; hanged. Friar Thomas, Carmelite; hanged July 6, Drogheda. Friar Angelus, Carmelite; killed Drogheda.

1643

Edmund Mulligan, Cistercian; slain near Clones by soldiers. Francis O'Mahony, Franciscan guardian at Cork; tortured and hanged, regained consciousness, was again hanged by his girdle. Peter, Carmelite lay brother; hanged Dublin.

1644

Cornelius O'Connor and Eugene O'Daly, Trinitarians returning from France; drowned at sea by Puritans. Hugh McMahon, Ulster noble, layman; executed, Tyburn, November 22.

1645

Patriot archbishop of Tuam, Malachy O'Queely, his priest secretary Tadgh O'Connell, and Augustine O'Higgin, both Augustinians; executed after the battle of Sligo, October 26. Henry White, secular priest, aged 80; hanged, Racconnell, Westmeath. Christopher Dunlevy, Franciscan; died at Newgate, London. Conor McGuire, Baron of Inniskillen, layman; hanged, drawn and quartered, Tyburn, February 20.

1647

Theobald Stapleton, founder of the college for the Irish at Madrid and former rector of the Irish college at Seville, secular priest, chancellor of the church of Cashel; stabbed while giving Communion. Theobald Stapleton (misnamed Edward) and Thomas Morrissey, secular priests, vicars choral; killed in Cashel massacre of 2000 Irish. Richard Barry, Dominican prior; killed in Cashel massacre. John O'Flaverty, Dominican; killed, Coleraine. Nicholas Wogan, Franciscan; hanged Dublin. Richard Butler, Franciscan, and James Saul, lay brother; killed in Cashel massacre. William Hickey, Franciscan of Adair convent; slain. William Boynton, Jesuit; killed in Cashel massacre. Elizabeth Carney and Margaret of Cashel, laywomen; killed in Cashel massacre.

1648

Gerald Fitzgibben, Dominican cleric and David Fox, Dominican lay brother; killed at Killmallock. Donal O'Neaghton, Dominican lay brother, Roscommon priory; killed. James Reilly, Dominican priest and poet; killed near Clonmel.

1649

Thomas Bath, secular priest, Dominic Dillon and Richard Overton, Dominicans, Peter Taafe, Augustinian, John Bath, Jesuit, and brother Thomas; all killed in Drogheda massacre of 3000 men, women and children. Brian Gormley, Franciscan; hanged, Drogheda. Richard Synnot, John Esmond, Paul Synnot, Raymond Stafford and Peter Stafford, Franciscans, and James Cheevers and Joseph Rochford, lay brothers; killed in Wexford massacre in which 2000 Irish perished. Eugene O'Teevan (O'Lemon?), Franciscan; killed in Donegal convent (1650?). Robert Netterville, Jesuit; beaten to death with sticks, Drogheda. Peter Costelloe, Dominican of Staid; killed.

1650

Boetius Egan, Franciscan bishop of Ross; taken by Broghill, his hands and feet cut off, hanged at Carrigadrohid. Heber McMahon, bishop of Clogher;

hanged, Inniskillen, September 17. Francis Ftizgerald, Franciscan; died in prison, Cork. Anthony Hussey, Franciscan; hanged Mullingar. Neilan Loughran, Franciscan; killed, Ulster.

1651

Terence Albert O'Brien, Dominican bishop of Emly; hanged, and head hacked off and impaled on St. John's Gate at Limerick. The pectoral cross which he took off and handed to his mother at the gallows is still preserved in the Dominican priory in Limerick. Roger Normoyle, secular priest, County Clare; hanged. Hugh Carrighy, secular priest; hanged with Normoyle, October 12. Myler McGrath, Father Michael of the Rosary, Dominican; hanged at Clonmel. Laurence and Bernard O'Farrell, Dominicans; killed, Longford. Ambrose O'Cahill, Dominican; killed, Cork. Edmund O'Beirne, Dominican; hanged, Jamestown. James Woulfe, Dominican; hanged after seige of Limerick. Gerard Dillon, Dominican; died in prison, York. James Moran and Donough Niger, Dominican lay brothers; killed. William O'Connor, Dominican; killed, Clonmel. John O'Cullen, Dominican of Athenry convent; hanged, Limerick. Thomas O'Higgin, Dominican; hanged, Clonmel. Denis O'Neilan, Franciscan; hanged, Inchicronin. Tadgh O'Caraghy, Franciscan; hanged, Ennis. Jeremiah MacInerny and Daniel MacClanchy, Franciscan lay brothers; hanged, Quin. Roger MacNamara, Franciscan; killed near Quin. Anthony O'Bruadair, Franciscan cleric; hanged, Turlevachan, County Galway. Donough Serenen, Augustinian; hanged. Raymond O'Malley and Thomas Tully, Augustinians, and Thomas Deir, lay brother; hanged (or 1652). Dominic Fanning, alderman and mayor of Limerick; Daniel O'Higgin, physician; Thomas Stritch, former mayor; Major General Patrick Purcell; Geoffrey Galway, member of Parliament for Limerick in 1634; Geoffrey Barron, nephew of Franciscan Luke Wadding, member of the Supreme Council and agent of the Irish Confederation to France, who, having obtained permission to dress for his execution, triumphantly climbed the steps of the gallows in white taffetie; all laymen; hanged after the seige of Limerick, October 29–30. Donough O'Brien, nobleman, layman; burned alive by Parliamentarians, County Clare. James, Bernard and Daniel O'Brien, brothers, laymen; hanged Nenagh. Louis O'Farral, layman; died in prison, Athlone.

1652

Eugene O'Cahan, high born youth of Thomond, Franciscan guardian of Askeaton, studied in Rome, taught philosophy in Naples, returned to Ireland in 1641; taken prisoner and beaten, hanged in County Cork. Brian Fitzpatrick, secular priest of Ossory; suffered for the faith. Phillip Flatisbury, Franciscan;

hanged, New Ross. Francis O'Sullivan, Franciscan provincial; shot near Derrynane. Anthony O'Feral, Franciscan; killed, County Roscommon. John Ferall, Franciscan; killed, County Roscommon. Walter Walsh, Franciscan; died in prison, Dublin. Donough O'Kennedy, Augustinian; hanged. Tadhg O'Connor, Sligo layman; hanged, Boyle. John O'Connor, Kerry layman; hanged, Tralee. Bernard MacBriody, layman; hanged. Edmund Butler, layman, son of Lord Mount-Garret; hanged, Dublin. Brigid D'Arcy, wife of Florence Fitzpatrick, laywoman; burned at the stake.

1653

Daniel Delaney, secular priest, Arklow; tied to a horse's tail, dragged to Gorey, hanged. Daniel O'Brien, secular priest, dean of Ferns; suffered with Delaney. Luke Bergin, Cistercian of Baltinglass; hanged with O'Brien and Delaney. David Roche, Dominican of Glenworth; sold as a slave to West Indies plantations in St. Kitts, died in captivity. Brian O'Kelly, Dominican lay brother; hanged Galway. Tadhg Moriarty, Dominican prior of Tralee; hanged, Killarney. Hugh MacGoill, Dominican; executed, Waterford. John Kearney, Franciscan; hanged, Clonmel. Theobald de Burgo, third viscount Mayo, layman; shot, Galway. Sir Phelim O'Neill, layman; hanged, drawn and quartered, Dublin. Honoria Magan and Honoria de Burgo, Dominican tertiaries; died of hardships while in flight from Puritan soldiers.

1654

William Tirry; Augustinian; hanged, Clonmel, May 12.

1655

William Lynch, Dominican of Straid; hanged (before 1655).

1656

Fiacre Tobin, Capuchin; died in captivity, Kinsale.

1659

Hugh MacKeon, Franciscan; died on release from jail (after 1659).

1661

Brian MacGiolla Choinne, Franciscan; died in captivity, Galway.

1669

Raymond O'Moore, Dominican; died in prison, Dublin.

1680

Peter Talbot, archbishop of Dublin; died in prison.

1681

(Blessed Oliver Plunket, in separate listing.)

1686

Felix O'Connor, Dominican; died in jail, Sligo, about 1686.

1703

John Keating, Dominican; died in prison, Dublin.

1704

Clement MacColgan, Dominican; died in Derry jail.

1707

Daniel MacDonnell, Dominican; died in Galway jail.

1708

Felix MacDonnell, Dominican; died in prison, Dublin.

1710

John Baptist Dowdall, Capuchin; died in prison, London.

1711

Father O'Hegarty (baptismal name unknown) secular priest; killed according to tradition by heretics near Buncrana.

1713

Dominic Egan, Dominican; died in prison.

Denis Murphy; *Catholic Encyclopedia*; *New Catholic Encyclopedia*; McManus; Brennen, p. 16.

VIII

Modern Irish Missionaries

Although technically, prohibition of the Catholic religion in Ireland ended in 1829, troubles were far from over for the Catholic Irish. The heritage of misery and poverty of the penal laws carried forward in long decades of unalleviated famine, landlordism, eviction to the roadside to starve or die in the workhouse. This was the era of wholesale emigration to Australia, to Canada, to the United States, to South America. But the faith survived and the Mass survived. Ireland's devotion to the Mass has been called one of the miracles of history.

Not all of the English were partisans of governmental oppression in Ireland. One of them wrote in the centuries past: "Such horrible spectacles there are to beholde, as the burning of villages, the ruins of the churches, yes, the view of the bones and the skulls of the dead, who partlie by murder, partlie by famyn, have died in the fields as in troth hardlie any Christian with drie eies could beholde."

In 1879, the Blessed Mother appeared at a little church in the most desolated county of Ireland, at Knock, in County Mayo. From time immemorial the Irish people had designated the Blessed Virgin the Queen of Ireland and in her apparition at Knock she wore a large and brilliant crown. With her were St. Joseph, St. John in bishop's robes and miter, an altar, a cross and a Lamb. The Blessed Mother spoke no word, no rebuke as in other apparitions. Her attitude throughout was one of prayer with upraised hands and eyes lifted to heaven. The Knock message has been interpreted as one of compassion and of consolation to an oppressed people and of inspiration to continued courage and prayer. It has also been interpreted as a mission to increase still further Ireland's devotion to the Holy Sacrifice of the Mass.

But if Catholic Ireland was poor in all else — long since dispossessed of all its endowments, colleges, hospitals, monasteries, churches — it emerged rich in the faith. Seminaries and convents reappeared to fan out all over Ireland and they were soon founding and staffing institutions all over the world placing Ireland, along with Holland, in the lead in sending missionaries to other lands — including America where today thousands of Irish-born priests and other religious enrich the work of the Catholic church. Inclusion of references to a few of the many great Irish modern day religious may serve to illustrate the vast contribution they have made to religion and education.

Honora (Nano) Nagle

1718–1784

The Penal Laws, so tragic for Irish ''Papists,'' were in force all of Nano Nagle's lifetime, 1718–1784. Nano Nagle's apostolate was dedicated to the alleviation of the man-made woes of the Irish poor, woes which in their remote beginning went back to the Anglo-Norman invasions in the time of Henry II. Nagle history projects a colorful saga of the evolution of Angevin adventurers who, as the saying goes, ''became more Irish than the Irish themselves.'' The brimming energies of the first Nagle (de Angulo then) won for him large grants of land out of which ill-gotten goods he hastened to provide for his soul's salvation by founding at Navan a priory for Augustinian Canons. As time went on the de Angulos made preference for the Irish way of things. They forgot their Norman French, adopting the Irish language and ways. In the time following Henry VIII the Nagle family, true to the ''papist'' faith and, accordingly, divested of their vast estates, managed somehow, perhaps with the connivance of friendly Protestants, to regain considerable property, proof of which are the still standing ivy-clad ruins of the castle of Nano Nagle's grandfather, David Nagle, at Monanimy. One of the greatest single influences in Nano Nagle's life was her father's brother, her doughty Uncle Joseph, whom she described as ''the most disliked by the Protestants of any Catholic in the kingdom.''

No Nagle was ever more doughty or more brimming with energy than the holy, heroic Nano. Even in her younger days, her mother worried about her high spirited, adventurous Nano. But Garret Nagle said fondly their little Nano would one day be a saint.

Nano was sent to France for her education. Later joined by her sister Ann, she spent a total of almost ten happy years in Paris. Nano and Ann had close ties with many of the prominent Irish émigrés and their descendants. Recruitment for the famous Irish regiments of France brought tidings from Ireland. And especially there was the Irish college in the rue des Carmes with its stir of Irish priests and seminarians coming and going and their harrowing details of the state of the church under the penal laws. From her portrait in the *New Catholic Encyclopedia* we know that Nano was a beautiful girl and her own writings tell us she loved the glamor and gaiety of Paris. But even there came reminders of Ireland. On her way home from a ball in the small hours of the morning, Nano saw a group of poorly dressed people waiting for a church to open for early Mass before they went to work, a right denied Catholics in her native land.

When Garret Nagle died in 1746, Nano and Ann returned to Ireland to live in Dublin with their widowed mother. Nano often told her family of religious that her own vocation to a religious life came about because of a seemingly trifling incident — the discovery that Ann had disposed of a piece of silk brought from Paris for alms for the poor. Ann died shortly afterward. This memory of Ann, more than anything else, determined Nano to devote her life to the poor.

But how even to begin. All about her were poverty and misery. The outlook was so bleak, the cause seemingly so hopeless, in despair Nano decided to return to Paris and become a nun in France. But France brought her no peace of soul. Once more she came back to Ireland. This time she would persevere no matter what the difficulties. In the meantime her mother had died and the family home in Dublin was gone. When her married brother Joseph and his wife asked Nano to make her home with them in Cork she accepted gladly. Hardly two miles away at Dundanion lived her Uncle Joseph whose support she knew she would need. He never failed her.

From the first, Nano was much given to prayer in the back lane chapel and in good works for the poor and the sick. She began her schools in 1755, or perhaps in 1754, in a mud cabin of two earthen floored rooms with 30 girls she had collected with the help of one of the Nagle housemaids, all in the greatest secrecy, even from her family. Then one day her brother Joseph came home with the laughable story about the poor man who had approached him to secure admission to Nano's school for his child. Joseph, although later reconciled, became very angry and reproachful that Nano should expose, not only herself, but all of them to the danger of retribution from the law.

Other Irish girls, some of them educated abroad like herself, came to help in Nano's schools. By 1769, seven of them ''had been in existence for some years,'' five for girls, two for boys. They were taught spelling, reading of the catechism or some other religious book, a little arithmetic and finally, writing. For the girls there were sewing and mending and other domestic skills. Twice a year Nano prepared a group for confession and Holy Communion in each of her seven schools, a privilege she reserved to herself. Her schools, she said, would never bring her to heaven, she found such delight and pleasure in them. After school hours she visited the poor, the sick and the dying. She is pictured going about in poor unfashionable dress, a lantern in one hand and a stick in the other, nothing so proper as a cane. Her annalist said there was not a garret in Cork that she did not know and did not visit. She exhausted her family inheritance; the generous allotment from her Uncle Joseph's estate went for ground and the building she erected and gave to the Ursulines on September 18, 1771, in a deed of agreement signed by Mother Margaret Kelly of the Ursuline Community and by Nano Nagle. Nano Nagle was acknowledged as foundress of the Ursuline Convent in Cork and entitled to certain spiritual favors. It was not a legal instrument — "Whereas 'tis yet doubtful in what form is most expedient to guard against penal laws . . . " In addition to all this, and in spite of ulcerated knees, almost as long as she lived, Nano Nagle "quested." In other words, she went about begging in order to keep her work going.

Nano Nagle never joined the Ursulines. The rule of enclosure and ministry to others as well as to the very poor were not for her. She remained in her little next-door convent in Cove Lane and with three others in June, 1776, received the religious habit, the beginning of the Presentation Order. Nano intended its members to be devoted exclusively to the very poor and especially to be free to seek them out and care for them in their homes. Twenty years after her death formal approbation of the Sisters of the Presentation of the Blessed Virgin Mary came from Rome — but with the addition of solemn vows and enclosure.

Nano Nagle died April 26, 1784, at the age of 65. Under the penal laws, a license from the Protestant bishop was required for a Catholic burial ceremony. The permission was not sought. A door was cut in an angle of the wall to give access to the Ursuline cemetery plot. Very quietly Nano Nagle was laid to rest in a tomb beside the boundary wall between the two convents, now in Presentation possession since 1827.

Today Nano Nagle's Presentation Sisters are found all over Ireland, in England, Newfoundland, Australia and New Zealand, India, Pakistan, California, New York, North and South Dakota, Iowa and the Philippines.

Enclosure did not preclude care for the poor. In 1847, when famine was raging and the English government assistance was so dilatory, a nun in the Youghal Presentation Convent, determined to find some way to alleviate the awful misery of the poor, discovered it in a piece of Italian lace in the convent at the time. She picked it out stitch by stitch and to her great delight was able to remake it perfectly. Gathering in young girls to teach them the process, she soon had a school of Irish Point Lace going that was not only the beginning of a new employment but of an industry of high perfection. It turned out award-winning ecclesiastical Irish Point. It made lace for queens. The magnificent court train commissioned for Queen Mary of England employed 60 workers for six months in fashioning nearly twelve miles of gossamer fine linen thread into the long yardage of fuchsias and roses. The train is four yards long and two yards wide at the bottom. Worked into one corner are the name and the date, "Youghal 1911."

Walsh, *Nano Nagle and the Presentation Sisters*.

Catherine McAuley

1781–1841

The foundress of the Order of Irish Sisters of Mercy with its more than 1500 convents throughout the world was Catherine McAuley. Gracious of manner with an easy gaiety and, above all, a high seriousness and an impelling motivation to care for and instruct needy girls and women, she had reached middle age when the opportunity for her life's work presented itself. In the beginning she had no special plan, no idea of a formal institution and, very definitely, no intention of having anything at all to do with nuns.

Catherine was born in 1781 in Stormanstown House in County Dublin, one of three children of Catholic parents, James and Elinor Conway McAuley, both of whom were well educated though records do not tell how or where. At their marriage Elinor was 22, James 55, a builder and woodworker who had built up a considerable fortune. He knew and never forgot the tragedies of the Catholic poor. Catherine, not yet two when her father died, could not have remembered his charity to the poor or his gathering in the Catholic children to instruct them in the faith, qualities that nevertheless reappeared in her own character. Pleasure and fashion were more to the talented, extravagant Elinor's taste. She gave up Stormanstown to live in Dublin and although never of her husband's staunch faith, she reared her children Catholic.

When Catherine was 17, her mother died. Her sister Mary and her brother James found a home with Protestant relatives, the Armstrongs, and Catherine went to live with her mother's brother, Owen Conway. That thoroughly Catholic home-life was to end in less than a year in sudden financial ruin to the point of actual want for the Conways. Brief though that interim was it gave her an acquaintance with Father Andrew Lube of Liffey Street, a lasting appreciation of her Catholic religion and a first-hand knowledge of what it meant to be poor.

The Armstrongs offered Catherine a home and although generous and warmhearted in every other way, Mr. Armstrong was a rigid Protestant and he expected all under his roof to share his religious views. Her sister and brother conformed to Protestantism and although it pained Catherine never to yield ground in the home that sheltered her for four years, she never faltered in her convictions, never attended a Protestant service. In this time of ridicule and scorn of her Catholic faith, Catherine sought out the counselling of the Jesuit

Father Thomas Betagh. He instructed her so carefully and so ably cleared up all her questions, she was to live out more than 20 years of bitter Protestant influence unshaken by the taunt of Catholicism, and to be otherwise held in the deepest affection by those with whom she disagreed.

Frequent visitors to the Armstrong home were a childless couple, Mr. and Mrs. Callaghan who took a great fancy to Catherine. Many years in India had impaired his wife's health and Mr. Callaghan suggested to Catherine that she come to live with them as a companion to her, an opportunity to provide for herself which Catherine gratefully accepted. Soon after, she went to the country with them to Coolock House with its own grounds of 22 acres in County Dublin. The bitter religious discussions continued ("imagine the insolence of Catholics pressing for religious emancipation") but provided she made no show of "popery" in their home, no display of a crucifix or other religious article in her room, the Callaghans suffered Catherine to go her way and to attend Mass in the village when she could. She found an outlet in the Catholic servants in the household and in the children in Coolock village whom she delighted in instructing.

Little by little the pendulum swung the other way. Catherine had the great happiness of bringing her sister Mary back into the Catholic church and of seeing Mary's five children choose the Catholic religion. Mrs. Callaghan, more impressed by Catherine's silent example than by any words, died a Catholic. Mr. Callaghan, who lived three years longer, was received into the church the night before he died. When his will was read, Catherine found herself sole mistress of Coolock House and a fortune of £ 25,000. That was in 1822.

Suitors had never been lacking to Catherine nor were they now. For her part she was free to devote all of her energies to the plight of the poor and the needy, to teach needlework, knitting and homecrafts in the Dublin Poor School and to open a shop in which to dispose of the pupils' work to her wealthy friends. She sold Coolock House and such furnishings not needed in her large lay social work building in the planning for the ample Dublin site she purchased on Baggot Street: large airy school rooms, dormitories to provide a home for girls and women, an oratory and some small bedrooms for herself and other resident workers. Always eminently efficient in all she undertook, Catherine studied teaching methods in the Protestant school system in Ireland and travelled to France to further observe and learn from the schools in Paris. Finally on the 24th day of September, 1827, Mary Ann Doyle came to live in the Baggot Street House, school commenced on that day and some women were given a home there. It was the Feast of Our Lady of Mercy.

Catherine continued in the belief that only a lay organization, unenclosed and unhampered, could reach out to urchins in back lanes and alleys, to convicts in penetentiaries, to outcasts in houses of correction. At the same time she and her little community were living an austere life of prayer after the manner of a house of strict observance. She provided a chapel and obtained a chaplain for daily Mass. She chose a simple uniform mode of dress and, not surprisingly, the House she had built looked for all the world like a convent.

Inevitably, Catherine's pattern of social welfare led to a new religious Congregation. Already a tried and seasoned ''Superior'' though she was, she entered upon a novitiate into the religious life as the humblest of postulants in Nano Nagle's Dublin Presentation Convent. Choosing not to rank herself and her two companions with patrons so exalted as Teresa, Clare and Angela, Catherine asked leave to decline the names so proposed for them and to be permitted to retain their own baptismal names with the addition of the name of Mary. Catherine McAuley's Order of Sisters of Mercy received formal sanction from Rome in 1835.

With plans laid for many others before her death in 1841, Catherine McAuley had founded ten houses in Ireland and one abroad in the Bermondsey district in London, over which she placed Mother Clare Moore from her Cork foundation. A 1955 survey of her Sisters of Mercy lists 198 convents in Ireland; in England, Wales and Islands, 108; Scotland, 7; South Africa, 5; New Zealand, 46; Australia, 252; South America, 12; Central America and West Indies, 6; Newfoundland, 14; United States of America, 861.

Mother Mary Francis Warde of the Carlow Sisters of Mercy came to Pittsburgh with seven Sisters, one of them a postulant, in 1843. Between that year and her death in 1883, Mother Warde opened 23 American foundations. In 1846, at the invitation of Chicago's first Bishop, Irish born William Quarter, the Mercy postulant, now Mother Mary Agnes O'Brien, opened the first permanent religious house in Illinois.

Catherine McAuley's nuns made up 20 of Florence Nightingale's nursing force of 38 in the Crimean war in 1854. On the way out, Mother Clare Moore and four Sisters from the Bermondsey Convent met Miss Nightingale in Paris in October. Fifteen Sisters from Dublin, Cork, Charleville and Kinsale under Mother Francis Bridgman of Kinsale joined them at the front in December. Two of the Sisters were victims of cholera. Sisters of Mercy archives preserve a letter of farewell from Florence Nightingale written to Mother Clare Moore then returned to England broken in health after the war had ended but leaving behind her the other Sisters until the troops could be brought home. Florence Nightingale, justly acclaimed the world over, concludes her letter to Mother Clare Moore ''You were far above me in fitness for the general superintendency in worldly talent of administration, and far more in the spiritual qualities which God values in a Superior; my being placed over you was my misfortune, not my fault. What you have done for the work no one can every say. I do not presume to give you any other tribute but my tears. But I should be glad that the Bishop of Southwark should know, and Dr. Manning, that you were valued here as you deserve, and that the gratitude of the army is yours.''

Belief in Catherine McAuley's sanctity began long before her death and after it her Sisters treasured with the greatest reverence her books, her letters, her clothes, her chair. Many of them sought her intercession with God — and smiled at what they believed to be the Reverend Mother's plan, to obtain the favor but in such a way no credit would seem to go to *her* prayer. When it was first discussed during the lifetime of her contemporaries, among friends of the Order to send an appeal to Rome to have their Foundress declared Venerable, several were of the opinion she would use her power in heaven to prevent it. Beginning in 1953, the cause for Sanctification of Catherine McAuley is now in progress.

Savage, *Catherine McAuley*.

Mary Aikenhead

1787–1858

All her life Mary Aikenhead, foundress of the Irish Sisters of Charity, would be admonished "It's never been done before" and her answer was always "That's no reason why it shouldn't be done now." Her motto for herself and for her Congregation was *Caritas Christi urget nos* — the love of Christ draws us onward.

Mary's father, David Aikenhead, was a Cork doctor of staunch Scottish Protestant descent, a man sympathetic to many of Ireland's grave problems but not to the Catholic faith. At the time of his marriage to a "dangerous papist," gentle Mary Stackpole, it was clearly understood that any children born to that union were to be brought up Protestant. However, when the first of three daughters, Mary, Ann and Margaret, was still a baby, Mrs. Aikenhead persuaded the doctor their too frail child needed good country air and so it happened that Mary was given into the care of the papist O'Rorkes just outside Cork. Mary lived in their home for six years, going to Mass with them, saying the rosary at night, one of the family except for her nicer clothing and the handsome couple who came in a smart carriage to see her or take her home for a visit.

On her return to Cork six year old Mary was placed in a school suitable for a life in society. The doctor decided it was time his daughter accompanied him to church. For a while she forgot the Catholic chapel and the rosary. To her grandmother Stackpole's offer of a rosary for her doll house she replied "No thank you, Grandmamma. All my dolls go the church except the kitchen maid and it's much too good for her."

But questions persisted, questions frowned upon by her father. And there were visits to her mother's Catholic family, visits that were happy times and when Mary was about twelve she secretly became a Catholic herself. It was the beginning of daily attendance at Mass. With the aid of a friendly housemaid and by slipping out quietly and hurrying home she could be back in time for the family breakfast. Her father, unwavering to the last, became critically ill in 1801 when Mary was 14. His minister duly attended him but still he was not at peace. He asked for a priest and became a convert to Catholicism on his deathbed.

Affluent Protestant Cork offered balls and beaus, all the gaieties of a young girl's dreams. But increasingly, Dr. Aikenhead's daughter devoted her time and her energies to the Catholic poor. Years later it was to be said of her, "Didn't we all know her as an angel of charity long before they made her a nun up in Dublin?"

Mary had corresponded with Bishop Murray of Dublin concerning his plans for a future community of Irish Sisters of Charity and concerning her own desire to join such a congregation. In 1812, when word came to report to him in Dublin, she made the trip in high expectations of meeting the other aspirants and especially the Reverend Mother. And then, the news of unbearable proportions — there were no others, no Reverend Mother, only herself.

The novitiate the Bishop chose for Mary Aikenhead and a companion, Alicia Walsh, was the Institute of the Blessed Virgin Mary in York, an unenclosed house whose members went out to visit the poor. Back in Dublin September 1, 1815, Sister Mary Augustine (Mary) and Sister Mary Catherine (Alicia) pronounced their vows to Bishop Murray. As secular ladies in secular dress "Mrs. Aikenhead" and "Mrs. Walsh" quietly inaugurated the Irish Sisters of Charity, a non-cloistered Order dedicated to charitable works of all kinds, the teaching of religion, industrial schools, caring for orphans, visiting and caring for the sick and the poor in their homes, in hospitals, in prisons.

In cholera-ravaged Dublin and Cork, heroic Sisters of Charity came daily "like ministering angels" their very presence a solace to the terror-stricken sick and dying. Their appalling plight convinced Mother Aikenhead that her dream of 18 years, a hospital for the Catholic poor, should now become a reality. Her first step was a fervent appeal to the Bank of Divine Providence. Then came a novice with a dowry of £ 3000 and an offer of medical services from that novice's physician brother, Dr. O'Ferrall. Forthwith, a mansion, providentially just then for sale on Stephen's Green, Dublin, was purchased and a blissfully confident Mary Aikenhead took up residence there. Although still without any hospital equipment or any visible source of income, in January of 1934 St. Vincent's Hospital was started on its distinguished career.

To Mary Aikenhead the suffering poor were God's own nobility and deserving of every care. One of them, a young widow dying of cancer, was distraught at the thought of leaving her three children. She could go in blessed peace with the promise the Sisters would take care of her orphans. Irish Sisters of Charity, pioneers of the active life among religious in Australia, had as their first post the convict settlement and prison ten miles from Sydney, helping and teaching those most destitute of souls how to live and how to die. At Mother Aikenhead's own death, she was borne to her last resting place by Dublin working men. The spokesman for the group who came to ask so great an honor was the now grown, once very frightened little boy she had held close in her arms when the doctor's scalpel pierced his badly infected leg.

For the last 27 years of her life Mary Aikenhead directed her Congregation from a wheel chair and finally from her bed, prostrate with spinal trouble. She was never to visit some of her institutions in person, even in Ireland. But amazingly, she managed to be familiar with even the smallest details of every project. Few of her convents but immediately branched out into houses or schools for every kind of care and uplift. Her many foundations dot Ireland. At least nine are enumerated for England, some 16 in Australia. Three Sisters of Charity in 1948 carried her work to Rhodesia in Africa. Others have labored in the United States since 1953. In 1965, 47 members staffed a convalescent home, four elementary schools and a secondary school of 41,000 students in the Los Angeles archdiocese. Mother Aikenhead said her Order would flourish after her death.

Benedict XV in 1921 signed the Decree for the introduction of the Cause for the Beatification of Mary Aikenhead. In 1958 the Irish Government issued a commemorative stamp in her honor, the first Irish woman to receive such recognition.

Butler, *A Candle was Lit.*

Dom Columba Marmion

1858–1923

The Benedictine abbot, Dom Columba, was Joseph Columba Marmion, the youngest of nine children of a prominent Dublin merchant and the daughter of the French Consul in Dublin. He studied at Belvedere College in Dublin, Holy Cross Seminary at Clonliffe, the Irish College in Rome, and the College of Propaganda.

Ordained in 1881 in Rome for the Dublin diocese, he spent five years in Ireland, first as a curate at Dundrum, later as Professor of Philosophy at Clonliffe College, Dublin. He became a novice in the Benedictine Abbey of Maredsous, Belgium, and in 1899 was appointed prior of the new Abbey of Mont Cesar at Louvain. In addition he held the Chair of Dogmatic Theology in the University of Louvain.

Along with writing, Marmion carried on an extensive apostolate, the guidance of a large Benedictine monastery, an enormous correspondence, hearing confessions and preaching retreats especially to priests and religious in Belgium, England and Ireland. He was one of those invited by the Anglican Community of Caldey to give them spiritual guidance before they joined the Catholic Church.

Dom Columba was elected abbot of Maredsous in 1909. With the invasion of Belgium in 1914 and German occupation of most of the country, the community was obliged to seek refuge. His nationality making Marmion the most suitable leader, the disguised religious made it through Holland, on board ship to England, finally to Ireland. It became the first step in his long cherished dream to reestablish the Benedictine Order in Ireland.

A year was to elapse before he succeeded in getting back to Maredsous. He found many of his older monks had been arrested and imprisoned for sheltering refugees. Many younger men he had released to serve in the Belgian Medical Corps had been killed at the front. All this time, although in failing health, Marmion did everything possible to help his friend Cardinal Mercier in the alleviation of hardships suffered by the Belgian people. In gratitude for his services, Queen Elizabeth of Belgium, on the feast of Dom Columba's patron in 1920, presented to Maredsous a beautiful chalice ornamented with intertwined gold shamrocks and roses made of rubies.

Dom Marmion prayed unfailingly for Ireland and, having gathered his community around him in July, 1921, when the country was rocked by the Black and Tan terror, he offered solemn pontifical Mass for his suffering countrymen at home. It happened that as that Mass ended, the Truce was signed, the forenoon of July 11, 1921.

Long recognized as a master of the spiritual life, Marmion's books since his death in 1923 have gone through numerous editions in ten languages. Two Benedictine monasteries have been placed under his patronage — Glenstall Abbey in Ireland, Marmion Abbey in Aurora, Illinois.

The veneration of Dom Marmion that began immediately after his death gave rise in 1954 to the opening of the process of his beatification.

New Catholic Encyclopedia, 9: 243.

Matthew Talbot

1857–1925

On June 7, 1925 in Dublin, a shabby elderly man fell in Granby Lane never to regain consciousness. He was taken to the Jervis Street hospital, then to the mortuary. No one knew who he was nor did he look as if he would ever be missed. And then they found his chains. Tied twice about his body was a cart chain held together with twine and hung with religious medals; around one arm was a smaller chain, around the other a cord of St. Francis; around one leg was a chain similar to the one on his arm and around the other leg a rope was tied tight. The chains were rusty and had sunk into his flesh but he was freshly shaven and scrupulously clean.

The man was Matt Talbot. His faithful attendance at services, his great devotion and piety had not gone unnoticed, but his comings and goings were so quiet his name was not known even in the churches he frequented. Once before he had been taken ill but in the hospital no tell tale chains were on him to give away his penances. In death he was surprised with the emblems of his austerities in place and suddenly every possible source of information concerning him was being minutely explored.

At the request of his friend Raphael O'Callaghan who knew him to have been out of the ordinary, Sir Joseph Glynn collected and published the outstanding facts of Matt Talbot's life in a pamphlet that within the next year or two was translated into more than a dozen languages. It was not easy to piece together his story. Matt was never one for talking about himself. Two priest friends that might have been helpful preceded him in death. One of them, the saintly Monsignor Hickey had said, it was recalled "Whenever I wanted a particular favor from heaven, I asked Matt to pray for it. His prayers were never refused."

Matt grew up in a Dublin in which the semi-feudal grandeur of a Protestant few mocked the stark poverty of the Catholic majority, in slums crowded with refugees and beggars from the famine-swept countryside, in an era in which an Irish paper could refer to the city's Catholic archbishop as "the son of a half-hanged traitor" and in which the combined impact of mass-hunger, coercion, emigration and proselytism threatened to destroy the structure and the faith of the nation.

Matt's early years were as drab as his background. His parents were very poor people, his education was neglected. When he did enroll at the age of eleven with the Christian Brothers, they did what they could for him in a special class but he was an indifferent student.

After about a year Matt quit school to go to work. His drinking began with his first job as a messenger boy for a firm of liquor merchants. It continued for some fifteen years.

The break came when he was 28. Out of work, without money or credit, he expectantly joined his drinking cronies on pay day. He could not believe not one of them would offer him a drink. Hurt beyond words, he went home. He told his mother he was going to take the pledge. None too hopefully, she prayed he would keep it. He took it for three months and kept it for 41 years.

Now he frequented churches instead of taverns. There slowly began his new life of penance, of prayer, of contemplation. He moved out to the privacy of a room of his own with a sister caring for his needs. After his father's death in 1899, his mother lived with him in the drab place in upper Rutland street, his home until he died.

Concealed under scanty bed clothes were wooden planks and the pillow of wood on which Matt slept. By two o'clock he would be up and kneeling in prayer until about four, time to get ready for daily Mass. He was very fastidious about cleanliness before entering a church. Long before six o'clock Mass he was waiting on his knees outside the church door, his overcoat covering the slits he cut in the knees of his pants so he could kneel unprotected on the cold pavement. He never rose from his knees during Mass, even for the Gospel, except to go to the Communion railing. He never used a prayerbook, kneeling there completely recollected and engrossed, "as rigid and upright as the candlesticks on the altar."

"Matt got to know two or three of us altar boys well," testified Sean T. O'Kelly, President of Ireland, who used to serve Mass at St. Joseph's Church. "He seemed as humble a type of man as one could meet. . . . I would say he was the nearest I could imagine to one in ecstasy; his fervour and recollection were extraordinary. . . ."

An equally interesting commentary on Matt Talbot is the list of books he read, spiritual classics such as *Writings of St. Alphonsus Liguori*, Faber's *Spiritual Conferences*, Blosius' *The Book of Spiritual Instruction*, *Leaves* from Saint Augustine; Church history, the encyclicals, books on social problems like Garriguet's *The Social Value of the Gospel* and Husslein's *Democratic Industry* — all that and more, thumbed and worn from use on the book shelf of a man who had had hardly enough schooling to learn to read and write.

Scattered through Matt's books were scraps of paper with notes he had jotted down on passages that impressed him or appealed to him: "The Kingdom of Heaven was promised not to the Sensible and the Educated But to such as have the Spirit of Little Children". . ."Liberty of Spirit is that freedom from self-love that makes the soul prompt in doing God's will in the least thing". . ."Sir Henry Wotton, a great authority on the point, Ambassador at Venice, tells us that an Ambassador is one sent to foreign

Courts to invent lies for his country's good"... ."God is the widsom of a purified soul"... ."The yc zcar czar of Russia his income is 20 mill year his demain is big as Ireland"... ."Man can fly from everything in nature but he cannot fly from himself."

Matt's charity was on the same scale as his prayers and his penances. Though the most he ever earned, usually much less, was about $15 a week, he gave away surprisingly large amounts. Outstanding among them were his contributions to the newly founded Columban Fathers, not all of them known. There is a clear record of over $200. The Columban Fathers are in possession of the only letter of his extant, written in December, 1924, six months before he died. "Matt Talbot have Done no work for past 18 months I have Been Sick and given over by Priest and Doctor I dont think I will work any more there one pound From me and ten Shillings From my Sisser." This last pound he had saved out of his $1.88 a week sick pay and his sister Susan said the ten shillings Matt paid himself to thank her for the care she had taken of him in his long illness.

Matt's cause is being considered in Rome. He rests in Glasnevin cemetery in a vault behind an iron gate over which is a marble plaque that is inscribed "Servant of God, Matthew Talbot." Attached to the gate of the vault is a framed copy of the prayer for his beatification.

O'Mahony; Glynn.

John Sullivan S.J.

1861–1933

In the hope that Father John Sullivan may one day be canonized a saint, ten volumes of documents dealing with his life are now at the Vatican awaiting examination by the Sacred Congregation of Rites. His father, a Protestant, had been Solicitor General, Attorney General, Master of the Rolls and in 1883 became Lord Chancellor with the title of Baron. Father Sullivan himself was brought up a Protestant, was a graduate of Trinity College, a scholar steeped in Greek classical culture, a lawyer, and a former Chancellor of Ireland.

To the astonishment of his family and friends, the young barrister known as the best dressed man in Dublin walked into the Farm Street Jesuit Church in London one day and asked to be received into the Catholic Church. Some time later on at the age of forty he entered the Jesuit novitiate.

In contrast to John Sullivan, Chancellor, the Jesuit Father Sullivan went about in clothes that were threadbare and ragged, giving almost everything he had to the poor, known to all as a holy priest whose prayers healed the suffering and helped the dying. He died in 1933 at the age of 72 in the Jesuit

College of Clongowes Wood, County Kildare. The preliminary process for his beatification was started about 1949. A film that depicts his life has since been produced in Dublin.

Peoria Catholic Register.

Edel Mary Quinn

1907–1944

Edel Mary Quinn was born on September 14, 1907, in Grenane, a village in County Cork. Her short life encompassed two years in school in England, family reverses, a business course and secretarial work in Dublin. Deep involvement in the Legion of Mary led to a religious vocation and acceptance by the Poor Clares in Belfast, a happy circumstance shattered by a medical report of advanced tuberculosis. After 18 months in a Wicklow sanitorium, Edel returned to Dublin, another secretarial job and Legion of Mary work in the Dublin headquarters.

Then came the call for establishment of the Legion of Mary in Africa, Africa with all the multi-lingual, tribal and social problems that must be faced. Edel enthusiastically volunteered and finally, in spite of her frail health, she was permitted to go. For the years 1936–1944, the standard bearer of the Legion of Mary in Africa was Edel Mary Quinn.

For seven and a half years, five of them unbelievably strenuous, slim, frail, tubercular Edel travelled the rough dirt roads of Africa. She is pictured going about in an ancient Ford driven by a frightening Moslem to penetrate the remotest corners of East Africa. Nothing, not weather, washed out roads and bridges, insufferable heat, malaria attacks, not even her chest malady could keep her from constant action and work. At Mother Kevin's Uganda convents the Sisters called her ''Our Lady's Little Lamp'' and Mother Kevin chided her for carrying out her daily schedule in spite of high temperature. Tuberculosis sent her to a sanitorium in Johannesburg for almost two years. As soon as the worst was over, she hurried back to Nairobi and her Legion of Mary work. Her single fear was that she might not live long enough to complete the work she knew could be done for Christ in Africa through the intercession of His Blessed Mother. Edel Mary Quinn died April 12, 1944, in the convent of the Sisters of the Precious Blood in Nairobi. She is buried in the little cemetery reserved for missionaries.

Of the Legion of Mary and ''Our Lady's Little Lamp,'' Bishop Heffernan of Nairobi said that after a year of Miss Quinn's work the atmosphere of his diocese had changed. That without any noise she brought a germ of life — Catholic action in its purity. Archbishop Antonio Riberi, Apostolic Delegate, who asked her to come to Africa, said "She has influenced the course of history."

Authored by Marius McAuliffe, O.F.M., teacher, lecturer and retreat master, is a record album, "The Interior Life of Edel Quinn," which tells the story of this remarkable modern Irish girl whose cause for beatification is now in progress.

Louis, 196; McAuliffe.

Mother Mary Kevin, O.S.F.

1875–1957

Petite, gay, charming Teresa Kearney seems never to have considered a religious vocation. She was eighteen and to all appearances there was a well thought of young Dublin bank clerk in her future. Suddenly it was all off. Very carefully Teresa evaded all questions. She said nothing about a strange, vivid, very compelling dream having to do with a terrifying country and dark skinned people who needed her help, the same dream three nights in a row.

The conviction grew upon her that God had intervened in her life and that He would show her what she must do. Shortly after the strange dream, Teresa left Dublin. Subsequently she put in what might be termed a ten year apprenticeship of teaching and nursing: three years of teaching in a school run by the Sisters of Charity in Essex, seven more years, most of that time as infirmarian, with the Mill Hill, London, Franciscan Congregation which had lately agreed to undertake work in the Negro Missions. Teresa was professed Sister Mary Kevin at Mill Hill in 1898.

On December 3, 1902, Sister Kevin in company with five other Sisters escorted by Bishop Hanlon, set out for Nsambya, 800 miles inland from the central east African coast.

There was a tumultuous welcoming throng with jungle drums, pipes and horns to escort the Sisters the last seven miles on foot. There was Benediction in the Mill Hill Fathers' church, all festive with great branches of golden bloom and green rushes on the earth floor. There was a little three room convent of sun dried brick and white washed walls, an oratory, a community room and a dormitory. The sisters arranged their scant belongings and thought their new home looked "almost rich."

There were to be many reminders of the warning of one of the Fathers that there was "more to it" than golden bloom and green rushes: the kitchen a mud hut with water two miles away; no bread ever for two years; evil-smelling wall-to-wall deterrent to flees and chiggers that infested, and prohibited, lovely floorings of green rushes; rats and snakes in the thatched roof, marauding monkeys; painful feet from chiggers that worked into the sisters' shoes; red ants, white ants, black ants, hordes of rampant mosquitoes. And as time went on the sisters battled sleeping sickness, plague, heat, weariness, malaria. "You just can't give in to illness."

Six months after their arrival the Sisters received the "Franciscan Accolade," no money anywhere for their support. Undismayed, Sister Kevin reminded them of the words of Teresa of Avila, "Teresa and a ducat can do nothing: God, Teresa and a ducat can do everything." "Let us do everything possible" she said "but let us make the good God our banker."

The Sisters tackled the language a word at a time. They treated the sick that came in droves to their open air dispensary. They started schooling of all ages. Half-kneeling, half-sitting, they wrote words in the sand for avid pupils whose wonderment knew no bounds at being able finally to make a piece of paper talk. From the first Sister Kevin worked to make her pupils bilingual in preparation for text books in the English language.

Thrity-seven years later, Mother Kevin opened the first Catholic Girls Senior School in the country. Among her pioneers were the first Catholic African woman to serve on the Legislative Council, the first African woman in East Africa to obtain a Bachelor of Science Degree, and the first African woman-doctor in East Africa.

In 1910, Mother Kevin was made Vicaress of the Franciscan Mission in Africa. In 1921, Dr. Evelyn Connelly came from Dublin for three years, stayed on permanently. In 1923, Mother Kevin founded the native African Congregation, the Little Sisters of St. Francis, and in 1927, 70 Little Sisters took possession of their new convent, Our Lady, Queen of Peace at Nkokonjeru. More than any other place, beautiful Nkokonjeru is Mother Kevin's monument. On his visit to Africa in 1943, Cardinal Spellman, with seeming foresight, built a little chapel in the Nkokonjeru cemetery.

When the African Province was made into a separate Franciscan Missionary Congregation in 1952, Mother Kevin was appointed the first Superior General.

With never any visible source of income, Mother Kevin was the founder of some 20 convents. Under her supervision they fanned out into home-craft centers; primary and secondary schools, teaching schools; schools for midwives, for pre-nursing, for general nursing; clinics; general and maternity hospitals; baby homes and orphanages; a school for the blind; two leprosaria; a rest home for Sisters.

And in 1929, Mother Kevin opened a Convent in northern England at Hohme-on-Spalding-Moor in Yorkshire. In 1935, Mount Oliver Convent in Dundalk in Ireland became her Motherhouse and Novitiate for Europe. Cardinal Cushing in 1953 presented to "the greatest missionary nun he ever met'' her Novitiate in Brighton, Massachusetts. In 1954, she opened a Convent in Paisley, Scotland, making a Franciscan house in each of the four countries from which the Congregation hoped to obtain vocations and funds.

On October 16, 1957, Mother Kevin wrote from Brighton to her African Sisters, ''I hope to be with you soon, God willing.'' The next morning she was found quietly asleep, her rosary in her hand, her bed unruffled. Cardinal Cushing flew her body to Ireland for burial. But the African people wanted their beloved Mama Kevina brought home to Uganda. Expense money flowed in from high and low, Catholic, Protestant, Muslim, Hindu, heathen. On December 3, 1957, she was laid to rest in the little chapel in the Nkokonjeru cemetery. It was 55 years to the day from the date she had first set out for the African mission.

The African people have raised their own monument to Mother Kevin, the identification of great good of any kind with their Mama Kevina. A hospital, a school, any charitable institution, is a kevin or a kevina. To do a kevina is to perform some act of great generosity. Even the giant American Dakota planes that dropped food to the troops in the Burma campaign were called Mama Kevinas by the African soldiers.

On February 23, 1968, an official prayer leaflet for the Beatification of Mother Mary Kevin, O.S.F., was authorized by Cardinal Conway of Armagh. She had lived her prayer ''For Thee, Lord.''

Sister M. Louis, O.S.F., *Love Is The Answer*.

Postscript

Cardinal Newman said the Book of Life alone contains the Irish multitude of saints. For America the missionary spirit that is the legacy of those saints has been a seemingly inexhaustible source of Irish priests and nuns. It is not surprising that an Irish born Mother Superior should be both close at hand and available when General Sherman was looking for two religious upon whom to bestow the honor of representing all Sisterhood at the unveiling of Lincoln's monument in Springfield, Illinois in 1874. The honor came to Mother Josephine Meagher of County Tipperary who led the Dominicans to Illinois from Kentucky. Her companion was Sister Rachel Conway, Canadian born of Irish descent. Reprinted, courtesy of the *Chicago Tribune*, is the following story of that occasion:

"On the morning of October 15, 1874, all was in readiness for the unveiling of the monument. Two magnificent star spangled banners, suspended by silken cords dropped gracefully in front of the monument. President U. S. Grant had requested that the honor of unveiling the monument be conferred on two members of some Religious Sisterhood as a token of gratitude for their faithful and self-sacrificing services during the Civil War. At the last moment the committee on arrangements announced that the Sisterhood in the immediate vicinity was cloistered and had declined the honor of unveiling the monument. There was real consternation manifested at this announcement, but General Sherman as in the war, was equal to this occasion. His memory went back to the days of campaign in Kentucky and to the appalling scenes in Memphis where the Sisters of Saint Dominic had ministered to the wounded and dying soldiers of his command, and he exclaimed, 'If I had my Sisters of Saint Dominic near they would not disappoint me.'

"The Reverend P. J. Macken, who happened to be within hearing, said: 'Why, I have Sisters of Saint Dominic from Kentucky teaching in my school but they are in Jacksonville. I am sure they would come with the permission of the Right Reverend Bishop Baltes.'

228

" 'Where is the Bishop,' asked President Grant. 'We'll get the permission. Sherman, order a special train while I wire the Bishop.' In a very short time President Grant received a telegram authorizing Mother Josephine Meagher, the Superioress of St. Patrick's School, Jacksonville, Illinois to take a companion and depart at once for Springfield, Illinois, where in compliance with President's request they should unveil the statue at the tomb of Lincoln. The Rev. P. M. Burke acted as an ecclesiastical escort on the thirty five mile journey to the capitol.

"In the procession, which preceded the ceremonies, the President with the attending Generals, dressed in full regalia, occupied the first carriage, while the second bore the unveilers whose humble, though peerless black and white garb formed a marked contrast to those about them. The ceremonies lasted several hours; finally, the oration of Governor Oglesby of Illinois was finished and the signal was given to the unveilers, and the banners parted revealing the statue of Lincoln. In the applause that followed the Sisters slipped away and were taken back to Jacksonville.''

Selected Further Readings

Barrett, William, *The Red Laquered Gate*. New York, Sheed and Ward, 1967.

Benedictine Monks, *Book of Saints*. New York, MacMillan Company, 1947.

Benn Blue Guide to Ireland, edited by L. Russell Muirhead. London, Ernest Benn Limited; Chicago, Rand McNally & Company, 1962.

Bieler, Ludwig, *Works of St. Patrick.*Westminster, Maryland, Newman Press, 1953.

Binchy, D. A., *Patrick and his Biographers, Ancient and Modern*, in Studia Hibernica, no. 2, 1962, pp. 7–173. Colaiste Phadraig, Dublin.

Brennan, Robert, *Irish Diary*. Westminster, Maryland, Newman Press, 1962.

Bulfin, William, *Rambles in Erin. Dublin,* M. H. Gill and Son, LTD., 1929.

Butler, Alban, *Lives of the Saints*.

Butler's Lives of the Saints, Edited, Revised and Supplemented by Herbert Thurston and Donald Attwater. New York, J. P. Kenedy & Sons, 1953.

Butler, Margery Bayley, *A Candle was Lit*. Dublin, Clonmore and Reynolds, 1953.

Canfield, Curtis, Editor, *Plays of Irish Renaissance*. New York, Ives Washburn, 1929.

Capuchin Annual. Dublin, 1948, 1959, 1960.

Carty, Francis, *Two and Fifty Irish Saints*. Dublin, James Duffy & Co. LTD., 1941.

———— *Irish Saints in Ten Countries*. Dublin, James Duffy & Co. LTD., 1942.

*Catholic Encyclopedia.*New York, Encyclopedia Press, 1907.

Catholic Encyclopedia, New. Washington D.C., Catholic University of America, 1967.

Columcille, *Father, Story of Mellifont*. Dublin, M. H. Gill and Son LTD., 1958.

Concannon, Helena, *St. Patrick*. London, New York, Toronto, Longmans, Green and Co., 1931.

———— *The Queen of Ireland*. Dublin, M. H. Gill and Son, LTD., 1938.

Corish, Patrick J., "St. Patrick and Ireland," from a Symposium held in Armagh, March 17, 1961. Dublin, Browne & Nolan, LTD., 1961.

Cotter, James A., *Tipperary*. New York, Devin-Adair Co., 1929.

Coulson, John, Editor, *The Saints*. New York, Hawthorne Books, 1958.

Curtayne, Alice, *St. Brigid of Ireland*. London, Methuen & Co., LTD., 1942.

Curtis, Edmund, *History of Ireland*. London, Methuen & Co., LTD., 1942.

Daniel-Rops, *The Miracle of Ireland*, Translated by the Earl of Wicklow. Baltimore, Maryland, Helicon Press, 1960.

de Blacam, Aodh, *The Black North*. Dublin, M. H. Gill and Son, LTD., 1942.

Donovan, C. F., *Our Faith and the Facts*. Chicago, Patrick L. Baine Co., 1927.

Dubois, Marguerite, *St. Columban*. Paris, 1961.

Fitzpatrick, Benedict, *Ireland and the Making of Britain*. New York and London, Funk and Wagnalls Company, 1922.

———— *Ireland and the Foundations of Europe*. New York and London, Funk and Wagnalls Company, 1927.

Flanagan, Urban G., *Our Lady of Grace of Youghal*. Cork Historical and Archaeological Society, vol. LV, 1950; vol. LVI, 1951.

Bleeson, Dermot F., *The Last Lords of Ormond*. London, Sheed and Ward, 1938.

Glynn, Sir Joseph, *The Life of Matt Talbot*. Dublin, Catholic Truth Society, 1925.

Gougaud, Dom Louis, *Gaelic Pioneers of Christianity*, translated by Victor Collins. Dublin, M. H. Gill and Son, LTD., 1923.

Graham, Hugh, *Early Irish Monastic Schools*. Dublin, Talbot Press Limited, 1923.

Green, Mrs. A. S., *The Old Irish World*. Dublin and London, 1912.

Gywn, Aubry, "St. Patrick and Rome," from a Symposium held in Armagh, March 17, 1961. Dublin, Browne & Nolan, Ltd., 1961.

Habig, Marion, *Franciscan Book of Saints*. Chicago, Franciscan Herald Press, 1959.

Hayes, Richard, *Old Irish Links with France*. Dublin, M. H. Gill and Son, LTD., 1940.

Healy, John, *Ireland's Ancient Schools and Scholars*. Dublin, Sealy, Bryers and Walker, 1902.

Henry, Francoise, *Irish Art in the Early Christian Period* (To 800 A.D.). Ithaca, N.Y., Cornell University Press, 1965.

———— *Irish Art During the Viking Invasions* (800–1020). Ithaca, N.Y., Cornell University Press, 1967.

———— *Irish Art in the Romanesque Period* (1020–1170 A.D.). Ithaca, N.Y., Cornell University Press, 1970.

Hoagland, Kathleen, Editor, *1000 Year of Irish Poetry*. New York, Devin-Adair Co., 1950.

Hughes, Phillip, Popular History of the Catholic Church. New York, MacMillan Co., 1950.

Jonas, *Life of St. Columban*. Bobbio, Italy, c. 643–659 A.D.

Joyce, P. W., *History of Ireland*. Dublin, Talbot Press, 1923.

Kahoe, Walter, *Saint Fiacre*. Moylan, Pa., Rose Valley Press, 1969.

Kenney, J. F., *Sources for Early History of Ireland*, vol. I, Ecclesiastical. New York, Columbia University Press, 1929.

Leask, Harold G., *Irish Castles*. Dundalk, Dundalgan Press, 1951.

Little, George A., *Brendan the Navigator*. Dublin, M. H. Gill and Son, LTD., 1946.

Louis, Sister M., *Love is the Answer*. Patterson, N.J., St. Anthony's Guild, 1946.

Macalister, R. A. S., *Tara*. New York and London, Charles Scribner's Sons, 1931.

MacGeogheghan, Abbe, *History of Ireland*. 1868.

MacLysaght, Edward, *Irish Families*. New York, Crown Publishers Inc., 1972.

MacNeill, Eoin, *Phases of Irish History*. Dublin, M. H. Gill & Son, LTD., 1937.

McCarthy, E. L., *St. Columban*. Society of St. Columban, 1927.

McKenna, Marion, *History of Catholicism*. Totowa, N.J., Littlefield, Adams and Company, 1962.

McLaren, Moray, *Shell Guide to Scotland*. London, Elbury Press, 1972.

McLoughlan, Helen, *My Name Day*. Collegeville, Minn., Liturgical Press, 1962.

McManus, Seumas, *Story of the Irish Race*. New York, Devin-Adair Company, 1944.

Montalembert, *Monks of the West*. Paris, 1863.

Moran, Cardinal, *Irish Saints in Great Britain*. Dublin, Brown and Nolan, 1879.

Mould, D. D. C. Pochin, *Scotland of the Saints*. London, Batsford, 1952.

——— *Ireland of the Saints*. London, Batsford, 1953.

Murphy, Denis, *Our Martyrs*. 1895.

Needham, Kieran, *Life of St. Patrick*. St. Patrick Fathers, 1963.

Neeson, Eoin, *Book of Irish Saints*. Cork, Mercier Press, 1967.

O'Byrne, "Irish Music." Irish World, October 1926.

O'Fiach, Tomás, "St. Patrick and Armagh," from a Symposium held in Armagh, March 17, 1961. Dublin, Browne and Nolan, Ltd., 1961.

O'Hanlon, John, *Lives of Irish Saints,* 10 vols. Dublin, 1875.

O'Kelly, J. J., *Ireland's Spiritual Empire*. Dublin, M. H. Gill and Son, LTD., 1952.

O'Mahony, Donal, "Matt Talbot." Columban Mission, April 1958.

——— Missionary Sons of St. Patrick. Jesuit Mission Magazine, March 1965.

O Siochan, P. A., *Aran, Island of Legend*. New York, Devin-Adair Company, 1962.

Porter, Arthur Kingsley, *The Crosses and Culture of Ireland*. New Haven, Yale University Press, 1931.

Rice, David Talbot, Editor, *Dawning of European Civilization*. New York, McGraw Hill Company, 1966.

Reilly, Robert., *Irish Saints*. New York, Farrar, Straus & Company, 1964.

Ryan, John, *Irish Monasticism*. Dublin, Talbot Press LTD., 1931.

Salmon, John, *The Ancient Irish Church*. Dublin, 1897.

Savage, Roland Burke, *Catherine McAuley*. Dublin, M. H. Gill and Son, LTD., 1955.

Sigerson, George, *The Easter Song*. Dublin, Talbot Press LTD., 1922.

Simpson, W. George, *Celtic Church in Scotland*. Aberdeen University Studies, 111, 1934.

Skene, W. F., *Celtic Scotland*, 3 vols. Edinburgh, 1875–80.

Stang, *Germany's Debt to Ireland*. New York, 1891.

Stokes, Margaret, *Early Christian Art in Ireland*. Dublin, Government Publications, 1932.

Sullivan, A. M., *Story of Ireland*. Dublin, M. H. Gill and Son, LTD., 1867.

Sweeny, James Johnson, *Irish Illuminated Manuscripts*. Collins in association with UNESCO, 1966.

Tommasini, Fra Anselmo, *Irish Saints in Italy*. London, Sands and Company LTD., 1937.

Toynbee, Arnold J., *Study of History*, Vol. II. New York, Oxford Press, 1951.

Walsh, T. J., *Nano Nagle and the Presentation Sisters*. Dublin, M. H. Gill and Son, LTD., 1959.

Zimmer, H., *Irish Element in Medieval Culture*, translated from the German, 1887.

Brochures

St. Bride's Church Fleet Street in the City of London, Saint Bride Restoration Fund at the Church. Leicester, Blackfriars Press LTD., 1969.

St. Wendel, History of the Town. Bishop's House, Trier, Germany.

St. Foillan. Booklet from Abbe Hennebert, Fosse-le-Ville, Belgium.

Feast Day Index

January

1. Fanchea, 23
1. Colman Muilinn (see Children of Miluic), 15
1. Dabeoc, 20
2. Munchin, 30
7. Kentigerna, 86
8. Erhard, 140
9. Fillan, 86
11. Ethna and Fidelma, 14
14. Kentigern, 81
15. Ita, 40
16. Fursey, 92, 129
18. Desle, 124
18. Ninidh, 37
19. Fillan, 86
19. Blaithmac, 87
20. Fechin of Fore, 59
21. Maolcalain, 159
23. Maimbod, 156
24. Guasacht (see Children of Miluic), 15
28. Cannera, 28
29. Blathe (see Brigid), 24
29. Dallan Forghaill, 47
30. Anmchadh, 163
30. Eusebius, 157
31. Aidan of Ferns, 54
31. Adamnan of Coldingham, 104

February

1. Brigid, 24
1. Ursus of Aosta, 114

2. Columban of Ghent, 159
3. Anatolius, 163
3. Ives, 90
4. Gillebert, 173
5. Fingen, 161
5. Indract, 109
5. Buo, 70
5. Vodaldus (see Erhard)
6. Mel, 17
7. Tressan (see Gibrian), 113
9. Marianus Scotus, Abbot, 165
9. Alto, 149
10. Erlulf (see Patto), 152
11. Gobnait, 35
12. Sedulius, 5
13. Domnoc, 19
16. Tanco (see Patto), 152
17. Finan of Lindisfarne, 99
17. Fintan of Clonenagh, 50
17. Fortchern, 12
18. Colman of Lindisfarne, 102
20. Colgu, 68

March

5. Kieran of Saigher, 4
5. Cadroe, 159
6. Fridolin, 116
8. Senan, 39
11. Aengus, 69
16. Abban, (also May 13), 1
17. Patrick, 6
18. Fridian, 115
20. Clement, 153

20. Cuthbert, 106
21. Enda, 29
21. Isenger (see Patto), 152
24. Caimin, 58
24. MacCartan, 15
26. Sinell of Killeagh, 16
27. Gelasius, 178
27. Rupert, 145
28. Tutilo, 158
30. Kortyla (see Patto), 152
30. Patto, 152
30. Riaghail, 78

April

1. Ceallach of Armagh, 171
1. Caidoc and Fricor, 128
2. Bronach, 48
7. Brenach, 90
10. Paternus, 163
12. Ailill of Cologne, 162
14. Tassach, 18
15. Ruadhan of Lorrha, 45
17. Donnan, 82
18. Cogitosus, 63
18. Laserian of Leighlin, 57
21. Maelrubha, 84
23. Ibar, 3
27. Asicus, 18
28. Cronan, 53
30. Forannan, 160

May

1. Brieuc (see Erhard), 140
2. Ultan of Fosses, 139
3. Conleth, 22
5. Diuma, 98
6. Colman of Cork, 60
8. Wiro and Plechelm, 146
8. Gibrian, 113
9. Beatus, 153
10. Cathal, 123
10. Comgall, 49
11. Cathan, (also May 17), 79
11. Lua of Killaloe, 60

13. Abben, 1
14. Carthage Mochuda, 56
15. Dympna and Gerebern, 135
16. Brendan of Clonfert, 42
17. Maildulf, (also April 18), 101
22. Boethian, 138
30. Maugille, 137
31. John Meagh, 196

June

1. Ronan, 117
1. Ruadhan of Cornwall, 92
2. Algise, 139
3. Kevin, 51
4. Buriana, 91
4. Breaca, 91
4. Concord, 181
5. Eoban and Adalar, 148
6. Jarlath, 36
7. Colman of Dromore, 37
8. Muirchu, 63
9. Colmcille, 73
12. Christian, 172
15. Vougay (see Erhard), 140
16. Berthold and Amandus, 113
17. Moling, 62
21. Diarmuid, 68
24. Rumold, (also July 3), 150
25. Moluag, 72
26. Mochae (see Children of Miluic), 15
26. Corbican, 145
30. Gobain, 132

July

3. Germanus, 91
3. Tirechan, 63
4. John Cornelius, 193
4. Patrick Salmon (see John Cornelius) 193
4. John Carey (see John Cornelius), 193
5. Modwena of Polsworth, 110
6. Modwena of Whitby, 109
6. Modwena of Edinburgh, (also Nov. 19), 22

7. Maelruain, 67
8. Kilian of Wurzburg, 142
10. Etto, 137
11. Oliver Plunket, 197
11. Droston, 80
11. Sigisbert, 125
12. Menulphus (see Erhard), 140
15. Harruch (see Patto), 152
16. MacDara, (also Sept. 28) 19
17. Fredegand, 144
17. Turninus, 139
18. Minborinus, 160
24. Declan, 4

August

1. Pellegrinus, 136
5. Abel, 147
8. Ultan of Craik (see Erhard), 140
9. Phelim, 38
10. Blane, 79
11. Attracta, 17
11. Lelia (see Munchin), 30
12. Molaise of Devenish, 40
14. Fachtna, 46
19. Cummian of Bobbio, 146
23. Eugene, 51
31. Aidan of Lindisfarne, 94
31. Fiacre, 133

September

3. MacNessi (see Dabeoc), 20
8. Disibode, 144
9. Osmanna (see Erhard), 140
9. Kieran of Clonmacnoise, 31
10. Finian of Movilla, 42
12. Ailbhe of Emly, 3
17. Roding, 137
23. Adamnan of Iona, 83
24. Mansuy, 2
24. Grimonia, 2
25. Finbarr, 52
27. Moengal, 157
28. MacDara, (also July 16) 19

October

6. Ceallach of Mercia, 98
11. Cainnech, 80
12. Fiacc, 13
12. Mobhi, 31
13. Comgan, 85
13. Colman of Stockerau, 162
16. Eliph, 2
16. Gall, 126
18. Monon, 129
21. Tuda, 100
21. Wendel, 116
22. Donatus, 155
24. Thaddeus McCarthy, 186
26. Albuin, 148
29. Colman of Kilmacduagh, 55
31. Bee, 105
31. Foillan, 131

November

2. Erc, 21
4. Malachy, 174
7. Florentius, Ch. IV, 686.
7. Patrick Fleming, 195
9. Benignus, 12
10. John of Ratzeburg, 164
12. Cummian of Clonfert, 59
12. Sinell of Cleenish, 38
13. Kilian of Artois, 135
14. Laurence O'Toole, 182
14. Sidonius or Saens, 143
15. Fintan of Rheinau, 156
18. Mawes (see Erhard), 140
18. Mombolus, 138
19. Modwena, (also July 6), 22
20. Autbodus, 139
23. Columban of Luxeuil, 118
24. Colman of Cloyne, 48
24. Marianus and Anianus, 148
27. Virgilius, 151
29. Brendan of Birr, 41

December

1. Martinus and Declan, 148

3. Eloquius, 132
7. Buite, 23
11. Two Emers (see Children of Miluic), 15
12. Finian of Clonard, 34
13. Colm of Terryglass, 35
14. Fingar, 90

18. Flannan, 61
19. Macarius, 170
19. Samthann, 64
20. Ursicinus, 125
22. Marianus Scotus, Incluse, 164
26. Tathai, 92

Alphabetical Index

A

Abben, 1
Abel, 147
Adamnan, Coldingham, 104
Adamnan, Iona, 83
Aengus, 69
Aidan, Ferns, 54
Aidan, Lindisfarne, 94
Aikenhead, Mary, 217
Ailbhe, 3
Ailill, 162
Albuin, 148
Algise, 139
Alto, 149
Anatolius, 163
Anmchadh, 163
Asicus, 18
Attracta, 17
Autobodus, 139

B

Beatus, 153
Bee, 105
Benignus, 12
Berthold and Amandus, 113
Blaithmac, 87
Blane, 79
Blathmac MacConbreton, 64
Boethian, 138
Breaca, 91
Brenach, 90
Brendan, Birr, 41
Brendan, Clonfert, 42

Brigid, 24
Brogan of Clonsast, 65
Bronach, 48
Buite, 23
Buo, 70
Buriana, 91
Burke, John, 193
Burke, Honoria, 196

C

Cadroe, 159
Caidoc and Fricor, 128
Caimin, 58
Cainnech, 80
Cannera, 28
Carey, John, (see John Cornelius), 193
Carthage, 56
Cathal, 123
Cathan, 79
Ceallach, Armagh, 171
Cealleach, Mercia, 98
Children of Miluic, 15
Christian, 172
Clement, 153
Cogitosus, 63
Colgu, 68
Colm, Terryglass, 35
Colman, Cloyne, 48
Colman, Cork, 60
Colman, Dromore, 37
Colman, Kilmaduagh, 55
Colman, Lindisfarne, 102
Colman, Stockerau, 162

Columban, Ghent, 159
Columban, Luxeuil, 118
Colmcille, Scotland, 73
Comgall, 49
Comghan, 85
Concord, 181
Confessors and Martyrs, 190
Conleth, 22
Corbican, 145
Cornelius, John, 193
Cronan, 53
Cummian, Bobbio, 146
Cummian, Clonfert, 59
Cuthbert, 106

D

Daboec, 20
Dallan Forghaill, 47
Declan, 4
Desle, 124
Diarmuid, 68
Dicuil, 97
Disibode, 144
Diuma, 98
Domnoc, 19
Donatus, 155
Donnan, 82
Drostan, 80
Dympna and Gerebern, 135

E

Eliph, 2
Eloquius, 132
Enda, 29
Eoban and Adalar, 148
Erc, 21
Erhard, 140
Ethna and Fidelma, 14
Etto, 137
Eugene, 51
Eusebius, 157

F

Fachtna, 46
Fanchea, 23
Fillan, 86
Fechin, 59
Fiacc, 13
Fiacre, 133
Finan, 99
Finbarr, 52
Fingar, 90
Fingen, 161
Finian, Clonard, 34
Finian, Movilla, 42
Fintan, Clonenagh, 50
Fintan, Rheinau, 156
Flannan, 61
Fleming, Patrick, 195
Foillan, 131
Forannan, 160
Fortchern, 12
Fredegand, 144
Fridian, 115
Fridolin, 116
Fursey, 92, 129

G

Gall, 126
Gelasius, 178
Germanus, 91
Gibrian, 113
Gillebert, 173
Gobain, 132
Gobnait, 35
Grimonia, 2
Guasacht (see Children of Miluic), 15

I

Ibar, 3
Indract, 109
Irish Confessors & Martyrs 1572–1713,
    200
Ita, 40
Ives, 90

J

Jarlath, 36
Jaruman, 101
John Dun Scotus, 185
John, Ratzeburg, 164

K

Kentigern, 81
Kentigernia, 86
Kevin, Glendalough, 51
Kevin, Mother, 225
Kieran, Clonmacnoise, 31
Kieran, Saigher, 4
Kilian, Artois, 135
Kilian, Wurzburg, 142

L

Laserian, 57
Laurence O'Toole, 182
Lelia (see Munchin), 30
Lua, Killaloe, 60

M

Macarius, 170
MacCartan, 15
MacCarthy, Thaddeus, 186
MacDara, 19
Maelruain, 67
Maelrubha, 84
Magan, Honoria, 196
Maildulf, 101
Maimbod, 156
Malachy, 174
Manisternenay, 191
Mansuy, 2
Maolcalain, 159
Marianus and Ananius, 148
Marianus Scotus, Abbot, 165
Marianus Scotus, Incluse, 164
Marmion, Dom Columba, 219
Martinus and Declan, 148
Maugille, 137
McAuley, Catherine, 214

Meagh, John, 196
Mel, 17
Minborinus, 160
Mobhi, 31
Modwena of Edinburgh, 22
Modwena, Polsworth, 110
Modwena, Whitby, 109
Moengal, 157
Molaise, 40
Moling, 62
Moluag, 72
Mombolus, 138
Monon, 129
Muirchu, 63
Munchin, 30

N

Nagle, Nano, 211
Ninidh, 37

P

Paternus, 163
Patrick, 6
Patto, 152
Pelligrinus, 136
Phelim, 38
Plunket, Oliver, 197
Potentin, 128

Q

Quinn, Edel, 224

R

Riaghail, 78
Roding, 137
Ronan, 117
Ruadhan, Cornwall, 92
Ruadhan, Lorrha, 45
Rumold, 150
Rupert, 145

S

Salmon, Patrick (see John Cornelius), 193
Samthann, 64

Sedulius, 5
Senan, 39
Sherlock, Robert, 191
Sidonius, 143
Sigisbert, 125
Sinell, Cleenish, 38
Sinell, Killeagh, 16
Sullivan, John, 223

T
Talbot, Matthew, 221
Tassach, 18
Tathai, 92
Tirechan, 63
Tuban, 149
Tuda, 100
Turninus, 139

Tutilo, 158

U
Ultan, Craik (see Erhard), 140
Ultan, Fosses, 139
Ursinus, 125
Ursus, Aosta, 114

V
Virgilius, 151

W
Wendel, 116
Wiro and Plechelm, 146

Y
Youghal, Our Lady of, 192

DATE DUE

DEMCO, INC. 38-2931